A Global Look At Business Education

NATIONAL BUSINESS EDUCATION YEARBOOK, NO. 29

Editor:
LONNIE ECHTERNACHT
University of Missouri
Columbia, Missouri

Published by:
National Business Education Association
1914 Association Drive   Reston, Virginia 22091

A GLOBAL LOOK AT BUSINESS EDUCATION

Copyright 1991 by

NATIONAL BUSINESS EDUCATION ASSOCIATION
1914 ASSOCIATION DRIVE
RESTON, VIRGINIA
$12.00

LIBRARY OF CONGRESS CARD NO. 91-061796
ISBN 0-933964-35-8

Any views or recommendations implied in this book do not necessarily constitute office policy of the National Business Education Association. References to and quotations from this publication are encouraged; however, no part of this book may be reproduced without permission of the National Business Education Association.

Preface

A global look at business education is a timely theme for the National Business Education Association's 1991 Yearbook. We live in a fast-changing world, and the role of the United States within the world is also changing. The United States is committed to giving leadership to and participating in the world, but in cooperation with other nations. With new transportation and communication technologies, the future will include increased international interdependence, intensified world-wide competition, and greater individual involvement in the global community.

Teaching and learning with a "global perspective" is needed in today's business education classrooms. No longer can we limit our teaching of business courses solely to American businesses, American ideas, American geography, and American lifestyles. Decisions that affect us as workers and consumers are often made in the economic arena by multinational corporations and other organizations outside the political and governmental systems. Traditionally, Americans have relied upon their schools to develop the skills, knowledge, and attitudes needed to meet new challenges and solve new problems. However, we must recognize that there are many educative forces in our society. Exchange programs, youth organizations, ethnic groups, and churches have long been involved in promoting international understanding and preparing newcomers for their roles as United States citizens.

Business education programs must realign their curricula to prepare workers and consumers for the world beyond our nation's borders—knowledge of how other countries affect us and how we affect the rest of the world is needed. International business concepts and procedures must be integrated into the business education curriculum so students are prepared for the global society in which they will work and live.

A *Global Look at Business Education* is a refereed yearbook. Due to the specialized theme of the yearbook, suggestions for chapter authors were requested from national, regional, and state business education association leaders; state and local business education supervisors; and business teacher educators whose names appeared on an NBEA mailing list. Chapter manuscripts were solicited by sending chapter descriptions and author guidelines to those business educators who had been recommended as potential authors. An editorial review board with representatives from each of the NBEA regions and the different levels of business education was established. Members were selected to serve on the editorial review board based on their commitment to and expertise in business education. Each chapter manuscript was reviewed and evaluated (using a rating scale supplied by the editor) by at least three reviewers. Members of the 1991 Yearbook editorial review board were:

Anna Burford, Middle Tennessee State University,
    Murfreesboro, Tennessee
Clarice Brantley, Woodham High School,
    Pensacola, Florida

R. Neil Dortch, University of Wisconsin-Whitewater,
   Whitewater, Wisconsin
Louis T. Harding, University of the District of Columbia,
   Washington, D.C.
Donna Holmquist, University of Nebraska at Omaha,
   Omaha, Nebraska
Colleen Vawdrey, Utah Valley Community College,
   Orem, Utah
Karen Waner, Central Missouri State University,
   Warrensburg, Missouri

The 18 chapters of this yearbook have been organized into four major sections. Part I, "Introduction: Global Perspectives in Business Education," presents the growing need for infusing the business education curriculum with a global and international business perspective.

Part II, "Developing an International Business Education Program," suggests strategies for building support for and marketing an international business education program. Practical approaches for internationalizing basic business and economics, business communications, information processing, and business management courses are discussed.

The authors contributing to Part III, "International Business Education Programs: Strategies and Organization," have described exemplary international business education programs at the secondary, community college, and university levels. The in-depth look at international business education programs at different levels demonstrates the need for interdepartmental collaboration and provides innovative ideas for planning, developing, implementing, and evaluating programs.

In Part IV, "Selected Foreign Business Education Programs," readers are provided a glimpse of how business education is being addressed in other countries. The four authors have been involved extensively in foreign travel and comparative studies of educational programs.

This yearbook represents a variety of thoughts about how business educators may internationalize the business education curriculum. Specific methods and techniques as well as program descriptions are presented. As you read the yearbook, I hope it helps you to recognize the need for a global perspective in business education, to examine your own program, and to consider strategies for internationalizing the curriculum.

I wish to thank everyone who contributed to this yearbook. Your constructive ideas, helpful suggestions, well-written manuscripts, and professional encouragement were appreciated. A sincere thanks is expressed to members of the editorial review board who so generously contributed their time and expertise in the review of the chapters. A special thanks is also extended to the National Business Education Association's Executive Board, Publications Committee, and Publications Staff. Working with all these professionals was a pleasant and rewarding experience.

Lonnie Echternacht, Editor

Contents

CHAPTER   PAGE

PART I
INTRODUCTION: GLOBAL PERSPECTIVES IN BUSINESS EDUCATION

1   Internationalizing the Business Education Curriculum 1
       LaNeta L. Carlock
       Westside Community Schools
       Omaha, Nebraska

2   The International Marketplace 8
       Jo Behymer
       University of Missouri-Columbia
       Columbia, Missouri

PART II
DEVELOPING AN INTERNATIONAL BUSINESS EDUCATION PROGRAM

3   Building Support for an International Business
     Education Program 19
       Carolyn Hagler and Sharon Abbott
       University of Southern Mississippi
       Hattiesburg, Mississippi

4   Marketing the International Business Education Program 30
       Wanda Blockhus and G. W. (Jim) Maxwell
       San Jose State University
       San Jose, California

5   Methods of Internationalizing Basic Business and
     Economics Courses 43
       Thomas B. Duff
       University of Minnesota, Duluth
       Duluth, Minnesota

6   Methods of Internationalizing Business
     Communications Courses 53
       Bobbye J. Davis and Donna H. Redmann
       Southeastern Louisiana University
       Hammond, Louisiana

7   Methods of Internationalizing Information Processing Courses 65
       Roy W. Hedrick
       University of South Carolina
       Columbia, South Carolina

8   Methods of Internationalizing Business Management Courses 74
       Chuck Coligan
       New Jersey Department of Education
       Trenton, New Jersey

PART III
INTERNATIONALIZING BUSINESS EDUCATION PROGRAMS: STRATEGIES AND ORGANIZATION

Secondary Level

9   What in the World Is Going On in Toledo, Ohio? 84
    SANDRA KRUZEL and EDWARD CHAVEZ
    Toledo Public Schools
    Toledo, Ohio

10 Integrating International Business Topics at the Secondary Level 93
    JAMES H. BEISTLE
    Unity High School
    Balsam Lake, Wisconsin

Community College Level

11 The International Business Education Program at
    Central Piedmont Community College 105
    RICHARD K. ZOLLINGER and JUDITH F. PATTERSON
    Central Piedmont Community College
    Charlotte, North Carolina

12 The International Trade Education Program at Waukesha
    County Technical College 113
    BARBARA MOEBIUS
    Waukesha County Technical College
    Pewaukee, Wisconsin

University Level

13 The International Business Education Program at
    Ball State University 122
    RODNEY E. DAVIS, J. LEE DYE, and ROBERT A. UNDERWOOD
    Ball State University
    Muncie, Indiana

14 The International Business Education Program at
    Illinois State University 131
    JEAN GREVER and IRIS VARNER
    Illinois State University
    Normal, Illinois

PART IV
SELECTED FOREIGN BUSINESS EDUCATION PROGRAMS

15 Business Education Programs in the United Kingdom 141
    JAMES CALVERT SCOTT
    Utah State University
    Logan, Utah

16	Comparative Business Education Programs in the European Community Countries...............................	153
	Albert G. Giordano Monterey Peninsula College (Retired) Monterey, California	
17	Business Education Programs in the U.S.S.R.......................	168
	Ray D. Bernardi Morehead State University Morehead, Kentucky	
18	Business Education Programs in Taiwan	181
	Larry E. Casterline State of Ohio Department of Education Columbus, Ohio	

Part I
INTRODUCTION: GLOBAL PERSPECTIVES IN BUSINESS EDUCATION

CHAPTER 1
Internationalizing the Business Education Curriculum

LANETA L. CARLOCK
Westside Community Schools, Omaha, Nebraska

How do business teachers educate for a new decade and a new millennium? What skills will students need to survive in a global society? Images of the world of the future should shape our curriculum planning. We cannot peer into the future and discern clearly where the world is headed or what its educational needs will be. However, we can make educated guesses based on past and current trends, facts, and observations. This introductory chapter of the 1991 NBEA Yearbook, *A Global Look at Business Education,* shows how the world is changing and how our nation represents an international society; reviews facts and observations; and discusses the impact on the business education curriculum at all educational levels.

CHANGING WORLD

Alvin Toffler stated in *The Third Wave* that "a powerful tide is surging across much of the world, creating a new, often bizarre environment in which to work, play, marry, raise children, or retire."[1] Some believe we are indeed in the current of this third wave. Turbulence, but also hope for progress, is evident in our changing world.

The role of the United States has changed from that of a dominating power, defining and maintaining the rules of the game, to that of a major player who must consider other players in the international system. Change is the constant in international economic, political, and social conditions. Values inherited from the past may now be inconsistent with human survival. The idea of a nation with inexhaustible resources is obsolete.

Explosive population growth continues to be increasingly dangerous. Improved medical care and the development of new wonder drugs have helped to extend the life span dramatically in recent years. By early in the 21st century, it is likely the global population will increase to between six and seven billion.[2] Though there are signs of declining birthrates, many of the less developed countries will see more and more children with frail bodies

---

[1] Toffler, Alvin. *The Third Wave.* New York: William Morrow and Company, Inc., 1980. p. 17.

[2] Rerschauer, Edwin. *Towards the 21st Century—Education for a Changing World.* Presentation paper, 1983.

and starvation-damaged minds. This situation places a growing moral burden on the United States and other more fortunate countries.

As one of the world's leading arms exporters, the United States has become a target for those who are alarmed over how, and against whom, these lethal weapons might be used. Widespread anxiety exists over damage to the biosphere, the dangers of nuclear plants, bombs in the hands of terrorists, and problems of waste disposal. Pollution and resource depletion are also having profound effects on our environment. There is an inability to reconcile extravagant lifestyles with the drain on the biosphere.

Coping with inflation, debt, and unemployment has become a worldwide phenomenon and is testing the capacity for economic innovation. People will be competing for the same diminishing living spaces, raw materials, and food for survival. Mounting governmental and personal debt concerns economists; however, it is politically difficult to moderate the governmental obligations. Global unemployment figures indicate between 800 and 900 million persons are now out of work or underemployed; and how to cope with this development is not clear.[3]

A rising level of global frustration will involve both domestic tranquility and international cooperation as rising human expectations are unrealized. Almost all of those born since 1950 have been exposed to the influences of television, computers and electronic communication. Television has become an especially powerful and mind-shaping force as it instantly transmits changes occurring in the world. Many individuals are unable to differentiate between the realities and the fantasies viewed on the screen. Exposed to global coverage of events everywhere in the world, people see only sensational bits and pieces—not necessarily the real world.

These are examples of the factors, forces, and developments of our changing world. It is by no means an all inclusive list. The speed of change today requires that individuals recognize the interdependence of human beings and world resources of an international society.

INTERNATIONAL SOCIETY

The world is now an international society. Human inventiveness has made it so. Yet many individuals seem to have difficulty accepting the concept of global interdependence. Examples: When a fire alarm sounds in Malmo, Sweden, a fireman puts the address of the fire into a computer terminal. A minute later a description of potential hazards at the scene is displayed on the computer terminal. The computer used to store that data is in Cleveland, Ohio.[4] In 1947, a trip across the Atlantic took seventeen and a half hours; today, it takes only three and a half—and a message may be sent across that distance by satellite in an instant. More than half of the United States' wheat, soybeans, and rice is sold abroad. On the other hand, the United States is

---

[3]"Business," *U.S. News and World Report.* March 19, 1990.

[4]Marx, Gary, and H. Thomas Collins. "It's a Big, Wide, Interdependent World," *American Association of School Administrators Research Data.* November, 1981.

either completely or almost totally dependent on imports for such key minerals as diamonds, tin, nickel, and cobalt.[5] International trade requires that a sense of world community and enhanced cooperation be nurtured.

Movement toward an international society is evident when we look at what is happening in the United States. Almost one-third of all U.S. corporate profits are now generated through international corporate business; and increasingly, other countries are locating their business firms in America. Japanese firms have at least 1,177 businesses in this country that directly employ 81,300 U.S. workers.[6] At least half of the leading corporations on the Fortune 500 list are foreign based and owned. One American in six now owes his or her employment to foreign trade. Over 100,000 Americans work on extended or permanent assignment overseas, and about 4 million annually take business trips abroad. Approximately 250,000 income tax returns are filed annually from Americans living in other countries.[7] American consumers purchase watches, shoes, televisions, stereos, automobiles, and other consumer goods that have been imported from other countries even though this balance of trade deficit affects each of us. State of the art communication systems, technology, and transportation have all fostered the globalization of business. Newspapers and newscasts carry daily news of international business. Advertising reflects the "think global, act local" watchwords of business.

Now, more than ever, international students are attending American educational institutions and exchange programs of students, teachers, and individuals are being encouraged. The American population is becoming increasingly multicultural. Some demographers say that by the year 2000, Hispanics will constitute nearly half of the population in the Southwest, and the numbers of Asians and other minority groups will significantly increase. Eighty-two percent of new workers in the year 2000 will be a combination of female, nonwhite, or immigrant. Minorities, most notably Hispanics, now make up 22 percent of the new entrants into the labor force, and this figure continues to rise. There will be a continuing need to educate non-English-speaking workers in the language of the workplace. The working age population is also changing, with fewer than half now under the age of 40.[8]

The changing demographics and family patterns will affect future lifestyles. The median age of the population continues to rise, and will soon reach 36.3 years. Americans over the age of 65 currently account for 12 percent of the population, but will soon reach 17 percent. The fastest-growing group in the population will be Americans over the age of 85; and by 2050, one in 20 Americans will be over 85.[9] One consequence of this graying of America will be greatly increased health, social, and economic needs. The graying of America will also impact on the international society.

---

[5] Ibid.

[6] Collins, H. Thomas. "East of Gibraltar, West of Japan: Questions and Answers about Global Education," *Principal*, page 16.

[7] "New Report Urges Global Perspective," *NAPSA Newsletter*. February, 1987.

[8] Lamy, Steven L. "Global Perspectives in Education." Presentation paper, Global Perspectives in Education, Inc. 1987.

[9] Ibid.

Because of changes in the family, more women will be employed. Today, almost 70 percent of adult women have jobs.[10] Many of these women work at home part of the time, using computers, telecommunications capabilities, and interactive cable television to communicate with their offices. Fathers are becoming more involved in the care of children, with some staying home to care for them. Divorce rates are leveling off, but with longer life spans, more than 50 percent of Americans will be divorced at least once.[11] There will be an increasing need for working parents to have flexibility in the workplace. The need for home management and child care will grow even greater.

Nontraditional families will become the norm. The high school graduating class of the year 2000 may have the following characteristics: 24 percent will live below the poverty line, one-third will be nonwhite, 18 percent will be born out of wedlock, 50 percent will live with a single parent, 66 percent will have mothers working outside the home, 30 percent will be "latchkey" children, over 15 percent will have physical or mental handicaps, and 20 percent of the girls will become pregnant during their teen years.[12] All of these predictions will also have an impact on the international society.

As the globalization of this international society continues to evolve, there will be increasing needs for broader skills in communicating across linguistic and cultural lines, and a much greater understanding of international problems by each of us. People communicate through the spoken or written word as well as through the way they act, dress, walk, and eat. People throughout the world may be essentially the same biologically, but culturally they are quite different. What is acceptable in one culture may not be acceptable in another. Students' understanding and knowledge of international relations are inadequate for present and future needs. The following facts and observations will reinforce the important role business educators can play in helping to respond to the needs of the international society.

FACTS AND OBSERVATIONS

This section will illustrate some of the facts and observations concerning America's need for developing international competence. Much of this compilation came from the American Institute for Foreign Study and the National Council on Foreign Language and International Studies.[13] National Geographic requested Gallup to conduct polls on international knowledge, and UNESCO conducted studies in many countries.

- In an international test of geographic knowledge, Americans ranked among the bottom third, and those aged 18 to 24 years of age came in last.
- Fewer than one-half of Americans are able to identify the United Kingdom, France, South Africa, and Japan on a map.

---

[10]Ibid.

[11]Ibid.

[12]Hodgkinson, Harold L. and Educational Research Service. Presentation paper, 1987.

[13]"Facts," American Institute for Foreign Study and the National Council on Foreign Language and International Studies, Research Findings, 1987.

- American students place next to last in their comprehension of foreign cultures.
- Almost 40 percent of high school students think Israel is an Arab nation.
- Many colleges have dropped language proficiency as an entrance requirement; thus, high schools have relaxed their teaching in these disciplines.
- High school teaching of basic geography and history has declined.
- Almost 20 percent of American students cannot even find the United States on a world map.
- Over one-half of the American population believe that foreign trade is either irrelevant or harmful to the United States.
- Fewer than three percent of all high school graduates achieve meaningful competence in a foreign language.
- The United States continues to be the only country in the world where a student can graduate from college without having had one year of a foreign language—either before or during the college years.
- The number of American students majoring in history has dropped by 62 percent since 1970. Students at 75 percent of American colleges can obtain a bachelor's degree without having studied European history.
- Less than 10 percent of college freshmen and seniors have taken a single course in international affairs.
- One American high school in five has no foreign language instruction, modern or ancient, for its students.
- Almost 10 million Soviets study English; only 28 thousand Americans study Russian. There are more teachers of English in the Soviet Union than there are students of Russian in the United States.
- Only seven percent of the people of the world speak English as a primary language, but nine out of ten Americans cannot speak, read, or understand any language but English.
- More than 700 million people speak Mandarin Chinese as a primary language, and more than 50 million rely on Cantonese. Fewer than 200 third-year high school students in the United States are studying Chinese.
- More than 134 million people speak Arabic, the language of oil, as a principal language, but only a few Americans can communicate in Arabic.
- There are 19 million Spanish-speaking people in the United States—making the United States the fourth largest Spanish-speaking nation in the world. By the year 2025, the United States could be primarily a Spanish-speaking country.
- Only about five percent of teachers in the United States are being trained or required to take bicultural courses for certification.

Clearly, global education must be integrated throughout the curriculum to ensure that citizens are adequately prepared to function intelligently in a global society. The last section of this chapter will address the impact per se on the business education curriculum.

IMPACT ON BUSINESS EDUCATION

What impact should the changing world have on the business education curriculum, and what are the implications for business educators? Today's international environment confronts U.S. educators with immense challenges. Teachers must provide students with an international perspective that reflects social, political, cultural, and economic reality. Students need international communication skills to enable them to think, behave, and work effectively in a global society. Research, technical assistance, study, and international service programs are needed to help confront and solve international problems. The business education curriculum at all levels is fertile ground for developing many of these knowledges and skills.

In the 1989 statement by the Policies Commission for Business and Economic Education, the need for global education was addressed. "America is a high tech, information, and service society with growing multicultural and international dimensions. This environment creates an opportunity . . . to prepare people to adapt to change."[14] Along with other American educators, business educators are beginning to respond to the curriculum changes needed for survival in this changing, international society. This 1991 NBEA Yearbook focuses on what can, and should be done to develop international education concepts within the business education curriculum at all levels.

Business departments may not be able to initiate a separate course in international education, but they can infuse the curriculum with significant experiences that will make a difference for students. First, business educators must read and study in this arena so they are knowledgeable and confident to share their knowledge with students. The business educators should do the following:

- Take advantage of every opportunity to learn more about the international society, different cultures, and the changing world.
- Establish an educational setting filled with such human values as acceptance of others, respect for all people's cultures, and an understanding of and competence in basic skills, productive work habits, and attitude development.
- Be future oriented.
- Pay special attention to the concepts of interdependence.
- Look outside the classroom and beyond textbooks for information, knowledge, and research pertaining to international education.
- Work with local businesses and chambers of commerce to bring reality to the global society concept for students.
- Establish a philosophy of lifelong learning in classes so students never stop thirsting for new knowledge of their changing world.
- Encourage travel and student/teacher exchange programs that provide first-hand experiences, and are the best way to learn of other cultures.
- Join professional organizations such as the International Society for Business Education to increase cultural awareness.
- Teach students the skills of decision-making, critical thinking, and communicating.
- Provide opportunities for creative problem-solving.

---

[14]"This We Believe About the Impact of Change Due to Information Technologies," Policy Statement No. 46, Montgomery, AL: Policies Commission for Business and Economic Education, 1989.

- Encourage students to examine the relationships between global issues and local issues or concerns.
- When reviewing, planning, and implementing curriculum changes, always keep in mind the global perspective.

Because change is constant, and because the world has indeed become an international society, ask the following question every day: "What do business students need to know for survival in the changing world?" Business educators have a responsibility to provide some of those basic survival skills.

CHAPTER 2
The International Marketplace

JO BEHYMER
University of Missouri-Columbia

The tastes and values of a new generation of Americans, new demographics, and rapid increases in international trade are likely to reshape most products, services, and jobs in the United States. The future of the country will be less affected than in the past by natural resources and more by what Americans choose to do as voters, consumers, investors, employers, and employees. Government regulations, incentives, and management of international affairs will also shape choices.

As the United States enters the 21st century, one of its toughest challenges will be to achieve economic growth. It will require a broadly shared vision of progress, including the belief that progress is possible. Economic growth must be measured ultimately by the extent to which the quantity and quality of amenities (anything that contributes to comfort, convenience, or happiness) has been improved and by the extent to which these improvements are shared across groups in America. International connections will increasingly influence the quantity and quality of amenities in the United States.

INTERNATIONAL MARKETING

The global corporation has replaced the multinational corporation. Although global corporations are beginning to emerge in Third World countries, they currently are mostly based in the United States, Japan, and Europe. Regardless of size and geographic scope, every company must become a global corporation to realize its potential and, in some instances, just to survive.

The evolving economic order shows a steady shift toward a geocentric orientation rather than an ethnocentric, home country orientation, or a polycentric, host country orientation. The shift to a geocentric orientation can be seen in the creation of worldwide product divisions and in the extent to which men and women from many nationalities are in positions of corporate and major product responsibilities.

The success of the global marketer depends upon the ability to perceive the similarities and differences of individuals and cultures of the world. Relevant differences are important, but the global marketer must also recognize similarities to avoid costly adaptations in marketing products, strategies, and programs. Products are adapted, if needed, to local market conditions. However, when possible, geocentric companies standardize products and marketing procedures to minimize costs of research, development, and manufacturing and to maximize gains from sale and consolidation of resources. The goal is to have a flexible product line that allows for local market conditions but is as standardized as possible.

BARRIERS IN INTERNATIONAL MARKETING

Government involvement ranges from simple guidance at one end of the spectrum to state trading at the other end, which can create obstacles in international trade. Japan, for example, uses administrative guidance in the form of a reward/punish approach to achieve implementation of its trade policies. A government achieves conformity by using tactics like licensing, foreign-exchange allocation, and quotas. Playing the role of consumer in trading arrangements, the government exhibits maximum involvement. Direct government business activities, or indirect activities by agencies under governmental control, are other ways governments get involved. The government/customer role is most common in communist countries, whose governments are responsible for central economic planning. However, active involvement of government in trade, control, and ownership is not limited to communist and developing countries.

Several forms of government subsidies protect local businesses or encourage exports: cash, taxes (value-added, corporate income, and sales), interest rates, insurance, freight, and favorable foreign-exchange conversion rates are examples. Less obvious subsidies include the training of workers, the building of infrastructures, and tax-sheltered profits, all of which are used regularly to attract foreign investors.

Another group of nontariff trade restrictions are customs and entry procedures: classification, valuation, documentation, licenses or permits, inspection, and health and safety regulations. Product classification, sometimes arbitrary and inconsistent because it may be based on a customs officer's judgment at time of entry, is significant because it determines the duty status. Each product must also be valued, which affects the amount of tariff assessed. Determined by a customs appraiser, the process is sometimes subjective, depending on whether foreign, export, import, or manufacturing costs are used.

At the least, long and complex document requirements slow down product clearance through customs. At the most, improper documentation may prevent clearance of goods through customs. Some products require a license or permit before they may be brought into a country. India requires a license for all goods imported; and to get foreign beer into Mexico, proof must be provided that Mexican brewers cannot meet their country's consumer demand.

Inspection of goods to determine quality, quantity, and health and safety hazards is sometimes used to discourage imports. Japanese customs agents require partial disassembling of imported cars to determine whether the serial number on a part matches the one on the shipping document. Japan, claiming that Japanese snow is different from other snow, set new ski equipment standards that are supposed to reduce accidents caused by the damper Japanese snow.

Countries set product requirements—which may apply to product standards, packaging, labeling, marking, specifications, and testing—for goods to enter the country. Product requirements may prevent or slow down importation of foreign goods. Japan's product standards are based on physical characteristics, rather than product performance, causing a repeat of the approval process when a slight physical difference occurs. The product performance may not change at all. Some products must be packaged according to specific standards. Businesses wishing to sell canned goods in Canada must pack them in specific sizes, and instructions on packages must be in English and French. Safety testing is also a trade barrier. Japanese companies gain enough time to develop competing medical equipment and pharmaceuticals by requiring safety testing that can take several years. Product specifications can be developed to favor local bidders over foreign suppliers. Frequently, meeting product specifications entails making expensive or lengthy modifications.

Quotas limit the quantity of foreign products that may be imported, thus protecting local firms and conserving foreign currency. Absolute quotas prohibit further shipments once a specified quantity is reached from all imports or perhaps only those from specific countries. Tariff quotas, conversely, permit entry of a limited quantity of a given product at a reduced duty rate. Any excess is subject to a higher rate. Tariff quotas discourage excessive quantities but permit needed imports.

Financial regulations control imports and capital flow thus restricting international trade. Exchange controls limit the amount of currency an exporter can receive for goods sold and the length of time it can be held. Multiple exchange rates also affect trade, encouraging exports and imports of some goods but discouraging that of other goods. Governments can require prior import deposits to make importation difficult. Importers often cannot afford to tie up their capital, and government credit or financing may be denied to them. Further, payments of earnings may be limited to a parent organization located in a third country that may or may not use a desired currency.

Other policies inhibit international trade. Some countries retain selected businesses and professions for their citizens; for example, Thai barbers must be nationals. A growing trend is for governments to require foreign firms to engage in specified activities that will benefit the country before permission to sell is granted. Such requirements include use of local raw products or exporting the host country's products.

Protectionism is on the rise, and trade barriers slow economic growth. Regardless of the inappropriateness of barriers, however, international marketers have no control over them. The best defense for marketers is to understand the barriers, to anticipate the results, and to use the information effectively.

FUTURE INTERNATIONAL MARKETING ISSUES

One of the foremost international marketing issues facing the world is the impact of unified actions of trading blocs like European, North American, and Pacific Rim blocs. These regional blocs likely will have significant implications for international trade. Whether such trading blocs would erase trade barriers against each other is not clear, but increased opportunity for trade within and outside trading blocs exists. Business in the 1990's will play a key role in this process and may need to pressure government leaders to change policies as necessary to sustain international trade.

Another future issue is the liberalization of the Eastern bloc, which could have an enormous future impact on buying, bargaining, and trading power. China, the Soviet Union, and the Eastern bloc countries are inhabited by millions of people who know that the standard of living of other countries has been denied to them. They are frustrated by pent-up consumer demand and the lack of means to improve their situations.

Japan's avoidance of a political leadership role in relationship to its dominant economic status is another future issue. At a time when Japan needs to assume more global responsibility for stabilizing the world economy, the country is hindered by a lack of well-developed international arrangements. As the world moves toward three major trading blocs—Europe, Asia/Pacific Rim, and North America—Japan will need to meet the leadership challenge.

Additionally, the explosive growth in technological sophistication that permits a constant flow of business information and transactions is an issue. Advances in technology have destroyed the traditional checks and balances.

TRADING BLOCS

Europe. Landmark events like the possibility of a united European Economic Community (EEC) in 1992 mark a growing trend toward global economic integration. Although the EEC is far from a single innovative unit, the "harmonization plan" draws upon a large home market in excess of 320 million people. The plan specifies achieving a single European market, which would be the world's largest unified free market, by facilitating trade of capital, labor, products, and services via the integration of political and economic policies.

Greater accessibility for American industry to world markets will result from European economic unification. Europe now has varied tariffs, quotas, and laws; bilateral agreements must be made with each country. Numerous local regulations encumber even simple product standardization efforts across national borders. An encouraging possibility exists that one currency will be established, followed by a consolidation of banks. However, with the establishment of the EEC a result of one currency will be a significant shift of banking power to European banks.

The effects of European unification extend beyond economics and into political arenas. Americans fret about a "Fortress Europe" as a potential outcome. European firms will be able to create political hurdles and influence

EEC policy to a much greater extent than the United States and other non-EEC counterparts. For the plan to succeed, governments and individuals of Western Europe will need to cooperate closely. In addition, some cultural issues must be resolved before the EEC's goals are achievable.

Continued U.S. export growth helps balance trade with Western Europe. Top markets in Europe for U.S. exports continue to be the United Kingdom, West Germany, France, and the Netherlands. The EEC plan will enhance further the United Kingdom's attractiveness as an export market absent of major trade barriers and as a point of entry for other European markets. Excellent prospects for expansion of U.S. exports to France continue because of a competitive exchange rate and high French demand. The French government recently further liberalized foreign direct-investment regulations, while the advance-notice requirement for foreign investors to establish new business operations has already been abolished. American manufacturers and suppliers increasingly seek European sales through the Netherlands. If a product or service sells well in the United States, then it will sell well in the Netherlands.

North America. On the other side of the Atlantic, the United States-Canada Free Trade Agreement parallels the EEC trade plan. U.S. and Canadian economies produce approximately $.5 trillion more in goods and services than the entire bloc of 12 EEC nations. The United States and Canada are the world's largest bilateral trading partners, and all trade barriers between them will be eliminated by the turn of the century as a result of the agreement. For Canada, the pact opens a market 10 times the size of Canada. For the United States, the pact destroys some of its protectionist reputation, illustrating its commitment to barrier-free world trade.

Mexico, the third largest trading partner for the United States after Canada and Japan, remains a strong market for exports. High demand for United States products results from a growing economy and a favorable exchange rate combined with liberalization of government trade policies.

Japan and other Pacific Rim countries. Unified by commonalities of the Pacific Ocean and economies oriented toward exports, the Pacific Rim includes a group of extremely diverse countries, from the economic giants of the United States and Japan to the dwarfs of the "island countries" like Fiji and New Guinea. Pacific Rim countries are economically, politically, geographically, socially, and religiously diverse. To illustrate the diversity, five major languages are spoken in the Pacific Rim—Chinese, English, Japanese, Cantonese Chinese, and Korean. However, about 25 percent of the population speak a language other than one of these five.

The economies of most Pacific Rim countries are growing more rapidly than those of the United States, some even more rapidly than Japan's economy. If this growth continues through this decade, there will be a noticeable change in the balance of economic power. However, the United States will continue to dominate economically the Pacific Rim throughout the 1990's.

Japan's cartel-like management system enables corporate executives to dominate the policy of Japan's major public companies. Cross-held directorates, creating interlocking boards, permit companies to reward one another with favorable contracts without consideration of the impact on shareholders. These relatively low-cost contracts help Japan achieve its goal of increased world-market share by undercutting global competition. Barriers to penetrating Japanese international markets are: (1) difficulty in hiring qualified staff, reflecting long-term employment customs in Japan, (2) long-time relationships between Japanese suppliers and customers, and (3) difficulty in entering Japanese distribution systems.

Manufacturing businesses in the United States are concerned because the Japanese are aggressively opening production facilities in this country. While they are shutting out American competition in Japan, they are exporting their system of cartels into United States manufacturing.

Japan's closed system is maintained by its corporate elite. However, the primary victims of a country's restricting trade policies are its residents. Japan provides an observable example. Japan is known as one of the world's richest countries; yet its citizens live only a little better than Third World citizens, and the first tentative rumblings from Japan's consumers are being heard. They are realizing that for their labor they do not enjoy an equitable share of Japan's wealth. If this movement escalates and Japan becomes more consumer oriented, a gradual decline of its trade surplus will occur.

Three of the economic dwarfs, Hong Kong, South Korea, and Taiwan, are now considered nearly industrialized countries because of their high rates of economic growth. In addition, the Asian group, comprised of Indonesia, Malaysia, the Philippines, Thailand, and Singapore, have had high rates of economic growth in recent years. In fact, Singapore's successes over the last decade put it near classification as a newly industrialized country (NIC). Conversely, the only market-oriented economy in the Pacific Rim that has not performed well over the past decade is the Philippines.

The Soviet Union, Vietnam, and other Southeast Asian states, and some Central and South American countries, like Mexico and Peru, have played a relatively insignificant economic role in the Pacific Rim. Nonetheless, their considerable physical presence suggests the possibility of a greater role for these countries in the future.

International trade fuels the economic boom of the Pacific Rim. Several examples are prominent. The United States leads the Pacific Rim in foreign trade, approximately 55 percent of which occurs with other Pacific Rim countries. The United States/Canada has the largest trade relationship, and the second largest is between the United States and Japan. The Pacific Rim countries with the most rapid economic growth trade extensively with the United States and Japan but relatively little with each other.

The model of export-driven economic expansion, often referred to as the Japanese model, has been credited for the economic progress of the most rapidly growing countries in the Pacific Rim. In this model, cooperation between government and business is emphasized, involving conscious national investment, subsidization, and trade-protection policies that stimulate selected privately-owned industries with the possibility of increasing foreign exchange through exports.

Future economic growth of the Pacific Rim could be impeded by potential roadblocks. As with any export-led economy, Pacific Rim countries are especially vulnerable to changing global economic conditions. To illustrate, changes in protectionist trade measures and economic slow-downs in industrial countries create economic chaos. In addition, an individual country's changes in consumer tastes make a difference. Pacific Rim countries are extremely sensitive to variations in international commodity prices because of their dependence on them. Pacific Rim political instability is a constant threat to economic growth. Some questions exist regarding the success of some economically advanced countries in maintaining their comparative advantage in the production of goods like textiles and electronics.

All of these are impediments to economic growth, but none are so great a threat to future regional prosperity than the combination of exclusionary regional trading blocs and protectionist policies in countries like the United States. The danger will be not only that Pacific Rim countries may be individually or collectively excluded from major world markets, but also that a lack of cohesion may prevent them from uniting and developing their own regional trading policies. However, free world trade is of such overpowering importance to Pacific Rim countries that they may be forced to join together and open their economic and political structure on a worldwide scale.

Although the United States and Japan dominate the Pacific Rim from an economic standpoint, the People's Republic of China is of growing economic importance because of its more than one billion population. China's significant policy change from that of isolationism toward a market-oriented economy has provided dramatic increased economic growth. China's plan is to enhance production by attracting foreign capital and technology. Imported raw materials will be processed, and semifinished products assembled in China's coastal areas will then be exported.

Despite China's amazing successes over a decade, increasing inflation and administrative corruption are slowing reform. The problems associated with inflation and corruption originate partly from unchecked power. The political reform program emphasizes decentralization of decision making to prevent abuses of power. Additionally, the market system is not fully operative. The reform program calls for abolition of special privileges and the two-tiered pricing system through which the state allocates scarce items at considerably lower prices than market. Other changes would encourage employer and employee initiatives. Many believe, however, that economic reform is not enough; political and cultural reforms must be coordinated with the economic reforms.

Eastern Bloc countries. No one knows what the new freedom in Eastern Europe means for business. Capitalism in the early 1990's is moving rapidly from west to east, creating new markets, new investment opportunities, and new headaches for American companies. When consumer goods were available in the Eastern bloc in the past, they were extremely costly. Long-denied demand for consumer goods presents what may be an unbelievable opportunity to sell everything from designer clothes to electronic luxuries. At the very least, the Eastern bloc is a major new market for reasonably priced consumer goods.

Actions of Soviet leaders in the early 1990's suggest that economic and political freedom are opposite sides of the same coin. The Soviets appear sincere in their efforts to abandon central economic planning and institute a program that will switch the country to a market economy, but the plan is expected to double food prices and lead to massive closures of inefficient factories.

President Gorbachev's proposed economic reforms include price liberalization on key commodities, a change from central planning control of investment to control through the banking sector, ruble convertibility, a massive boost of consumer goods into the economy, and programs to support low wage earners and the unemployed. The Soviets are expected to turn to Western countries including the United States for short-term purchases for immediate needs, particularly consumer goods. Negotiations have begun between the United States and the Soviet Union on an investment agreement, a trade agreement, and a new tax treaty.

This desperate reform is in response to a low standard of living that is worsening. Even inferior consumer products are in short supply, and food shortages are widespread. Life expectancy in the Soviet Union is decreasing, which is unheard of in an industrialized country. Economic observers inside and outside the Soviet Union fear that the new plan will create an economic panic.

Capital will be required to modernize and expand factories in Eastern Europe. For example, the 1990's will see the opening of the Eastern bloc's first stockmarket in Budapest. General Electric has already made major investments in Hungary, and Kodak not only made investments in Hungary but is also working on even larger ones in Poland. Not to be left out, individual Eastern European investors are buying West German and Austrian stocks. Most experts agree that East Germany and Czechoslovakia have the best potential for trade. In addition to investments from several large corporations, smaller firms are also showing interest. Some smaller companies have made large investments, taking a much bigger gamble.

After years of producing only for the Eastern Europe and Soviet Union economies, Eastern European countries will now have to find their niche in the world market, producing high-quality products at competitive prices. Even if Eastern European countries are able to modernize, they will still have the problem of nonconvertible currency. For example, Pepsico must receive payment in the form of vodka because the Soviet ruble is not convertible to dollars. Despite the vast opportunities for Western investment, large industrial investments will probably be delayed until the currency problems in Eastern Europe are alleviated. In the meantime, many Western companies prefer to invest in the service industries.

Understandably, advocates of East-West trade advise proceeding with caution. Doing business in Eastern Europe is still a risk. Uncertainty is part of the risk because business regulations have not yet been completely developed. Just as significant, these regulations are being decided by politicians interested in their own national interests, rather than by business representatives. The United States already has many regulations to live with, but quite possibly the European ones will be added rather than replace the United States ones. Consideration must be given to political risks, currency fluctuations, red tape, and economic uncertainty. Because most of these nations have insufficient hard currency, returns on investments will be difficult to collect; short-term profits will be limited to very few firms. Many companies will delay action until they see the success of modernization and reform, which will determine return on investments.

ADAPTING TO THE GLOBAL ECONOMY

Adaptability may be the key because changes are going to occur at different speeds, depending on the businesses involved. Adaptability in other nations may mean following the lead of the United States in relying upon small businesses to provide new job opportunities and to bring new products and services to international markets. Third World countries in particular have tended to invest most of their resources in big projects that frequently do not meet expectations. In many ways the small business is the most adaptable, resilient, and creative part of the economy in the United States. Adaptability will mean the difference between those businesses that profit and those that suffer from the changes.

Success in international marketing will depend on advanced marketing tools and techniques including market segmentation, quality and service management, and sales automation. Markets need to be watched closely to identify profitable niches and customized products and product/service packages must then be developed for relative advantage in targeted market segments. Value may be added to traditionally nondifferentiated products through delivery scheduling, packaging, and other services. Suppliers are embracing a "just-in-time" delivery philosophy of defect-free products and services.

The use of computers can help achieve greater efficiency for sales and marketing systems. For example, laptop microcomputers streamline sales reports and paperwork, freeing salespeople to cover larger territories. Electronic messaging will become even more popular in the process of cultivating customers. Telemarketers arrange appointments for sales representatives and conduct follow-up after on-site calls thereby reducing the size of the field sales force. Automation permits joining information in a way never before possible, allowing marketers to overcome internal barriers and integrate all their data bases to gain a comparative advantage. By closing the information loop between marketing and sales, companies can react to customers' real needs rather than perceived ones.

Many American companies are seeking to form joint ventures to attract capital, technology, and new markets. A catchall term, "joint venture" describes all cooperative business arrangements that involves foreign companies, except the corporate acquisition. Joint ventures, of course, include an interest in growth opportunities, but sometimes the reason is survival. Nontariff barriers and import restrictions make direct exporting to some countries difficult if not impossible. Market access to these countries may depend upon opportunities to form joint ventures.

International joint ventures permit partners to share expenses, minimizing risks. Small- and medium-sized partners can combine skills and resources that allow economy of scale in manufacturing, distribution, and research and development. If the joint venture involves potential competitors, each partner may be able to increase market share and prevent undermining the current markets or future markets. Through the international joint venture, partners can put new technology on the market sooner and pierce distribution channels in markets that might otherwise be impenetrable.

Companies forming joint ventures immediately face additional complications and risks. For example, labor laws may require provision of fringe benefits like social security, medical insurance, housing, vacations, and clothing allowances. In countries where termination of an employee is possible, termination payments may be required. Particular attention must be paid to the respective immigration laws so that managers have the ability to move people abroad. Staff must be selected carefully; in addition to other necessary attributes, a company entering into a joint venture must be able to adapt to the host country's culture.

GLOBALIZATION OF TECHNOLOGY AND HIGH-TECH FINANCE

"Global trading" has been in the media frequently in recent years, but only now through technology and change in structures of the world's market does the ability to "shop the world" become a reality. World market structures have been significantly affected by deregulation in Asia and Europe, and world markets are no longer the exclusive domain of their respective exchange members. Trading is now conducted in an international marketplace without regard to geography.

Some financial experts predict that the financial services industry is entering a period of growing prosperity and that companies that survive on Wall Street during the 1990's may enjoy the fruits of a boom. Forces at work causing optimism are—

- Japanese liquidity (Enormous investments in non-Japanese assets and securities may create a multiplier effect.)
- Mergers and acquisitions
- Additional specialized firms
- United States financial technology transferred to the overseas markets
- United States alliances with Japan and Europe
- Decrease in defense spending worldwide
- Technological revolution.

A dominant force in the financial services industry, technology increases revenue through new products and services and simultaneously permits domestic cost reductions. Technology is making financial markets more efficient, services more creative, and operating services more productive. The problem, however, is combining hardware, software, and communication technology that are compatible. Incompatible technology can prevent the integration of information coming from multiple business activities. Technology has become so important to the financial industry that a clear business plan cannot exist without serious consideration of emerging technology.

In recent years the world has experienced a change in international macroeconomics. In the past, a creditor country's monetary policies, by manipulation of interest rates, influenced the stability of international capital markets. Although the United States will continue in the near future to exercise influence on worldwide interest rates, Japan could also influence interest rates and stock prices on Wall Street. For the first time, the United States, the leading international financial market, is also a net foreign debtor. Japan's rise as the dominant creditor nation, coupled with the change of the United States to a large debtor nation while retaining the dominant currency, has changed the nature of Japan's global responsibilities. The Japanese policy that is best for its domestic economy may not be best for international financial stability. This situation may be the biggest challenge that the United States and Japan face.

CONCLUSIONS

Although it is possible in theory for trade to improve living standards throughout the world, such a dream is unlikely to occur because of the realities of nationalism, protectionism, and distrust. The overarching objective of international marketing policy should be to make trade a winning combination for all participants including the United States. No one country can achieve this objective; only global action is likely to come close to success. To accomplish this objective United States leadership is crucial.

With the global marketing trend well on its way, U.S. corporations are scrambling to establish relationships in foreign markets. The flip side of how to forge these ties is the question of who is able to do so. As the world moves toward globalization, profiles of chief executive officers will look quite different from those of today. Tomorrow's global manager will likely be a liberal arts graduate with a joint MBA/technical degree, will have begun in research rather than in finance, will be fluent in one or more foreign languages, will have held several positions, and will have traveled extensively.

The global manager will be able to build relationships based on respect for the culture and its idiosyncrasies. The distinct American style cannot be maintained if business operations abroad are to succeed. International executives must demonstrate knowledge of the different methods of doing business. For example, business in Spain is typically transacted over at least a two-hour lunch, but not discussed until after cognac and cigars. Western style eating is considered bad manners in France, and Japanese are hesitant to speak first in a meeting. The French and Japanese prefer a formal style of address.

Decision makers in competing global markets need flexibility—the ability to manage new, conflicting situations; the recognition that numerous ways to solve a problem may exist; and negotiation skills. Of course, expertise in areas like finance, law, and manufacturing are important for business with foreign companies, but personal characteristics will determine whether there will even be a relationship.

PART II
DEVELOPING AN INTERNATIONAL BUSINESS EDUCATION PROGRAM

CHAPTER 3

Building Support for an International Business Education Program

CAROLYN HAGLER and SHARON ABBOTT
University of Southern Mississippi, Hattiesburg

With the global marketplace a reality, diverse work forces at home and abroad, and business education's history of preparing students for and about business, the time has arrived to internationalize business education. Business educators, along with other U.S. citizens, must expand their perspective from an insular economy to a global one with the United States as a supporting member of the world-trade community.

Modification of business education programs to reflect globalization of the workplace will require widespread support both internally and externally. This chapter will present a support model for international business education programs, along with a plan to actuate the model and suggestions to modify the curriculum. A list of resources at the end of the chapter will be helpful to those persons interested in learning about internationalizing and in globalizing their local programs.

SUPPORT MODEL FOR INTERNATIONAL BUSINESS EDUCATION

A common-sense approach to internationalizing business education is to develop a strong network of knowledgeable persons who can and will contribute to a support system. The composition of a support model will greatly aid the transition of business education into a more global context. The participants needed for an operative model should play an active part in developing an international business education program whether by assisting in identifying needed curricular changes, helping to develop methods for implementing these changes, upholding the program by encouragement, or contributing to funding as a means of continuing the program.

The following model consists of both internal and external support:

Internal support. Business education must build an infrastructure with four basic constituencies: (1) students, (2) all business educators, (3) administrators, and (4) teachers in other disciplines.

Students are the principal recipients of the educational tools to be developed and utilized in the international arena. As a basic component of the internal support structure, students should be exposed to international topics and other cultures. Various vehicles can be used to expose students, such as student organizations, conferences and conventions, guest speakers from other cultures, media presentations, class discussions and assignments, study-abroad tours, international festivals, and exchange programs.

Many business educators are aware of the need for an international approach to business education. Acceptance of the need for intercultural literacy and multilingual communication and recognition of global interdependence will spearhead the drive to update the curriculum to meet the needs of the global business community.

Business educators can receive active support and encouragement for the international approach through professional associations' planning conferences and programs on the topic, international material in textbooks, and teacher education methods courses that incorporate units on international business. Furthermore, encouraging researchers to investigate international business education and disseminate the findings through professional journals could help to develop all business educators into a strong support base.

Curriculum changes usually require the approval of administrators above the departmental level, and the support of the appropriate administrative unit should be elicited in the early stages of considering an international program. Strong administrative support, with appropriate funding, can be instrumental in making an international element a major priority for the total education program and in encouraging efforts to modernize the curriculum.

International education provides an opportunity for linkages between and among all school disciplines. Disciplines such as history, geography, foreign languages, and international studies are already global in nature. Teachers in these areas could serve as important allies to business educators interested in internationalizing and could provide support for business education's entry into that domain. A cooperative approach cutting across all disciplines would result in a marriage of all components of an international curriculum to prepare students to compete in a global economy, one of the educational goals of the nation's governors.

External support. External support for an international business education program should reasonably and naturally stem from a number of sources. These sources include: (1) educational institutions, (2) professional organizations, (3) the business and lay community, and (4) governmental agencies and foundations.

Every rung on the education ladder has a responsibility to prepare students for productive roles in an international marketplace. Failure of one segment of the educational system will transfer the responsibility to another segment and thereby decrease the effectiveness of the system in achieving its goals. Communication and cooperation from all divisions within the educational system are essential to implementing an international business education program.

The role of professional organizations as a support component should be threefold: to provide leadership and direction in developing international business education programs, to coordinate efforts to avoid duplication, and to pursue appropriate funding from governmental organizations at all levels. Collaboration among groups like NBEA, DPE, ISBE, PSI , and OSRA, for example, could provide a major impetus to business educators in developing international programs. Also, groups like the Coordinating Council for Business Education, Business Education Advisory Council, and the Foundation for the Future of Business Education could be used to coordinate efforts.

Business education should forge mutually beneficial partnerships with the business community and lay community (including parents) to develop and sustain a viable international business education program. Citizens of these communities and business people, in particular, could be used in a variety of ways:

1. To provide expertise in identifying critical elements of an international program
2. To help in designing a curriculum tied to international workplace skills
3. To serve on advisory councils
4. To teach international units or courses
5. To work as tutors and mentors
6. To provide cooperative work stations where students could be exposed to elements of international business
7. To expose students to the expectations of the business world in today's economy.

Governmental agencies, foundations, school boards, state departments of education, legislators, and governors have a vested interest in international business. Because governmental bodies have a major impact on business education through funding and decisions on curriculums and programs, these agencies should be a part of the support model.

A PLAN OF ACTION TO BUILD SUPPORT FOR INTERNATIONAL BUSINESS EDUCATION

The vision of international business education is the beginning; a strategic plan of action built upon that vision must then be developed. A plan for building support should be a multifaceted approach including research, education, involvement, commitment, and leadership.

Research. The academic rationale for internationalizing business education should begin with thorough research into the current and future needs of students and the needs of the business world.

Little research has been conducted in the international arena by business educators; yet sound research can make business education's entry into this area a credible and worthwhile pursuit. Change for change's sake is questionable. Research, however, can provide the basis to make business education more relevant in an international business environment.

Education. One of the difficulties in building support for international business education may be a lack of awareness of the need for such a program. Therefore, an integral part of the plan of action is education of all who make up the internal and external components of the support model.

The United States has a parochial perspective, a narrow view that permeates individuals, schools, businesses, and the government. Until individuals and groups recognize that the global community exists today and that the new marketplace will not be led by the United States, a lack of support will exist. Therefore, education is the primary mode of attack in building support for any international program.

Involvement. One can recognize the need for international business education, but without involvement by many internal and external support groups, internationalizing will be a vision—never a reality.

Involvement is the key area where advisory committees can be used. Representatives selected from the various internal and external constituencies should be involved in planning an international business education program, implementing the program, and evaluating the program.

Local, state, and national advisory committees, which should be representative of a cross-section of the internal and external support components, could be instrumental in developing and adapting an international curriculum in business education. Business educators should involve specifically those individuals and businesses that are interested in and involved with international business, such as utility companies, world trade centers, international corporations, port authorities, airlines, banks, mining companies, import/export firms, ship lines, telecommunication firms, and energy companies. By involving and using an advisory committee as a liaison between the business education program and the business community, business education will reflect the needs of the immediate community as well as the region, the nation, and the global market.

Commitment. For business education to meet the needs of students and businesses in a global economy, a deliberate commitment to incorporating an international dimension in business education must be a part of the plan of action. Business educators, administrators, employers, political leaders, and the American public must be committed to educational reform in general and to business education reform in particular. Business education is a part of the broader goal of internationalizing education, and, as such, a commitment is necessary to establish priorities, to assign resources and personnel, to coordinate activities, and to evaluate progress.

A specific commitment to international business education must be made by business education teachers, administrators, leaders, and professional groups. That commitment could be revealed through a statement on internationalizing business education by the Policies Commission for Business and Economic Education, the creation of international advisory groups, the establishment of a national clearinghouse for international business education, and alliances with other groups dedicated to international education.

Leadership. Only through leadership will the plan of action function efficiently. To avoid a fragmented approach with few benefits and much duplication of effort, internationalizing business education requires a united effort involving many groups.

One of the obstacles that business educators face is a lack of knowledge of resources that can help develop a background in international education and programs in the area. Leadership at the national and regional levels could help overcome this obstacle by providing a network of interested groups that could coordinate efforts in research, education, involvement, and commitment and would serve as a repository of information.

INTERNATIONALIZING THE BUSINESS EDUCATION CURRICULUM

With a support model and a plan of action for building support in place, the business education curriculum can be revised and updated. With the incorporation of appropriate pedagogy and curricula changes, the necessary global perspectives can be achieved.

Just as writing across the curriculum is the approach for improving writing skills, internationalizing across the curriculum is the best approach for improving global literacy. An international component is essential in virtually every aspect of education, but it is even more crucial for business education to adjust to the demands of an international economy.

In general the curriculum should provide all students with a respect for all peoples and an awareness of the increasing global interdependence among peoples and nations, of the diversity of cultures, and of world conditions and developments. In addition, students need an understanding of the relevance of developments in other countries to their profession, business, and/or local economies; a knowledge of societal movements that are resulting in goals and values that are international in scope; and a knowledge of ethical questions and issues resulting from global conditions. At least two years of a foreign language is also needed.

Goals and objectives. Goals and objectives embodying an international dimension and a global perspective must be established at all levels of education from kindergarten through graduate school. Even though most business educators are not involved with elementary education, the curriculum at this level must articulate with all other levels.

Elementary schools. Beginning with the early grades, objectives concerning international literacy should be established and global education integrated in classes such as social studies. The primary international goal in elementary schools is to develop an awareness of world cultures and world geography.

Middle/High schools. With a primary goal at the secondary level of awareness of global economy and respect for other peoples, international business education should become a part of every school in one or more of the following ways:

1. Infusion method, in which international aspects are introduced and integrated in every business education course where feasible
2. Development of a new course or courses dealing with international business topics, such as an introduction to international business
3. A vocational program for students interested in international business.

With the already crowded curriculum at most secondary schools, the infusion method may be the only approach available to most secondary business education programs. Classes in typewriting could use materials on other countries and cultures for timed writings; classes in consumer economics could study consumer problems and issues relating to the global economy; and an economics class could investigate other countries' economic structure.

Postsecondary. Working and living in a global community requires a knowledge of geoeconomic and intercultural customs, education in foreign practices, skills in acceptable behavior, and competency in a foreign language. All postsecondary institutions should provide for international and multicultural experiences for the students, depending upon the resources and size of the institution.

At this level, awareness is still an objective, but more indepth training will be necessary. International aspects must be infused in every business education course. Not all students need to be international experts, but all students must have a working knowledge of international issues and an understanding of world interdependence. An important aspect of international education at this level is a narrowing of focus to a specific country so that students will have opportunities to learn more about a country of choice.

Another aspect will be international business study tours in which students can receive a first-hand view of business practices in the countries visited and can develop an appreciation for the cultural differences in other countries.

Of even greater benefit are study-abroad programs in which students study in a country of choice. These programs give students realistic experiences and opportunities to put classroom knowledge into practice.

For a student to become truly competitive in an international workplace, graduate programs will most likely be necessary to provide in-depth study with opportunities to develop conversational skills and to adapt to a particular environment.

Specific objectives and goals at the postsecondary level are as follows:

1. To accept and respect customs of diverse cultures
2. To understand other cultures and adapt to other cultures
3. To apply skills and knowledge in business education to an international setting.

Guidelines for changing to an international business education curriculum. Based upon the global marketplace that exists today and the need for business education to adapt to the needs of the business world, the following guidelines are presented:

1. Infuse intercultural components into all business education classes to expand awareness and to reduce xenophobia (fear of foreigners).
2. Establish advisory committees at local, state, regional, and national levels. These committees should include persons who are knowledgeable in international education and international business.
3. Encourage business educators to become knowledgeable in international education by planning seminars, conferences, and conventions dealing with the topic.
4. Develop a refereed journal devoted to international topics to encourage researchers to become involved in the area.
5. Establish a clearinghouse for storing and disseminating information and publications on international business education to avoid duplication of effort.
6. Unite all interested business education groups into a consortium to build support, to coordinate efforts, and to guide the development of international business education.
7. Build support for an international business education program through research, education, involvement, commitment, and leadership.

CONCLUSION

The question is not whether or when to build support for an international business education program—the question is how. Only through research, education, involvement, commitment, and leadership can a support system succeed in globalizing business education. The Chinese have a word for crisis that can mean either danger or opportunity. The changes that business educators are facing are not dangerous; rather opportunities abound for them to meet the needs of students and businesses by adapting to the international marketplace.

RESOURCES FOR DEVELOPING AN INTERNATIONAL BUSINESS EDUCATION PROGRAM

Many resources, in the form of both publications and organizations, are available to help develop a background of knowledge in international education and international business education. Some of these resources are as follows:

Publications.

Abraham, Yahannan T.; Loveland, Terry L.; Bunn, Radie G. "The Value of International Business Study Tours in Business Education and Internationalization of the Business Curriculum." *NABTE Review* 15:36-38; 1988.

The Admissions Strategist/Recruiting in the 1980s. New York, NY, The College Board, 1987.

"An American Vision for the 1990's." *Fortune Magazine.* March 26, 1990, pp. 14-158.

Blockhus, Wanda. "Research in International Business Education." *Business Education Forum* 44:35-37; February, 1990.

Border, Gretchen K. "The Business Future and its Effect on Business Education." *The Balance Sheet* 70:11-12; May/June 1989.

Callahan, Madelyn, R. "Preparing the New Global Manager." *Training and Development Journal* 43:28-33; March 1989.

Conway, Carol. "Internationalizing Southern Business Degree Programs." *Southern International Perspectives.* Winter 1985.

Conway, Carol. "Setting a Southern International Agenda for 1990-95." *Southern International Perspectives.* February 1990.

Educating Americans for Tomorrow's World: State Initiatives in International Education. National Governors' Association, July 1987.

Federal Register. Government Printing Office. Washington, DC. A daily publication.

Feig, John and Blair, John G. *There is a Difference.* Washington, DC: Meridian House International, 1980.

The Foundation Directory, The Foundation Center, New York, NY.

Giovannini, Mary, and Riley, Connee. "Schools and Business: Forming Productive Partnerships." *The Balance Sheet* 69:4-6; March/April 1988.

Gomez, Adelina M. "Developing Intercultural Communication Skills for the Global Business Community." *Facilitating Communication for Business.* Twenty-sixth Yearbook. Reston, Virginia: National Business Education Association, 1988. Chapter 10, pp. 92-102.

Guidelines for College and University Linkages Abroad. American Council on Education, Washington, DC, 1984.

Guidelines: Incorporating an International Dimension in Colleges and Universities. American Association of State Colleges and Universities, Washington, DC, June 1988.

Hackett, Susan. "Meeting World Marketplace Needs." *Balance Sheet* 66:15-16; March/April 1985.

Hanamura, Steve. "Working with People Who are Different." *Training and Development Journal* 43:110-114; June, 1989.

Harris, Phillip R., and Moran, Robert T. *Managing Cultural Differences,* Second Edition. Houston, TX: Gulf Publishing Co., 1987.

Hoopes, David S., and Ventura, Paul, Eds. *Intercultural Sourcebook: Cross Cultural Training Methodologies.* Chicago, IL: Intercultural Press, Inc., 1979.

IIE Educational Associates Directory. First Edition. Washington, DC: Institute of International Education, 1989.

Institutions and Individuals in International Educational Exchange. National Association for Foreign Student Affairs, Washington, DC, 1989.

"Internationalizing the Curriculum." *National Forum* 48:1-34; Fall 1988.

The International Dimension in U.S. Higher Education: New Directions in Business School/Liberal Arts Cooperation, Proceedings of American Assembly of Collegiate Schools of Business and Association of American Colleges, Washington, DC: Association of American Colleges, 1988.

International Funding Guide. American Association of State Colleges and Universities, Washington, DC, 1985.

The International Responsibility of Higher Education. American Association of State Colleges and Universities, Washington, DC, 1975.

Internationalizing the Curriculum and the Campus. American Association of State Colleges and Universities, Washington, DC, 1983.

Kiplinger, Austin H., and Kiplinger, Knight A. *America in the Global '90s.* Washington, DC: Kiplinger Books, 1990.

Kruzel, Sandra. "Business Education with an International Flavor," *Balance Sheet* 69:10-12; May/June 1988.

LeSourd, Sandra. "Curriculum Development and Cultural Context." *The Educational Forum* 54:205-216; Winter 1990.

McLean, S. Vianne. "Early Childhood Teachers in Multicultural Settings." *The Educational Forum* 54:198-203; Winter 1990.

National Telecommunications and Information Administration. "Comprehensive Study on the Globalization of Mass Media Firms." U.S. Department of Commerce: *Federal Register* 55:5792-5805; February 16, 1990.

Redmann, Donna H., and Davis, Bobbye J. "Ideas for Developing International Literacy." *Business Education Forum* 44:20-22; December 1989.

Rhinesmith, Stephen, and others. "Developing Leaders for the Global Enterprise. *Training and Development Journal* 43:24-34; April 1989.

Storlazzi, Giacinta Bradley. "Cross-Cultural Business Environment." *The Secretary* 44:8-9; Nov./Dec. 1984.

Watters, Kathleen and Conway, Carol. "Internationalizing Education in Southern Universities." *Southern International Perspectives* 15; June 1989.

Willis, David, and Enloe, Walter. "Lessons of International Schools: Global Education in the 1990's." *The Educational Forum* 54:169-183; Winter, 1990.

Without a Nickel: The Challenge of Internationalizing the Curriculum and the Campus. American Association of State Colleges and Universities, Washington, DC, 1983.

Organizations.

Agency for International Development (AID)
320 21st NW
Washington, DC 20006

American Assembly of Collegiate Schools of Business
605 Old Ballas Road, Suite 220
St. Louis, MO 63141-7077

American Association of State Colleges and Universities
One Dupont Circle, Suite 700
Washington, DC 20036

American Council on Education
One Dupont Circle, Suite 800
Washington, DC 20036

Association of American Colleges
1818 R. Street, NW
Washington, DC 20009

Bureau of Educational and Cultural Affairs
U.S. Information Agency
301 Fourth Street SW
Washington, DC 20547

Canadian Association for Future Studies
#302, 100 Gloster Street, Ottawa
Ontario K2P OA4, Canada

Center for International Business
Suite 184
World Trade Center
Dallas, TX 75258

Center for International Education
U.S. Department of Education
Room 3053, 400 Maryland Avenue SW
Washington, DC 20202

Continuing Higher Education Review (Continuum)
   National University Continuing Education Association
One Dupont Circle, NW, Suite 420
Washington, DC 20036

Educational Resources Information Center
U.S. Office of Education
Washington, DC 20202

ERIC Clearinghouse on Adult, Career and Vocational Education
Ohio State University
1960 Keeny Road
Columbus, OH 43210

The Foundation Center
79 5th Ave., 8th Floor
New York, NY 10003

Institute of International Education
809 United Nations Plaza
New York, NY 10017

International Communications Association
Balcones Research Center, 10
100 Burnet Road
Austin, TX 78758

International Council on Education for Teaching
One Dupont Circle, NW
Suite 616
Washington, DC 20036

International Federation of Training and Development Organizations
The Institute of Management Education
7 Westbourne Road
Southport PRS 2HZ England

International Reference and Coordination Centre for Educational Facilities
17 Rue du Cendrier
1201 Geneva, Switzerland

National Association for Foreign Student Affairs
1809 19th Street, NW
Washington, DC 20009

National Governors Association
Hall of the States
444 No. Capital St., NW
Washington, DC 20001

Society for Intercultural Education, Training and Research (SIETAR)
1414 22nd Street
Washington, DC

Society for International Development
1346 Connecticut Ave., NW
Washington, DC 20036

Southern Growth Policies Board
5001 South Miami Blvd.
PO Box 12293
Research Triangle Park
North Carolina 27709

United States Trade Center
Centro de Comericio Estados Unidos
Liverpool 31
06600 Mexico, D.F.

U.S. Department of Commerce
14th St. and Constitution Ave., NW
Washington, DC 20230

U.S. Department of Defense
Department of Defense Dependent Schools (DODDS)
Room 152, Hoffman Building #1
2461 Alexandria, VA 22331

U.S. Department of State
1345 E Street NW
Washington, DC 20520

World Trade Center
2 Canal Street, Suite 2900
New Orleans, LA 70130

World Trade Center Institute
2990 Mesa Verde Drive East
Costa Mesa, CA 92626

World Trade Institute, The
One World Trade Center, 55th Floor
New York, NY 10048

CHAPTER 4
Marketing the International Business Education Program

WANDA BLOCKHUS and G.W. (JIM) MAXWELL
San Jose State University, California

Last year, Frederic Chavé, Jean-Philippe Debeaudoin, Olivier Delbosc, and Frederic Farre, students at INSEEC, a collegiate business school with sites in both Bordeaux and Paris, organized a humanitarian mission to Poland. They enlisted 10 other business schools to join in collecting and distributing 300 tons of food, clothing, and medicine. They persuaded companies including Shell, Renault, and Nestlé to donate gasoline and transportation as well as goods. In March 1990 the students delivered 18 truckloads of food such as corn, peas, tomatoes, paté, biscuits (cookies); baby foods; medicine; and clothing including trousers and rainwear. Seventy students accompanied the goods to Poland and stayed with Polish families for a few days. Three months later two of the student organizers studied for the summer at San Jose State University. When they told their classmates about their project, the American students asked if the French students spoke Polish or if the Poles spoke French. The answer was no; however, they were able to communicate . . . in English.

This story demonstrates that globalization, the buzzword of the eighties, has become a reality in the nineties not only in America but also in far away places with strange sounding names. In a special issue of *Business Week* that focused on "Innovation, the Global Race," the U.S. Department of Commerce pointed out:

> Globalization, of course, means different things to different people. To some, it means exporting products and services. For others, it means new partners in distant markets. Or it can mean shifting asset investments offshore. Now, as information and capital leap across oceans and through time zones at the speed of light, the business and financial worlds have truly become one interlocked global entity.[1]

To meet the challenges of globalization, more and more schools are developing international business education programs. This chapter will discuss how to market such programs—a complex task since there are so many components to consider.

---

[1] *Business Week*, June 15, 1990, p. 9.

RATIONALE FOR INTERNATIONAL BUSINESS EDUCATION PROGRAMS

Communications, transportation, politics, and economics continue to reshape the world. The Bedouin in Saudi Arabia, the television technician in Beijing, and the college student in Australia share at least one thing in common with the people who live and work in the White House. That common element is Cable Network News (CNN). A stock market plunge in Tokyo, an earthquake in San Francisco, an invasion in the Middle East, or an assassination in Columbia is simultaneously telecast around the world. Communications and transportation have shrunk the world. In today's world it seems the only constant is change itself. And the rate of change has accelerated.

PLACE	EVENT	DATE
Germany	Reunification of Germany	1990
USSR & Eastern Bloc	Movement toward market economy	1990's
South Africa	Modified stance on apartheid	1990
Middle East	Iraqi invasion of Kuwait; continued tension	1990
Japan	Search for world markets in new technology	1991
Europe	Free trade among 12 countries: Belgium, Denmark, France, Germany, Greece, Ireland, Italy, Luxembourg, Netherlands, Portugal, Spain, United Kingdom	1992
	Common currency and language predicted	2000
Hong Kong	Colony reverts to People's Republic of China	1997
North America	All trade barriers dropped between Canada and the United States	1998

U.S. products and services are marketed around the world but so are products from other nations as well. Labels on products we buy may read, "Made in China (or Costa Rica, or Madagascar)." The plane we take may be an American carrier such as Delta, TWA, or United, or a foreign carrier such as British Air, Cathay Pacific, or Varig.

In a recent analysis of the Global 1000, *Business Week* ranked companies from Australia, Austria, Belgium, Britain, Canada, Denmark, Finland, France, Hong Kong, Ireland, Italy, Japan, the Netherlands, New Zealand, Norway, Singapore/Malaysia, South Africa, Spain, Sweden, Switzerland, the United States, and West Germany. South Korea, Taiwan, Mexico, and Brazil were excluded only because their stock markets are mostly closed to foreign investors, and their major corporations are often privately owned.

Using market value of stock as the criterion, the analysis revealed the top 10 companies in the world included six Japanese, three American, and one British/Dutch company. The top 10 were Nippon Telegraph and Telephone, IBM, Industrial Bank of Japan, Royal Dutch/Shell, General Electric, Exxon, Sumitomo Bank, Fuji Bank, Toyota Motor, and Mitsui Taiyo Kobe Bank. (Hisashi Shinto, the former chairman of Nippon Telegraph and Telephone, the world's largest company, was convicted in 1990 of accepting bribes for his part in the recruit scandal, the stock and influence peddling case that shook Japan for more than a year and ultimately forced the resignation of Prime Minister Noboru Takeshita. Thus, no country seems immune to scandal.)

Using sales and profits as the criteria, the world's top ranked business firms currently are:

SALES Billions of U.S. Dollars		RANK	PROFITS Billions of U.S. Dollars	
Mitsui	$128	1	IBM	$5.26
Marubeni	123	2	General Motors	4.22
Mitsubishi	122	3	General Electric	3.94
General Motors	110	4	Ford	3.84
C. Itoh	105	5	Daimler Benz	3.80
Sumitomo	97	6	Exxon	2.98
Exxon	95	7	Philip Morris	2.95
Royal Dutch Shell	85	8	British Petroleum	2.92
Ford	83	9	AT&T	2.70
Nissho Iwai	75	10	Fiat	2.65

Business Week, July 16, 1990, p. 111.

The global village looks more like an industrial park according to *Fortune* in its 1990 Global 500 issue. *Fortune* says that we live in an expansive new world of economic interconnections where business roars through borders and time zones. Kenichi Ohmae talks about the Interlinked Economy (ILE) of the triad countries—the United States, Europe, and Japan. Well over half of *Fortune's* Global 500 revenues are from petroleum production and refining, automobile manufacturing, electronics manufacturing, and food processing. Oil companies generated higher revenues and earnings than any other group. Out of the 500 companies, 167 were from the United States and 111 were from Japan, as shown on the chart at the top of page 33.

The United States is No. 1 in 14 out of the 25 industries in the Global 500 including aerospace, computers, and electronics. Impressive as the numbers are, U.S. dominance is slowly eroding. In 1980, 23 U.S. companies made the top 50, compared to five Japanese companies. In 1990 there were 17 American and 20 Japanese companies on the list. The electronics category is particularly noteworthy; of the 46 electronics companies, the United States has 16 and Japan has 15 companies on the list. Two of the top 50 companies are South Korean; Samsung and Daewood. Kotkin and Kishimoto point out that this rise in Asian power generates unease in the West.

COUNTRIES WITH BIGGEST COMPANIES BASED ON SALES

COUNTRY	COMPANIES ON LIST	LARGEST COMPANY
United States	167	General Motors
Japan	111	Toyota Motors
Britain	43	British Petroleum
West Germany	32	Daimler-Benz
France	29	Renault
Sweden	15	Volvo
Canada	13	Canadian Pacific
South Korea	11	Samsung
Australia	10	Elders IXL
Switzerland	10	Nestlé

Fortune, July 30, 1990, p. 265.

EDUCATION FOR BUSINESS

The American Assembly of Collegiate Schools of Business (AACSB) is the professional association and sole accrediting agency for collegiate schools of business and management in the United States. More than 800 organizations belong to AACSB including approximately 650 U.S. colleges and universities, 70 schools overseas and in Canada, 60 major corporations, and a variety of related academic and trade groups. *Management Study Abroad 1989-91*, published by AACSB and the Institute of International Education, indicates that AACSB-affiliated business and management study abroad is offered in the following countries:

EUROPE		AFRICA, SOUTH OF THE SAHARA	WESTERN HEMISPHERE
Austria	Monaco		Argentina
Belgium	Netherlands	Kenya	Brazil
Denmark	Norway	Liberia	Canada
Finland	Poland	Zimbabwe	Columbia
France	Portugal		Costa Rica
Germany	Spain		Ecuador
Greece	Sweden		Mexico
Hungary	Switzerland	**MIDDLE EAST AND NORTH AFRICA**	Panama
Ireland	USSR		Paraguay
Italy	United Kingdom		Peru
	Yugoslavia	Cyprus	Puerto Rico
		Egypt	Venezuela
ASIA AND OCEANIA		Israel	
Australia	Nepal	Turkey	
China/Hong Kong	New Zealand		
India	Singapore		
Japan	Sri Lanka		
Korea	Thailand		

International business education is not limited to AACSB-affiliated collegiate schools, secondary schools, or postsecondary schools. It may include exchange programs, programs within business, travel, overseas periodicals or books, or the lead story on the 6 o'clock TV news.

STUDENTS TO BE SERVED

Developing and marketing a program for international business education is a complex task because of the multiplicity of components to consider. The setting for business education may be secondary (likely grades 9-12), postsecondary, and college-university. The setting may also be in business or in community programs. Developing a marketing strategy involves two steps: (1) determining the target market, and (2) developing the marketing mix, that is, the product (type of education), price (how it will be funded), place

	\multicolumn{7}{c	}{INTERNATIONAL BUSINESS EDUCATION: FOR WHOM? HOW?}
	\multicolumn{2}{c	}{SECONDARY}	\multicolumn{4}{c	}{COLLEGE/UNIVERSITY}	\multicolumn{2}{c	}{BUSINESS/INDUSTRY}
	Unit	Course	Unit	Course	Several Courses	Major	Seminars	Other
American student studying in U.S.								
American student studying abroad								
American student working abroad								
Foreign student studying in U.S.								
Foreign student studying in home country in U.S. program or with U.S. teacher								

(where it will be offered), and promotion (how it will be promoted). The simple matrix below shows there are several groups that are potential clients of international business education, and these are also multiple delivery systems.

If each category of students is linked with each type of delivery system, there are 40 decision points on this matrix. The facets of business education are numerous and complex, making it difficult to approach business education as a singular topic.

International education has been well entrenched in the educational fabric of America for many years. Although international business education came later, it is no newcomer. For example, the International Society for Business Education (ISBE) was founded in Switzerland in 1901. Prominent American business educators attended the annual meetings in Europe long before the U.S. Chapter was formed in 1948.

George Stauss, business professor emeritus at San Jose State University, studied in Germany before World War II at a time when the magnificent Berlin railroad station handled more traffic than any other in all Europe. The division of Germany put the train station in the East, and it became just a hollow shell of its past glory. It remains to be seen whether the reunification of Germany will mean a rebirth for the station.

For many years, the American Church in Paris has served as a home away from home for generations of American students. Overlooking the Seine at 65 Quai d'Orsay, the church is located a short walk from the Eiffel Tower. It was founded so that students and expatriates could have not only a church but a community center. At noon on Sunday, lunch is available and attracts not only Americans but French who are practicing their language skills.

Both authors of this chapter are advocates of international business education and have taught overseas. Jim Maxwell taught in Pakistan, where he was invited to the home of one of his students in a remote village. The student, Akram Chowdry, subsequently studied in the United States and earned an M.B.A. at San Jose State University and a Ph.D. from the University of California, Berkeley. Subsequently, Chowdry founded his own high-tech firm in Silicon Valley, now a successful manufacturer of motherboards. Wanda Blockhus was an exchange professor of business at Queensland University of Technology in Brisbane, Australia. Truly, international business education spans both continents and generations.

Study abroad seems to be on the rise everywhere. Instructors and students across the country participate in international or global education, with business ranking among the top five subjects studied. In a 1988 survey by the Institute of International Education, 707 colleges and universities reported over 48,000 U.S. students had studied abroad. Thirteen colleges and universities reported over 400 students studying abroad, and two, Syracuse University, Syracuse, New York, and Beaver College, Glenside, Pennsylvania, reported over 1,000. The 13 schools with over 400 students are Arizona State, Tempe; University of Arizona, Tucson; Stanford University, Stanford, California; Northern Illinois University, DeKalb; University of Massachusetts, Amherst; University of Minnesota, Minneapolis; Duke University, Durham,

North Carolina; Friends World College, Huntington, New York; Russell Sage Junior College, Albany, New York; Miami University of Ohio, Oxford; Temple University, Philadelphia; Southern Methodist University, Dallas, Texas; and University of Wisconsin, Plattville.

STUDENTS SERVED

School levels. Programs in international business education can be found in the same schools and on the same levels where other programs of business education are currently offered. For example, an increasing number of schools of business in four-year universities, sensing a growing realization of an impending expansion in the global economy, are offering concentrations in international business. Schools of business (among a number of others) that have developed strong emphases in this field are the University of South Carolina in Charlotte, Georgia State University in Atlanta, the University of Michigan at Ann Arbor, and San Francisco State University in California.

Community colleges, private business schools, and high schools, because of their respective roles in the educational pattern, do not tend to offer full-blown programs in international business education. However, courses related to international topics, may be found in many community colleges. Some specialized, innovative programs in international trade or business education are being offered in community colleges and secondary schools.

Three kinds of students are interested in international business education programs: (1) foreign students in U.S. schools; (2) U.S. students in foreign schools; and (3) students, regardless of residence, enrolled in U.S. international business education programs.

Foreign students in the United States. It comes as no surprise that no other country in the world has received more immigrants than has the United States. Currently, the number of persons of all ages moving to the United States exceeds 600,000 annually; and the number has been increasing since the end of World War II in the mid 1940's. Various immigration movements have been observed for over a century. The last one, taking place during the 1970's and 1980's, saw about half a million Vietnamese people enter the United States. The next big immigration wave, during the nineties, could be people from Eastern European countries.

The number of foreign students in U.S. schools is also on the increase. In 1989-90 the Institute of International Education reported that about 386,000 foreign students were enrolled in American schools. The number has been growing steadily since 1954-55 when there were about 34,000 foreign student enrollments. Yet, foreign students account for less than 3 percent of the enrollments in U.S. institutions of higher learning. More than half (about 52 percent) of the foreign students come from Asia. The five countries sending the most students are China, Taiwan, Japan, India, and Korea.

The leading fields of study for foreign students are business and management with engineering a very close second. Third and fourth on the list are mathematics and computer science, respectively. A little over two thirds (68.9 percent) of the foreign students studying in the United States are male; 31.1 percent are female.

A demographic study of foreign students in the United States shows that, in many cases, they are from families of high socioeconomic status. About 73 percent of the foreign students receive their primary funds from personal and family sources. This is probably particularly true for foreign students who come to the United States temporarily for purposes of education rather than for permanent immigration. Many parents of these students believe that American education is superior and that America offers education in fields not readily available overseas. For example, U.S. education in engineering and medicine has a worldwide reputation for excellence.

Profiles of foreign students based on both psychographic and demographic data are complex. The motivations that cause foreign students to study in the United States are varied. Large numbers of students in our unsettled world may be trying to escape something—unstable government, economic poverty, blatant racial discrimination, mistreatment, or political persecution.

Foreign students must make many adjustments when they come to the United States. One adjustment, for example, is to our American system of education. Our system, in contrast to many of those in foreign lands, includes greater local-school participation by teachers in setting standards and preparing examinations. Our system strives to encourage creativity in students. We may "forgive" students who do poorly at many grade levels by permitting them to continue to higher grade levels of education (at least through a bachelor's degree). We tend to utilize instructional delivery systems that emphasize classwork as opposed to the emphasis on individual study is often used in many foreign educational systems. We attempt to educate "all of the students of all the people."

Foreign students must also, of course, adjust to American mores. Adjustments of this type can be relatively minor for students coming from countries similar to the United States, such as Canada, the British Isles, Australia, New Zealand, and possibly Western Europe. On the other extreme, learning to fit into our lifestyle can border on being traumatic for students from Asia, Africa, the Middle East, and South America; these students may experience a distinct culture shock.

English has increasingly become the worldwide universal language. But students from countries where English is not the primary language obviously face a monumental task in learning to speak, read, and receive instruction in English. The English language is difficult to learn with its many rules and seemingly even greater number of exceptions. Add to this the need to learn slang expressions that are universally spoken by Americans, and the result can be a formidable challenge for foreign students. One foreign student having heard an overworked American lamenting that he was "snowed under" also became overworked and was heard lamenting that he was "under the snow!" However, students from most foreign countries have developed the ability to speak English (with various levels of proficiency) as well as their own language. Most foreign students have a "running start" on English.

Foreign students tend to be very polite, especially to teachers, often exceeding American students in this aspect.

Although progress could probably be described as uneven, it appears to be a fair statement to say that American women have progressed in the treatment they receive and the opportunities they have gained during the past two decades. Their status appears, at the very least, to be superior to that granted women in many foreign countries. Attitudes toward women by foreign students may therefore differ markedly from attitudes held by U.S. residents.

Religions differ throughout the world. In the United States, most church members belong to either Catholic or Protestant denominations. Although visitors from other lands may very well be Catholic or Protestant, they are perhaps more likely to profess Buddhist, Muslim (Islam), Hindu, Jewish, or other religious faith.

U.S. students in foreign schools. Many U.S. students engage in foreign study by enrolling in undergraduate and graduate programs sponsored by U.S. collegiate institutions. Others enroll directly in foreign schools, either in those schools' regular undergraduate and graduate degree programs or in special programs established just for foreign students. Overseas secondary school programs are also available, mostly during summers.

Whatever form of foreign study a student may contemplate, it is well to investigate carefully the merits of the various institutions being considered. Particularly determine whether credits from foreign institutions are accepted by the U.S. institution from which a degree is sought. And, quite obviously, it is necessary to determine whether time deadlines established by foreign schools as well as their stated entrance requirements can be met.

The number of U.S. students attending school in foreign countries has risen dramatically during the past two decades. In 1988, the Institute of International Education, while granting that data was not available for all American students studying abroad in all types of schools, found that a total of 48,483 students received academic credit in U.S. institutions after returning from study abroad.

- Most students (77 percent) studied in Western Europe. The leading host countries were United Kingdom (29 percent), France (14 percent), Spain (9 percent), Italy (8 percent), and Germany (6 percent).
- The most prevalent fields of study were liberal arts (18 percent), foreign languages (17 percent), social studies (14 percent), business and management (11 percent), and humanities (8 percent).
- Most (37 percent) of these students stayed for one semester, the summer only (28 percent), or a full academic year (18 percent).
- About two thirds (64 percent) of these students were female; about one third (36 percent) were male.

Why do American students study overseas? Some wish simply to experience living and studying in a foreign land—to observe foreign mores, living styles, language, historical sights, religion, music, recreation, holidays, and economic standards.

Some wish to prepare for careers in foreign lands. They may wish to work for a U.S. business firm in a foreign country, a foreign business firm, the U.S. government in a foreign land, or a foreign government. Other students, having discovered the increasing importance of international relationships and involvements in the world (especially in the world of business), wish to gain a greater understanding and knowledge about these developments.

When U.S. students study overseas they should be aware that they are truly ambassadors for the United States. Our country is generally admired throughout the world, even if we are not universally loved/liked. Students' behavior has the potential of improving attitudes toward the United States.

For all students studying overseas the importance of becoming proficient in the language of the country being visited must be stressed. The value of foreign study may very well rest on students' abilities to understand the lectures, read the assignments, and engage in discussions with other students. And needless to say, residents of host nations are favorably impressed by visitors with good language skills.

A number of other general matters that should be investigated carefully by students contemplating foreign study are: costs (including fluctuating exchange rates); types of housing and meals available; scholarships available; passports as well as any visas and vaccinations needed; health insurance; transportation; and information about mores and lifestyles in the foreign land. Generally it is not recommended that students attempt to obtain employment while studying overseas.

Students enrolled in U.S. international business education programs. A U.S. school that offers an international business education program at any school level will very likely attract both foreign students and U.S. students interested in some aspect of foreign business. This factor of two types of student enrollments can have major implications in setting goals for the program. Consideration must therefore be given to the needs, challenges, and goals of both types of students.

STRATEGIES FOR ACHIEVING AN INTERDISCIPLINARY PROGRAM

If an international business education program is to be successful, it needs widespread support within the school. One way to generate that support is through an interdisciplinary program. At the secondary school level that would mean involving teachers in areas outside business education such as foreign languages, English, math, and social studies. At the college-university level, it could mean instructors in almost every discipline across campus. If a new program of international business is to be set up, then representatives from as many disciplines as possible should be a part of the planning process. If an existing program is being expanded, key people should be invited to informational meetings, asked to serve on committees, and/or provide input in other ways. Besides teachers and administrators, other stakeholders in an international business education program could be tapped for advice and assistance. Examples of resources in a community might include service clubs such as Rotary Club, city or town officials involved in sister city programs, and foundations that could provide seed money. Other consultants might be business people, athletes, or musicians who have lived, traveled, or performed abroad.

RESOURCES

Early in the planning and development stages of an international business education program, existing agencies should be studied for mutual goals and the assistance they may be able to provide. The U.S. Department of Commerce has a wealth of useful data, and a starting point might be a visit to one of its district offices located in 68 U.S. cities to sort through the vast amount of data on overseas business climate, worldwide publications, overseas trade shows, regional seminars, and other pertinent information.

AGENCIES INVOLVED IN INTERNATIONAL EDUCATION

Many agencies are involved in international education. Some are large, operating in many countries around the world. Most are nonprofit. Some have large staffs, others have more limited resources. Five such agencies involved in international education are described below.

Institute of International Education (IIE) is a private, nonprofit educational institute founded in 1919 with headquarters at 809 United Nations Plaza, New York. It also has offices in Washington, D.C., Atlanta, Chicago, Houston, San Francisco, and overseas in Hong Kong, Jakarta, Mexico City, Harar, and Barbados. IIE has over 600 U.S. college and university members. IIE assists the U.S. Information Agency in administering Fulbright grants for both U.S. and foreign graduate students at the predoctoral level. It manages some 200 educational programs that benefit approximately 10,000 men and women from over 150 nations each year. IIE publications serve as standard guides to international study, and its research reports are widely read. IIE collaborated with the American Assembly of Collegiate Schools of Business in publishing *Management Study Abroad*.

Council on International Educational Exchange (CIEE) was founded in 1947 to actively promote and sponsor international educational exchanges and provide services to academic institutions and youth-serving agencies. CIEE is located at 205 E. 42nd Street, New York. It administers several study programs in cooperation with member institutions including language programs in the USSR, China, Japan, Indonesia, and several places in Europe. It sponsors exchange programs between secondary schools in the United States and schools in England, France, Germany, Israel, Japan, Spain, Venezuela, Italy, Austria and Costa Rica. It arranges low-cost flights for groups and individuals to Asia, Europe, and Latin America. Over 200 opportunities world-wide for 12- to 18-year olds are described in *The Teenagers Guide to Study, Travel, and Adventure Abroad*. Additional programs are listed in *Vacation Study Abroad*.

American Field Services Intercultural Programs (AFS), located at 313 E. 43rd Street, New York, promotes international understanding primarily through an exchange of secondary school students. It conducts a variety of exchange programs that provide family living experiences to enhance the impact of intercultural experiences, program quality, cultural training, and global education.

International Society for Business Education (ISBE) is affiliated with the National Business Education Association, 1914 Association Drive, Reston, Virginia. The international secretary is Erik Lange, Hunderupvej 122A1V DK 5230, Odense, Denmark. Members include educators involved in economic training, heads of in-company training programs, firms, universities, and schools at various levels. ISBE aims to promote the international exchange of ideas and experiences in business fields. The 1991 annual meeting will be held in England in 1992, British Columbia, Canada in 1993, Germany and Norway in 1994.

Experiment in International Living/School for International Training, located in Brattleboro, Vermont, was founded in 1932. EIL provides educational experiences combining predeparture orientation and intensive language training, homestay living as a member of a family abroad, and a period for travel through the host country. It conducts summer programs in 27 countries of Africa, Asia, Europe, Latin America, and the United States.

PROMOTION OF THE PROGRAM

When promoting the international business education program, one should consider international events as well as utilize both internal and external methods. A local advisory committee of individuals who are knowledgeable, committed, and reflect the international business education needs of the local community as well as the region, nation, and global market may be utilized. Student interaction with local businesses involved in international trade can bring reality to the concepts of international business.

International events. The geographical location of the school as well as the nationality makeup of the students can suggest international events to use as a focus for promotion. For example, although foreign students can be found just about everywhere in the United States, special nationalities seem to be attracted to certain areas—many Asians and Hispanics to California and Texas, Scandinavians to Minnesota, Czechoslovakians and Irish to Illinois, Puerto Ricans to New York, and Cubans to Florida. Ethnic holidays can be highlighted through promotional efforts aimed at international business education programs. For example, Hispanics' Cinco de Mayo, commemorating Mexico's victory over an invading French army, is celebrated May 5 with colorful festivals. On July 14 the French celebrate Bastille Day, the day in 1789 when the people of Paris attacked and captured the Bastille; this holiday is equivalent to our own Independence Day, July 4. Each spring Muslims observe Ramadan, the holy month of fasting, when they must not eat or drink from dawn to sunset. A three-day Festival of the Breaking of the Fast comes at the end of the fast. People in the British Commonwealth observe Victoria Day on May 24, the birthday of Queen Victoria.

As major business and political developments occur, they can be a focus for publicity. During 1990, for example, many Eastern European countries, as well as the Soviet Union were moving away from communism and toward democracy and capitalism. Even major day-to-day news events can serve as points of reference for publicizing the international business education program.

Internal forms of promotion. Many internal media are available for promoting the program within the school, for example, the school newspaper, posters (handmade or commercial travel posters from travel agencies and airlines), contests, t-shirts, tables with information and staffed by students, and brochures.

External forms of promotion. An open house featuring various facets of the international business education program can be very effective, especially if a strategy is developed with the goal of in-depth contact with the public. Attractive brochures can be developed and mailed to a strategically targeted audience, including parents and community leaders.

REFERENCES

American Assembly of Collegiate Schools of Business, *Management Study Abroad.* New York: AACSB and Institute on International Education. 1989-91.

Dickey, Christopher, *Expats: Travels in Arabia from Tripoli to Teheran.* As reported in "At Play in the Garden of Allah," *Image,* a supplement to the *San Francisco Examiner.* October 7, 1990.

Encyclopedia of Associations. Detroit: Gale Research, Inc. 1990.

"Ex-NTT Chairman Found Guilty in Recruit Company Case," *Wall Street Journal.* October 10, 1990.

"Global 500." *Fortune.* July 15, 1990.

"Global 1000." *Business Week.* July 26, 1990.

"Innovation, the Global Race," (Special issue). *Business Week.* June 15, 1990.

Institute on International Education, OPEN DOORS 1988-89, *Report on International Education Exchange.* New York: IIE. 1989.

Kotkin, Joel and Yoriko Kishimoto, *The Third Century, America's Resurgence in the Asian Era.* New York: Ivy (Ballantine Books). 1988.

Ohmae, Kenichi, *The Borderless World.* New York: Harper. 1990.

Porter, E. Michael, *Competitive Advantage of Nations.* New York: Free Press. 1990.

Toffler, Alvin, *Power Shift.* New York: Bantam Books. 1990.

Zikopoulos, Marianthi, Editor, *U.S. Students Abroad.* New York: Institute of International Education. 1988.

CHAPTER 5
Methods of Internationalizing Basic Business and Economics Courses

THOMAS B. DUFF
University of Minnesota, Duluth

The rationale for the current focus on internationalizing the business curriculum is to help graduates be prepared to function as effective producers, consumers, and citizens in the global economy of the 1990's and beyond.

While it may be tough to come up with ideas for discussing international topics or integrating international units in some components of the business education curriculum, that is not a problem in the basic business and economics component. In fact, the general business, consumer economics, and economics textbooks used in business education courses have contained one or more chapters on international trade or other international topics for years. However, these chapters were almost always at the end and, no matter where they were presented in the text, were the ones most likely to be left out by the teachers. That has changed in recent years and basic business and economics teachers use these chapters and the wealth of other materials now available to enrich their courses with international topics.

Many different topics and approaches can be used to internationalize activities in basic business and economics courses. The focus of this chapter will be on how teachers might use one of these general topics—international trade—as the basis for many learning and teaching activities. Therefore, this chapter will present thoughts, ideas, and suggestions related to using international trade as a topic for internationalizing basic business and economics courses. First, there will be a brief discussion of the development of international trade and the global business community. The second section presents suggestions as to which international trade concepts need to be taught. The source of most of these ideas is a chapter written by the author in *Business in an Information Economy*, a 1990 textbook developed for high school basic business and economics courses.[1] The third section presents ideas and identifies sources of other ideas on how to teach international trade concepts effectively.

---

[1] Graf, David; Church, Olive D. and Duff, Thomas B. *Business in an Information Economy.* New York: Gregg Division, McGraw-Hill Publishing Company 1990. pp. 93-111.

DEVELOPMENT OF INTERNATIONAL TRADE AND THE GLOBAL BUSINESS COMMUNITY

Although nations of the world have always traded or bartered goods, there has been a significant increase in international trade during the years since the end of World War II. Currently, more nations than ever before are involved in trading with each other. In addition, these nations are trading more goods and services than ever before. It is because of this active international trade that many people today prefer to focus on the global economy rather than on any single national economy.

Developing world trade. As you may recall from your study of world history, one of the reasons countries financed explorers was their hope that the explorers would find new products and trading partners. Marco Polo's expeditions to China and the other areas of the Far East were responsible for the beginning of trade between Europe and that area. Others sailed the seas in search of new trade and ended up discovering new territory. One of the primary benefits of finding and claiming new territory was the fact that the resources from the new area could be used at home or traded for other items. Today, nations still send representatives to other parts of the world to discover trade possibilities. In fact, many nations are developing world trade centers specifically designed to encourage and help set up world trade. There are currently over 50 such centers either completed, under construction, or in various stages of design in major population centers such as Beijing, Moscow, and New York, and even in less heavily populated areas such as Cedar Rapids, Iowa, and Toledo, Ohio. Although modern trade representatives do not discover new lands, they continue to explore for new trading partners.

World trade now easier. During the 20th century there has been a rapid increase in the number of independent nations established in the world, adding to the complexity of political and trade relationships. During the century four general developments, involving both technological advancements and political agreements, have made it easier for nations to conduct international trade.

First, **technological advances** have made it possible to transport large quantities of natural resources and finished goods rapidly and safely. Second, **improved communication technology** of the 20th century has made it possible for nations and business firms to communicate quickly and accurately. Electronic and satellite technology makes it possible for the over 170 nations of the world to communicate with each other in a matter of seconds or minutes.

Third, world trade has increased this century because **political agreements** specifically designed to achieve this goal have been signed and honored. Perhaps the most significant is the General Agreement on Tariffs and Trade (GATT), which was originally signed by the United States and 22 other countries in 1947 but now has been agreed to by over 75 countries. More recently signed agreements will establish free trade between the United States and Canada and will set up a single European Economic Community in 1992.

These other similar agreements breaking down political barriers have been very positive influences in increasing the amount of international trade. Finally, the **gradual thawing of the "Cold War"** relations between non-communist and communist nations has helped increase international trade between these nations. It is expected that the recent dramatic political and economic changes occurring in many of the former communist nations will be a stimulus for even more international trade.

The global business community. The increased emphasis on international trade that has occurred over the years has affected business activity in the United States and other nations of the world. Many farmers and business firms now sell their goods and services to foreign countries. Our nation now faces stiff competition for world sales of food, clothing, automobiles, electronic components, and many other goods and services from countries such as Japan, Korea, Taiwan, West Germany, Canada, and some of the South American countries. New business firms dealing solely in international trade have been developed. Large business firms have taken over firms located in other countries or have established separate firms in other countries. And many firms now have special divisions or departments for conducting their international trade activities.

Business firms that manufacture motor vehicles, agricultural equipment, and electronic equipment have been some of the most active international traders in the world. General Motors Corporation, John Deere & Company, Caterpillar, Inc., IBM, and General Electric Company are among U.S. firms participating in these activities. Firms that sell agricultural or petroleum products and other natural resources in raw form or that process them in some way before marketing them are also active international traders. U.S. firms leading the way in these areas are Cargill Inc., Pillsbury Co., Exxon Corp., and Texaco Inc. And firms providing communications, banking, utilities, and transportation—services required to support the international exchange of goods—have also had increased activity in the international arena. The leading U.S. companies in these areas are American Telephone and Telegraph Co., ITT Corp., Citibank, and Bank of America. Based on total dollars of sales revenue, some of the leading foreign firms in these markets are Toyota (Japan) and Daimler-Benz (West Germany) in motor vehicles, Phillips (Netherlands) and Matsushita Electric (Japan) in electronics, Royal Dutch/Shell Group (Netherlands) and British Petroleum (Great Britain) in petroleum, NTT (Japan) and Tokyo Electric Power (Japan) in communications and utilities.

The United States has spent billions of taxpayer dollars to support international trade activities between U.S. firms and organizations and their trading partners throughout the world. Large amounts have been spent in direct foreign aid to the governments of the nations that are our trading partners, but even more has been spent to set up and operate government units here and abroad to encourage and monitor international trade. Clearly the United States has played a dominant role in international trade for many years. Even though other nations are now providing much stiffer competition, and our share of exports into the international market is slipping, the United

States is still among the export leaders in the world. Further, the U.S. market is still considered to be the major market for consumer goods by other nations of the world. And, while the overall balance of trade and the trade balance with some specific nations is negative, there will continue to be a great deal of emphasis put on international trade by the U.S. government and U.S. business firms. Therefore, it is important that today's high school graduates be familiar with and understand some basic concepts related to international trade.

WHICH INTERNATIONAL TRADE CONCEPTS NEED TO BE TAUGHT

Generally speaking, teaching and learning about international trade consists largely of teaching and learning how basic economic principles apply to international activities. Since the foundation or core of the basic business and economics curriculum is teaching and learning about basic economic principles and how they are applied to various situations, activities related to international trade can be included as simply another step or twist to these areas. Choosing which of the many concepts related to international trade should be taught is in itself an exercise in applying the basic economic principle of opportunity cost and tradeoffs. The amount of time available for focusing on international trade is usually scarce relative to the amount of content one might want to teach. Therefore, teachers must make choices about which international trade concepts to teach in the limited time available.

Total agreement does not exist among basic business and economics educators about how much time to use or what to teach about international trade in the business curriculum. However, there seems to be general agreement that, at a minimum, students should be familiar with and understand each of the concepts identified and discussed in the following sections. Wanda Blockhus presents several ideas related to this subject as she discusses what students know, what they need to know, and presents some other ideas about what should be taught in international business in a February 1990 article in *Business Education Forum*.[2] Since there is only room for a brief discussion of the four basic concepts included here, the reader who needs more explanation and examples to illustrate the concepts should read one or more of the references identified throughout the chapter.

Why international trade occurs. International trade occurs for exactly the same reason that two individuals might trade things with each other. Both parties believe they will benefit or acquire some advantage from making the trade. The same principle holds true for exchanges between businesses, states, and nations. They will not normally trade with each other unless they believe that what they receive will benefit them more than keeping or consuming the good or service they possess. Students should understand this concept and the fact that the exchange of goods and services in international trade is discussed in terms of exports and imports. They should also be familiar

---

[2]Blockhus, Wanda. "Research in International Business Education." Business Education Forum 44:35-38; February 1990.

with what types of goods and services account for the largest share of U.S. exports and imports and which nations are our major trading partners for them. All nations actively seek opportunities to export and import, but the individuals who make decisions about what will be exported and imported carefully weigh the advantages and disadvantages involved and base their final decision on whether or not the trade will benefit their citizens.

When economists discuss why trade takes place between nations or different regions in a nation, they use the concepts of absolute and comparative advantage to explain it. Basic business and economics students should learn about these concepts as well. When one nation or a region can produce goods or services at less cost than another, it has an absolute advantage in producing them. The absolute advantage might be present because of climate or soil conditions, proximity to natural resources, the quantity and quality of the labor supply in the area, availability of transportation links or power supply. Comparative advantage is a bit more subtle. A nation is considered to have a comparative advantage when it can produce several goods or services more efficiently than another nation but has a greater advantage in producing one rather than others. Stated another way, nations should only produce those items they can make less expensively than others; they should not produce those items they can buy more cheaply elsewhere. For example, Japan produces electronic goods and leaves the production of jeans to the United States even though it can produce both products more cheaply than the United States. Japan has a greater margin of efficiency over the United States in producing electronic goods than in producing jeans; therefore, the opportunity cost of diverting resources away from producing electronic goods and into producing jeans is very high. The Japanese have a comparative advantage in producing electronic goods and a comparative disadvantage in producing jeans.

Students should be able to identify examples of absolute advantage and to explain that nations will usually specialize in producing as much as possible of the goods or services for which they have an absolute advantage. Similarly, they should be able to explain the principle of comparative advantage, understand that most international trade occurs because of this principle, and identify examples of such trade situations. Further, they should understand that, from a purely economic perspective, it would be best if there were no barriers to free trade in the world. If this condition existed, each nation could specialize in producing and exporting the goods and services in which it had either an absolute or comparative advantage and could import goods and services in which its advantage was either nonexistent or less than that of other nations. If there were free trade among all nations, then world production, world economic growth, and efficiency in the use of the world's limited resources would be maximized. As a result, everyone in the world would have access to more goods and services.

How U.S. companies conduct international trade. U.S. companies have several options for conducting international trade. Students should be able to describe these methods, to identify advantages and disadvantages related to each, and to give examples of each. They should know that some of the companies involved in international trade are based solely in the United

States; others are based solely in a foreign country; and still others involve a combination of these two possibilities. Among the most popular methods of international trade used by firms located only in the United States are exporting, foreign licensing, marketing agreements, and joint ownership. Companies may export directly to overseas importers, or they may participate indirectly by selling their goods to local buyers who specialize in exporting. The major soft drink and fast food firms have entered into licensing agreements with companies in other nations, permitting them to manufacture one or more products abroad. A company can also keep its production facilities in the United States but set up marketing agreements for selling its products in other nations. Finally, some United States companies set up partnerships with foreign companies or governments because some nations such as Japan and Mexico will not allow companies controlled by foreigners to be physically located there. However, they will allow joint ownership arrangements if the foreign company does not hold controlling interest.

Multinational companies are defined as those that manufacture and sell their products in foreign countries. Many U.S. firms are multinationals today because there are lucrative opportunities for international trade if they are willing to locate a part of their organizations abroad. Companies that are multinational organize their production so they specialize in producing different product lines in different countries. Because they are able to locate their manufacturing facilities near both raw materials and people or companies that will buy their products, they are able to decrease transportation and other costs. Today's basic business and economics students should know what is involved in offshore manufacturing, why companies use it, and some of the social issues it raises. A definite move is evolving toward the production of services as well as goods through offshore arrangements. Foreign companies also use offshore manufacturing. For example, Toyota and Nissan employ U.S. workers at plants in the United States.

How international trade is financed. Although export and import activities are referred to as international "trade," very little actual barter or trade of goods and services takes place. Almost all exports and imports are actually exchanged for payment rather than for other goods and services.

To help understand how international trade is financed and to prepare themselves to make personal consumption decisions as tourists in foreign countries, students should be familiar with foreign exchange and foreign exchange rates. They should know that the foreign exchange rate for the various currencies is generally determined by supply and demand just as prices are determined for other commodities in a free market situation. Thus, the values of currencies are constantly changing, and making decisions about when and how to make or receive payment for international trade can be very complicated. Daily reports of the foreign exchange rate for the U.S. dollar and other selected currencies from around the world are reported in the financial section of most daily newspapers. Students should be familiar with these reports on the value of the dollar and be aware of the importance of such reports to business persons and others interested in the financing of international trade.

Students also need to learn how a nation's balance of trade is determined, how and why trade surpluses or deficits occur, and the difference between a nation's balance of trade and balance of payments. They should know that the U.S. balance of trade has been unfavorable for more than 10 years, some of the consequences of this prolonged trade deficit, some of the reasons for the situation, and some of the steps that are available for decreasing the size of the deficit. Finally, students should be aware that the balance of trade lets a nation know how it is doing in trading goods and services with the rest of the world. While that is important, many business and financial persons feel the balance of payments is more important since it provides information on the demand for and supply of currencies in foreign exchange markets.

How nations restrict and encourage international trade. While most economists agree that there should be unrestricted or free trade among the nations of the world, that is not the case. Students should realize that the world market for goods and services is similar to that within the United States; it is not a completely free, competitive market. All nations of the world have policies related to exports and imports. These policies almost always restrict imports and encourage exports. Competition from imported goods should benefit consumers by providing them more choice, better quality, and lower prices. However, when consumers buy imported goods rather than similar goods produced at home, economic activity is increased abroad rather than at home. Students need to know that there are individuals or groups in all nations who feel there should be restrictions on importing certain goods and services in order to protect the companies and workers who produce similar goods or services at home. They should also be made aware of the fact that the United States and other nations sometimes restrict imports from or exports to nations because of political differences. The United States and other nations have restricted trade with South Africa because of its apartheid policy, for example; and the United States has limited trade with the Soviet Union, Cuba, and Panama in recent years as a result of political disagreements. Students should be asked to discuss and analyze the tradeoffs related to restricting trade of certain goods and services in order to protect home industries or to achieve political goals, so they begin to see that international trade involves some complicated social issues.

In addition to knowing why nations restrict or encourage trade, students should know some of the ways this is accomplished. They should be familiar with and understand how tariffs, quotas, special labeling, detailed tests and inspections, customs delays, and embargos are used to specifically prevent or discourage trade. They should also know that several hundred free-trade zones have been developed throughout the world to create designated areas within these countries where foreign goods can be assembled, processed, or stored free of tariffs in order to encourage international trade. Similarly, they should be aware that some nations actively work to encourage international trade by making political agreements, such as the GATT, the United States-Canadian free trade agreement, and the agreement to create a single European economic community and market by 1992. Students should understand that some barriers to international trade are the result of cultural differences rather than planned efforts to restrict trade. Differences in languages, customs, and political climate are all factors that tend to restrict trade among nations.

While studying and learning about these and any other topics related to international trade students should be helped to recognize that costs and benefits are always hard to measure and evaluate in both the short run and the long run, and that this is an even more difficult task when analyzing issues related to world trade. There may be valid logical, social, political and national security reasons for national leaders and policymakers to make decisions restricting trade in various ways despite the recommendation by economists that they should always act in ways that support free world trade.

HOW INTERNATIONAL TRADE CONCEPTS CAN BE TAUGHT EFFECTIVELY

Deciding what to teach about international trade is only the first step. The next step is to decide how to teach the concepts selected. As is the case with all teaching, a variety of methods need to be used to teach about international trade. Although there are others to be sure, three of the better sources of ideas for teaching about international trade are the instructor's manuals accompanying basic business and economics textbooks, the limited number of basic business and economics teaching methods texts available, and publications from the Joint Council on Economic Education (2 Park Avenue, New York, NY 10016).

Prior knowledge of economic concepts is helpful but not required of students as they learn about international trade. The basic concept of economizing, which includes many basic assumptions of economic analysis, can be used as a tool throughout the study of this topic. Economizing has to do with making choices in various situations. Simply stated, economizing is the process of identifying and evaluating tradeoffs among the costs and benefits related to various alternatives, and choosing the one alternative that is judged to provide the greatest benefit-to-cost ratio in a given situation. This basic concept can be applied in more subtle and complex ways depending on the situation, but it can be used consistently by students as they study about the economic choices involved in international trade activities.

As suggested earlier in the chapter, basic business and economics teachers could quite naturally extend the use of economic analysis to help students learn about international trade. In an introductory section of a Joint Council on Economic Education publication on international trade, Ankrim states that the "basic structure" of economic analysis "can be broken into three parts: terminology, theory, and data."[3] He goes on to suggest that all three parts are needed; none can stand alone. Ankrim believes that before analyzing any problem it is necessary to have a basic understanding of the terminology or words used to define the problem. Students cannot begin to analyze the causes of the U.S. balance-of-trade problems if they don't know what the term

---

[3]Ankrim, Ernest D. "Understanding World Trade—An Economic Perspective." *Master Curriculum Guide in Economics Teaching Strategies, International Trade* (Secondary). New York: Joint Council on Economic Education, 1988. p. 3.

"balance of trade" means and how it is different from "balance of payments." While learning definitions does not equate to understanding, knowing terminology will enable students to better understand what others are telling them and to explain exactly what they want to say to others about international trade.[4]

Ankrim, like most other economic educators, believes that there are some basic "clusters" of economic concepts that form the basis for nearly all of the teaching strategies one might use to help students learn about international trade. He suggests that using illustrations from scarcity and choice, opportunity costs, rationing and incentives, laws of supply and demand, and gains from voluntary exchange can be used to analyze and better understand much of human behavior. Focusing on individual economizing behavior will help students to understand why individuals make the choices they do and will enable them to better understand why groups of people engage in international trade. Finally, students need to learn how to find, analyze, and use data to measure what is happening in world trade. In Ankrim's words, "basic information about the existence, nature, and magnitude of world trade is necessary to appreciate why the economic way of analyzing this activity is valuable."[5] Data and information are needed to help anyone who is interested know the dimensions of world trade.

Anyone who is teaching any aspect of international trade should obtain a copy of the *International Trade (Secondary)* publication from the Joint Council on Economic Education's Master Curriculum Series. It contains 23 separate lessons related to world trade, global economics, and economic reasoning. Each lesson includes all the necessary student materials, and teachers may reproduce them without violating copyright protection laws. A variety of instructional techniques are used in the lessons including debates, case studies, simulations, worksheets, class surveys, writing projects, graphing exercises, data analysis, and class discussions. The lessons vary in the level of economic sophistication required of the students, but warnings to the teacher at the start of each lesson indicate what, if any, prior learning is required for the lesson. Finally, "most lessons require students to be both active participants in the learning process and reflective thinkers about what has taken place."[6] An additional source of ideas is a chapter in the *1987 NBEA Yearbook* by Manzer. One part of this chapter is devoted to a discussion of "what new teaching strategies are available to accommodate the increasing complexity of economics facing teachers of business education courses."[7] In this part of the chapter Manzer presents teaching-strategies updates for teaching fundamental economic concepts, microeconomic concepts, macroeconomic concepts, and international economic concepts.

---

[4] *Op. cit.* pp. 3-7.

[5] *Op. cit.* p. 5.

[6] *Master Curriculum Guide in Economics Teaching Strategies, International Trade (Secondary).* New York: Joint Council on Economic Education, 1988. 171 pp.

[7] Manzer, John P. "Economic Awareness for a Changing World." *Business Education for a Changing World.* Yearbook No. 25. Washington, D.C.: National Business Education Association, 1987. Chapter 11, pp. 122-133.

The preceding paragraphs present some ideas and sources for other ideas related to how to teach basic business and economics students about international trade. While it is not discussed here, it is recognized that there are also many opportunities to integrate the use of computer-based teaching and learning activities into the teaching of international trade. As is true for teaching any topic, the major factor determining the effectiveness of any activity will be the teacher. Anyone who is interested in and enthused about international trade, has a relatively good understanding and appreciation for economics, is willing to try new and different activities in the classroom, and is not easily discouraged or deterred by some minor problems that will invariably occur when using activities for the first time will be successful at teaching international trade.

SUMMARY

While it may be difficult to integrate the teaching of international topics in some parts of the business education curriculum, it is a natural to include them in the basic business and economics component. Although there are many topics to choose from, international trade can be used as the central theme for teaching and learning about the global economy in this component of the curriculum. Most of the tried and proven teaching methods used to teach basic economics concepts can be used to successfully teach about international trade.

CHAPTER 6
Methods of Internationalizing Business Communication Courses

BOBBYE J. DAVIS and DONNA H. REDMANN
Southeastern Louisiana University, Hammond, Louisiana

Effective communication in our global, interdependent, multi-cultured world is very involved and requires skills possessed by very few people. To address this need, many institutions throughout the country are requiring that international communication be incorporated into their curriculum. In addition, the American Assembly of Collegiate Schools of Business (AACSB) now requires that the business curriculum be internationalized.

The intent of this chapter is to provide strategies for incorporating international concepts into a business communication course by offering suggestions on what to teach, how to integrate, how to instruct, and how to evaluate.

CONTENT FOR INTERNATIONALIZING BUSINESS COMMUNICATION

There is an enormous amount of information available for use in internationalizing the business communication course. A teacher will have to make decisions on what to teach based on students' needs and interests, considering class time constraints. After presenting the rationale for including international topics and analyzing the United States culture, instructors may choose from among a variety of topics in the areas of cultural differences, language differences, and nonverbal communication.

Rationale for learning international communication. Introducing students to the necessity of acquiring international business communication skills can be accomplished easily by stressing the current status of global interdependency among nations. In an international situation, cultures, customs, and ways of thinking play a major role in effective communication. In addition, the influence of international trade on business communication and vice versa, the problems that may occur when communication skills are lacking, and the effects of various subcultures within a country will reveal a sound rationale for pursuing the topic.

The degree of U.S. business involvement in other economies and the level of involvement of other countries in the United States substantiate the requirement for the study of international business communication. During the past twenty years, world trade expanded from billions to trillions of dollars. Lack of sensitivity to other cultures and inadequate training for those who communicate with people from other cultures can cost a company thousands and sometimes millions of dollars in negotiations and purchases, sales and contracts, and customer relations, thereby possibly weakening both productivity and profitability.

An abundance of information relating to international business activity is supplied by daily newspapers, periodicals, radio, and television. Alerting students to the extent and importance of international trade issues through the use of these media should not only motivate them to study the topic but provide sources of current information as well.

Americans are already involved in cross-cultural communication. In recent years, immigrants from Latin America, China, Vietnam, Korea, the Caribbean, and Mexico have entered the United States either legally or illegally—all bringing their own unique culture. Miscommunication can occur easily in this "melting pot" of cultures when the communicators are assumed to be products of similar cultures.

Synonyms for *international* are *global, multinational, global village, intercultural, cross-culture, globalization,* and *transnational.* Related terms include *sharing the code, ethnic culture, macroculture, microculture,* and *subculture.* A knowledge of these terms relating to international activities improves students' understanding of reading materials and media messages.

Understanding the United States culture. Effective cross-culture communicators must be able to analyze another culture and compare that culture with their own. To make such a comparison requires that communicators must first know their own culture and the perceptions others have of that culture.

Even though the United States is a multicultural society, there are some generalizations used that depict the American character: (1) goal/achievement oriented, (2) materialistic and capitalistic, (3) competitive and aggressive, (4) highly organized, time conscious, work and efficiency oriented, (5) impatient and independent, (6) friendly and informal, (7) sense of humor, (8) business relationships not dependent on personal friendship, (9) generous, (10) English speaking, (11) direct and polite manner of communicating, (12) eye contact valued, (13) adequate personal distance, (14) personal touching limited in public, and (15) democratic. This limited analysis of the American culture can be helpful in cross-cultural communication.

People throughout the world use positive and negative stereotypes of other people to understand the messages those people are sending them. Americans are perceived positively as friendly, laughing and smiling frequently, time conscious, independent, individualistic, and materialistic. Americans demonstrate a need for personal space and are a no-contact society. Traits perceived as negative are that Americans are affluent and wasteful, impatient, aggressive, status seeking, and very blunt.

Cultural differences. Identifying real and perceived traits of Americans will help us to relate more easily to those from other cultures. Care should be taken, however, to assure that ethnocentrism—the tendency to believe that the standards in one's own country are superior—plays a minor role in business relationships. Ethnocentrism can lead to limited effectiveness and even to cross-cultural conflict. Better business and personal relationships can be developed by respecting the cultures and customs of others.

Culture may be defined as the knowledge, values, beliefs, customs, and practices of a society that provide the society standards of behavior and feelings of identification. A member of a society is an offspring of a culture that shapes actions and thinking.

A plethora of cultural differences can be identified. Some of these differences are in power, role, and status of individuals within a society; decision-making procedures used in the society; social behavior; work attitudes; and the importance of the individual vs. the group.

Power, role and status. The display of power and the demonstration of leadership qualities differ from culture to culture. The aggressive, take-charge American may be looked upon with distaste in some cultures. Some cultures believe that people should occupy their "proper place." Americans display a limited respect for rank and authority while other cultures are very conscious of position and power.

Another major difference among cultures is the role of women. The status of women is not the same everywhere. While Americans are adapting to the use of *businessperson* rather than *businessman,* this change occurs much more slowly outside the United States.

Women in some cultures play a less prominent role in business than do men. Female administrators may dine with the wives of Arab businessmen, while the male executives eat together. Women executives in Latin America may not be granted the respect accorded the men executives. In some Middle Eastern countries, men may balk at working with women; even women executives with excellent qualifications are definitely not welcome.

Status symbols also differ by culture. American top executives perceive a large corner office with windows and carpet located on the top floor as a status symbol; yet in many parts of the world large offices are for clerical workers and smaller ones are for executives who do not need much space for thinking and planning. The high-level executives in France sit in the middle of the work area. Business affairs are conducted in cramped quarters in the Middle East, not in the spacious surroundings to which most Americans are accustomed.

Decision-making procedures. The way decisions are made in other cultures can be very frustrating to many Americans. In this country, decisions are made as quickly as possible by key people; in other cultures, decisions are often made by a team of people. Japan uses this method of decision-making, and all members of the team must agree with the decision made. There is no majority rule. The use of team decisions and total agreement dictate long decision-making procedures. Like the Japanese, Latin Americans prefer that their business decisions be made slowly and only after long discussions.

In the United States agreement is reached on major points, and the working out of minor points is delegated to others. The Greek businessman considers this practice highly suspect because he thinks this routine is evasive and that the decision maker is untrustworthy. The Greek executive believes that every detail of an agreement must be scrutinized very carefully in order to show good faith.

Social behavior. Social behavior includes manners, etiquette, greetings, bribes, and gifts. All of these actions, though considered social amenities, can have serious consequences in business relationships.

One of the greatest difficulties in communicating interculturally is the difference in ideas about what is considered polite. Americans are considered rude by many cultures in Asia and the Pacific, while Americans think those culture standards are unreasonable. Americans often use first names as a greeting; many other cultures are more formal. In Europe first names are never used without an invitation, and academic titles and degrees are used as a form of respect. West Germans are especially diligent when applying this rule. But in Iceland calling people by their last name is impolite. Eye contact, considered impolite in some cultures, is expected in the United States.

The method of greeting others varies from culture to culture. The firm handshake with a pumping action expected in the United States is considered impolite in France. In some countries, the handshake is sometimes accompanied with a light kiss, and in Saudi Arabia males will kiss both cheeks after the handshake. A hug and a kiss on both cheeks is used by the Greeks; and in Thailand, placing both hands together in prayer position at the chest and bowing slightly is the common greeting.

Americans' refusal to pay money or present gifts, a particularly sensitive situation, is considered improper in some cultures, for in some cases both the gift and the money requested are used for the benefit of the American and cannot be used for anything else in that culture. Many Americans view these actions as dishonest and unethical while the other culture views them as the normal way business is conducted.

Small gifts are sometimes helpful although knowing the customs of the culture is necessary so as not to offend the receiver. The color of the gift could offend in some cultures. Since cows are sacred to the Hindu, gifts made of cowhide should not be given. Clocks are symbols of death to the Chinese, and pairs of anything are not acceptable gifts in a West African culture. Studying the culture before giving presents is fundamental to appropriate gift selection.

Work attitudes. Most Americans subscribe to the Puritan work ethic, a belief in hard work and accomplishing one's desires. Americans believe that they can make things better, and they take pride in their work. Often work is the topic of conversation at social gatherings, and many Americans take work home.

But these beliefs and practices are not adhered to in other parts of the world. In Australia the person is admired who can appear to be working hard but is actually doing very little. In Moslem countries the belief is that Allah controls everything, and there is therefore no need to plan or work diligently for the future. Nepotism, discouraged in America, is widely practiced in many parts of the world.

Individual vs. group orientation. Some cultures emphasize the value of individual effort, while others stress the merit of working for or with the group. Group-oriented cultures include the Oriental, Russian, and Latin American ones; the American culture represents an individual-oriented culture. Recognizing this cultural difference identifies two distinctly different value systems.

The individualistic American perspective stresses the importance of individual effort; the importance of self; the necessity of questioning, of developing individual opinions, and of solving problems; the freedom to achieve; and aggressiveness or at least assertiveness.

In group-oriented cultures, the family, the group, and the organization take precedence over the individual. The rights to question or to have individual opinions are sometimes interpreted as disrespect for authority.

Recognizing and studying cultural differences can become intriguing and revealing as the learner realizes the necessity of understanding different cultures in order to communicate properly.

Language differences. The most obvious area of concern when dealing with a business person from another country is language. A Japanese prime minister has said that his country's success in trading can be attributed to the Japanese knowledge of the language and culture of the country with which they are doing business.[1] When he was asked the most important language in world trade, a Japanese executive replied, "My customer's language."[2] Another expert expressed the idea this way: "You can buy in any language. But to sell, you'd better speak the buyer's language."[3] Written communication is considered easier to handle than oral communication.

Semantics and translation problems. While English is becoming a global language, many know English as a second language and will have some difficulty in understanding it. People do not think in a second language the same way they do in their native language. Language usage will mirror the outlook of the speaker, and this outlook or perspective is dependent upon the speaker's culture and native language.

Communicating when a language barrier exists requires the awareness that the receiver of the message may not understand all that is said or written. The biggest problem occurs when dealing with people who speak no English. When this predicament occurs, the communicator can learn the other person's language, teach the other person the communicator's language, or use a translator. The most reasonable approach appears to be using a translator.

Translators can be an invaluable asset when communicating with people from other cultures. However, even translators are likely to be victims of cultural barriers because they must listen to one language, mentally reword the message into another language, and then speak those words. This is a difficult task.

American businesspersons have found that problems can be caused by incorrect translation of advertisements and product names. Translation is not a simple matter of matching word for word; accurate translation requires

---

[1]Gould, John W. "For Doing Business Abroad, How Much Foreign Language Proficiency is Enough?" *Bulletin of the Association for Business Communication* 49:26; September 1986.

[2]Pearce, Glenn C.; Figgins, Ross; and Golen, Steven P. *Business Communication Principles and Applications.* Second edition. New York: John Wiley & Sons, 1988, p. 635.

[3]Wells, Walter. *Communications in Business.* Fifth edition. Boston: PWS-KENT Publishing Co., 1988, p. 571.

an understanding of a country's culture. Some of the exact translations of advertisements are amusing. An example is the Otis Engineering Company's poster shown in Russia that promised its oil well equipment would improve people's sex lives. Other examples include "Come alive with Pepsi" translated as "Come out of the grave" and "Body by Fisher" translated as "Corpse by Fisher." When analyzing the sales of the Nova automobile in a foreign market, a company found that "no va" in Spanish means "it won't go," and the company finally understood why no one in the country wanted to buy the new automobile. Experts in translating should be employed to alleviate such events.

Subtle differences need to be taken into consideration also. Japanese executives are looking for intention in what is not said while Americans rely on the actual words conveyed. The Japanese use an indirect method of communicating while Americans use the direct method.

Oral communication/listening. Oral communication has been identified as the most important human relations skill. Both words and tone of voice used are signficant when communicating orally. Russians speak in flat, level tones, a practice Americans might consider indicative of boredom. Speaking in loud tones, a trait of Middle Easterners, could be construed by Westerners as emotional. And the Japanese habit of speaking in soft tones exhibits humility or courtesy. Voice usage can cause misunderstanding unless the communicators understand the differences.

Americans should be especially careful to avoid the use of slang and idioms when speaking (or writing) to internationals. Americans also should avoid the use of superlatives such as "fantastic" and "terrific" since these words are considered by foreigners to be unreal and overly dramatic. Word usage should be simple and straightforward.

Words should be pronounced clearly and slightly slower when communicating with those speaking English as a second language. Asking "Am I going too fast?" will provide feedback, as will careful observation of the person to whom the message is being given. "Is that clear?" is another significant question. Questions and careful observation can be invaluable in increasing accurate communication. When misunderstanding does occur, rephrasing the message is better than repeating the same words louder. Also allowing correspondents to ask questions and to finish their own sentences is helpful.

Astute listening skills allow both Americans and internationals to improve pronounciation of foreign languages and thus increase understanding when communicating. The international communicator must listen very carefully to what is said and what isn't said. Japanese people think before making responses. Americans, too eager to make their point, will sometimes interrupt a Japanese speaker before the message is completed and misinterpret the meaning.

Silence, a form of communication, seems to elude Americans, who like to keep oral communication flowing and do not like periods of silence. Someone has said that Americans will agree to anything if the negotiating party is silent long enough.

When negotiating in other countries, the following guidelines are helpful.

(1) Use a team of negotiators; don't send just one person. (2) Learn key words in the language in which you will be negotiating, and use an interpreter. (3) The "checking with the home office" strategy is useful in some cultures. (4) Expect to spend more time negotiating; most cultures are less time conscious than Americans. (5) Adjust your negotiating strategy to include reserving one or two points to be used as concessions late in the negotiations. (6) Abide by the local customs relative to status and business procedures, such as how to address those at the bargaining table. (7) Recognize that silence is used as a powerful bargaining tool. (8) Ask questions, and then request a recess or another meeting. (9) Expect full discussion on any issue. (10) Know that a signed contract in the United States means one thing, and in another culture it means something else.

Written communication. The most widely used languages in international communication are English, Spanish, and French. Even though interpretation problems occur in business correspondence, these difficulties are often inconsequential when communicators exert efforts to overcome them.

Writing style differences include longer and more complex sentences in the German culture, and no paragraphing in Chinese and Japanese cultures. Germans omit the familiar buffer in negative messages, but the Japanese present negative messages in such a positive manner that recognizing them is difficult. Japanese letter openings begin with concerns about the weather and the prosperity of the business. A typical German salutation might be "Very Honored Mr. Professor Jones." Comparing and contrasting American writing styles with those from other cultures reveal some drastic differences.

Writing out the name of the month is especially important in international correspondence. A date written 4/2/91 would be interpreted in the United States as April 2, 1991; in other countries it might be interpreted as February 4, 1991.

Several suggestions for improving intercultural communication are: (1) Write short, clear sentences, and try to limit each sentence to one idea; (2) Avoid the use of slang, idioms, jargon, and overstatement; (3) Be precise when selecting words; (4) Use graphics and illustrations when possible; (5) Use numbers for figures—preferably the metric system.

Nonverbal communication. The nonverbal aspects of international communication are perhaps more important than the verbal component. In our culture it can account for as much as 90 percent of a message. There is as much variation in the meanings of nonverbal signals in international business communication as there is variation among language. Communication can be affected by nonverbal subtleties in behavior, such as the length of time a person holds on while shaking hands, the color or type of dress, and posture. Lack of understanding of cultural differences in nonverbal messages can cause miscommunication.

Students will enjoy studying the effects of nonverbal communication in cultures different from America's. Interesting topics in nonverbal languages include space, touch, dress, time, facial expression and emotions, eye contact, gestures, posture, and body movement.

Space. The amount of physical space people require to feel comfortable will vary from culture to culture. Americans prefer to stand 3 to 5 feet apart when conducting a business conversation, but are willing to stay within 12 to 18 inches of friends and relatives for intimate conversations. In many countries, close contact is the norm. In Latin America, the Middle East, India, Japan, and the Far East, the people are comfortable with very little distance between them during conversation. An example of misinterpretation related to the nonverbal language of space is the "conversation tango," which can occur when a North American engages in a conversation with a Latin American. The Latin American moves in for almost nose-to-nose conversation and the North American steps back; the Latin American steps forward and the North American steps back. Back—forward—back—forward. The cha-cha-cha dance of conversation.

Touch. Touching can be a source of misunderstanding in international communication. In most Latin countries, the hug is as commonplace as the handshake. The French sometimes kiss each other on the cheeks. Touching someone while conversing is customary in the Middle East. Americans tend to limit personal touching of each other in public, and the Japanese have an aversion to casual body contact. The Japanese prefer the traditional bow from the waist but will make the concession of shaking hands with Westerners.

Gestures, posture, and body language. We often use the silent language of gestures, posture, and body language to miscommunicate or convey negative messages. Certain gestures that have positive meanings to us can be negative to others. In many countries, hitchhiking with a thumb stuck out is a very rude gesture. Thumbs-up is considered vulgar in Iran and Ghana. Some gestures have a variety of meanings. The American "okay" sign is an obscene gesture in Greece and Brazil, while in France it means zero and in Japan it signifies money.

Posture is another form of silent language. How you stand, sit, cross legs, and look can make good or bad impressions. Americans' casual way of sitting—slouching in a reclining position, tilting back in the chair, crossing one's legs—can offend people in Saudi Arabia and Japan. Arabs find it offensive to allow the soles of one's shoes to be seen by others. In Japan, sitting straight is the mark of a person in physical and mental control.

Head movement can have the opposite meaning in different cultures. In America, the up and down nod indicates agreement or yes. In other countries, the nod indicates only that the person heard what was said. In some Eastern European countries, the up-and-down head motion means 'no' and the side-to-side motion 'yes'—just the opposite of our meanings.

Dress. The type of dress can send the wrong silent message. Conservative style and dark or subdued colors are advisable for business and social purposes. For males or females, the Western business suit is generally considered acceptable dress for business. Blue jeans, too, have become an acceptable international uniform for young people. Color should be a consideration when dressing for business abroad, because in some cultures certain colors are worn only by royalty, and others convey grief. Therefore, in Malaysia do not wear yellow, blue, or white; in Thailand do not wear black, purple, or solid white; and in Japan do not wear mauve. Sometimes what you wear or don't wear can be a problem. Shoes are among the biggest offenders in the East. They are forbidden in Muslim mosques and Buddhist temples. It is customary to remove one's shoes before entering a Japanese, Indian, or Indonesian home.

Time. The language of time has a different perspective throughout the world. For some populations, time is viewed as linear, progressing from past to present to future; for others it is cyclical. In the American society, time is viewed as a scarce resource; while in other cultures time is considered abundant. Clock-watcher Americans are known as time-conscious people who like strict schedules and who are somewhat inflexible. Many cultures have a looser idea of time, where delays in meeting visitors or answering letters is acceptable or even the norm. In some cultures the more time that elapses before a reply, the more important it is. Therefore, Americans should not interpret these delays as a lack of interest.

The length of the work day and the days of the week worked have great diversity in different countries. Many countries have business hours similar to those in the United States; however, some (generally those in warmer climates) close their businesses for two to four hours during the middle of the day for the main meal and/or for taking a siesta. The work week varies throughout the world. In Muslim countries like Saùdi Arabia, Thursday and Friday are the days off with Friday reserved for a day of worship. The Korean work week is Monday through Saturday and possibly even Sunday. The time differences due to the international time zones also have an impact on communication.

Emotional expression. The degree of emotional expression varies all over the world. Americans seems to be a center of an emotional spectrum that extends from the effervescent Latin Americans at one end to the subdued Asians at the other end. Americans are seen as hot-blooded, impulsive, and emotional by the Asians, while Latins view Americans as cold and controlled. By American standards, the British appear aloof, the French condescending, and the Arabs emotional. In contrast to American ways, Arab men weep openly and Asians often giggle or smile when told bad news or when embarrassed. For some cultures, kissing is not done in public, and for most cultures anger is not expressed in public.

Eye contact. In many Western cultures, a person who does not maintain good eye contact is considered untrustworthy. Americans also label people who avoid eye contact as unfriendly, insecure, inattentive, and impersonal. Eye contact is not so important for cultures of the South Pacific and Japan, where lack of eye contact is a sign of respect. Arabs use direct eye contact as a means to judge the tone of a conversation. They believe that when people are interested in a topic, their pupils dilate; and when they hear something they dislike, their pupils contract. To hide their feelings, Arabs wear dark glasses.

APPROACHES TO INTEGRATING INTERNATIONAL CONCEPTS IN BUSINESS COMMUNICATION COURSES

The business communication course should include relevant instruction in international communication. Three specific techniques for integrating this instruction are presented below:

First, a unit, a chapter, or a block of time can be devoted to international concepts. This arrangement signals the importance of the topic; however, many instructors lack knowledge and training in the area and are ill at ease teaching the material. A separate unit also requires additional time.

Spreading international communication concepts throughout the course offers an answer for teachers who feel unprepared to teach a unit. Small amounts of relevant information can be taught when the teacher feels comfortable with it. For example, teaching the differences in letter openings United States style vs. letter openings Japanese style adds interest to this topic and imparts valuable international information. Other brief discussions held at appropriate points throughout the course provide an answer to internationalizing the course for both the teacher and the student. A disadvantage of the spread approach is that most textbooks are not written in this manner.

A combination of the two approaches—a unit and the spreading-when-appropriate method—is a third approach. Setting aside a block of time to cover the topic will stress the importance of the topic, and spreading it throughout the course will allow students to see the global nature of business.

STRATEGIES FOR TEACHING INTERNATIONAL CONCEPTS

Action learning or learning by doing is a recommended strategy for teaching international concepts. This strategy presents an exciting and relevant topic in a nontraditional way and is usually used after a formal class lecture or training session.

Student/team projects. Assigning an individual or team research project on a topic related to international business requires action learning, for these projects will require library research to complete. In some instances, primary research might be incorporated into such projects. For example, a student studying correspondence could very easily talk with international students on a college campus and get firsthand information relative to business letter styles. These individual or team research projects could be presented as written reports to the instructor and then as oral reports to the other class members. All of these activities are legitimate exercises for any business communication class.

Using instructor-prepared structured study guides, students could prepare a culture profile on a specific culture. Factors that may be included in the culture profile are greetings, gestures, dress, language, work environment, employment trends, work attitudes, education, history, government structure, food customs, symbols of status, religion, time consciousness, and do's and don'ts. Oral reports based on the prepared culture profile provide additional communication opportunities and add more international information for the class.

CulturGrams, prepared by the Center for International Studies at Brigham Young University, may be purchased for a small fee. These prepared studies of different cultures may be read by students and then used as a basis for class discussion.

Role playing/culture shock projects. Students may role play several different situations to emphasize the difficulties involved when an American settles in an overseas country and when a foreigner attempts to settle in the United States. Role play may be considered for the following: (1) A Haitian migrant worker manages to bring his family north to settle in Iowa. (2) A Russian family resettles in Houston, Texas, where the father is a professor at a university. (3) A female executive travels to South America to negotiate the location of a new factory. (4) A manager must move his family, which includes a teenage son and daughter, to a country in Africa for at least one year.

Role playing activities may be found in simulations and game books written to help understand reactions to intercultural experiences. These role playing exercises can alert the students to the feelings of internationals in this country as well as Americans in other countries and thus prepare them for communicating. Class discussion after the role play situation is essential to the effectiveness of this activity.

Case studies. International case studies are presented in some business communication textbooks and teacher's manuals as well as other books written especially for the purpose of providing case studies. Using case studies will allow students to analyze a problem and to make suggestions for solutions. In the process of searching for solutions to the problems, students find their own understanding and knowledge lacking. Thus, students can reach their own conclusion that more study is needed in the area of international communication.

Critical incidents. Teachers using this strategy will find that searching newspapers, journals, television news, or talking with friends will provide ample incidents for class use. The point is to present a situation and have students indicate how they think different cultures will interact in this situation. Using small groups to make these decisions, followed by class discussion, is required in this strategy.

Assignment/discussion of readings. Newspapers, journals, and magazines supply an abundance of relevant material for assigned readings and follow-up discussion. Instructors may decide to ask students to read a major newspaper on a specified day, or for a specified period of time, or for a relevant article on international business communication. Occasionally the instructor may provide an outstanding article for the entire class to read and discuss on an announced day. The timeliness of the readings will be evident, and students often become intrigued with international business from this activity.

Guest speakers. Guest speakers from other countries, from the international business community, and from government agencies dealing in international affairs, where available, add interest and often a fresh insight into international affairs. Foreign-born adults may enjoy talking about their culture, and these people could very easily ask students questions relative to the United States that have been taken for granted by the students. Such an interaction could clarify some misunderstandings as well as point out areas needing more study by Americans.

Differences in customs and business practices among countries could be discussed. Interpretations of American customs by other countries would serve to identify differences to which Americans would have to defer when doing business with the country under discussion.

Traditional/electronic communication exercise. Students need an understanding of the ease with which communication can be accomplished in the world today. Means of global communication include not only the traditional mail and telephone but also satellite, microwave, electronic mail, and facsimile machine.

Modern technology has made communication to other countries uncomplicated and relatively inexpensive. Students can investigate how to accomplish the various types of international communication and compare cost factors, speed of transmission, clarity, accuracy, etc.

Audiovisual media. Television, radio, films, video and audio-tapes, and records are available for use in instructing students in international communication. Using media appears to appeal to today's student as a strategy of learning. The media should be previewed before being used in the classroom.

EVALUATING STUDENT ACHIEVEMENT

Evaluation is an on-going process in teaching. It has the potential for strengthening a student's self-image and can be a motivating force for continuing learning. It is necessary to identify the evaluation criteria before instruction begins. Several methods can be used for evaluating students' performance, which can include objective tests, short answer tests, and discussion questions. An evaluation checklist or similar instrument will provide uniformity in evaluation to ensure that students' learning is being measured according to the competencies and evaluation criteria identified.

CONCLUSION

In whichever job or profession American citizens choose to enter and in whatever locality they are situated, communication remains an essential skill for their existence. In an interdependent world consisting of many cultures, communication becomes difficult because of differences in cultures, in language, and in nonverbal characteristics. Among all the intercultural differences affecting international communication, one nonverbal message appears to mean the same across all cultures—a smile. This communication form, utilized and understood by every culture in every country, can improve personal and business relationships and become the most useful form of communication.

CHAPTER 7
Methods of Internationalizing Information Processing Courses

ROY W. HEDRICK

University of South Carolina, Columbia, South Carolina

The time is now for educators to provide education and training with a global scope. It is not enough to teach current information processing technologies and trends; we must provide the information processing experiences our students need to participate effectively in a global economy. In any of the component courses in information processing, certain methods of internationalizing the curriculum will be common. Examples include developing vocabulary skills and apprising students of the differences in cultures. A detailed study of appropriate cultural variations might be necessary as a preliminary course to the development of multi-cultural differences in the components of information processing.

The intent of this article is to provide explanations of current trends of curriculum development integrating international concepts in information processing and to provide suggestions for implementing this integration. The chapter also provides a discussion of teaching information processing to students with limited English skills and how information processing, often called "informatics," is taught in other countries.

COMPONENTS OF INFORMATION PROCESSING

Several subjects in the curriculum make up the information processing core. They include accounting as well as courses dealing with administrative support, electronic communication, records management, reprographics, and courses dealing with word and data processing or, simply, information processing. A thorough search of the literature has revealed that, presently, only two of these subjects (accounting and information processing) have incorporated the unique opportunities and problems of international concepts.

Accounting. Accounting is one of the core elements in any business curriculum, whether at high school or college level. The development of generally accepted accounting principles is the goal of these basic courses. In these beginning courses, there are several international concepts that can be integrated into the course material. One is the value that different cultures place on setting standards for generally accepted accounting procedures. The importance of various financial statements will have different meanings in different countries. For example, in Switzerland, bankers are the principal users of financial statements; however in Sweden, the government is the principal user of these statements.

Another important concept in the accounting course is that generally accepted accounting principles of the United States are not necessarily better than those of another country. Students will understand the differences when they are explained and discussed. Could the reason or differences be that of political philosophy, the influence of unions, or the importance of employees' welfare? Different cultures have different views on the social responsibilities of businesses.

Still another element of the international accounting course is the importance of foreign currency translation. So many of the large U.S. corporations have branches in other countries. The development of consolidated financial statements must take into consideration the differences in the U.S. dollar, the British pound, the German mark, and the Japanese yen as well as currencies of other countries.

On the collegiate level, a separate course in international accounting has been proposed. Bloom describes the content of the course to include the following topics:

1. The differences in setting standards in various countries and the underlying reasons for those differences. For instance, what roles do the International Accounting Standards Committee and the International Federation of Accountants play in setting these standards in individual countries?
2. The differences in the generally accepted accounting procedures in selected countries.
3. Financial reporting issues such as transactions between countries, currency translation, changing prices, and consolidation of financial statements.
4. The managerial accounting issues of transfer pricing and performance evaluation.
5. Auditing a multinational corporation.
6. A comparison of the educational requirements for accounting certification among countries.

Information Processing. At the University of South Carolina, a special course has been developed in international information systems: Multinational Information Systems. The course, developed and taught by Dr. Douglas Durand, is a part of the Master of International Business Studies degree. The purpose of this course is to "focus on the competitive strategies, tactical uses, and technical constraints facing firms with a global presence." Since the students take this course after their internships (discussed later in this chapter), they bring insights of the real world into the classroom.

The topics of office automation, transaction processing, and decision support, among others, are discussed in class. The following are critical issues which the course addresses:

1. The strategic role of information technology in international business
2. Technological hurdles: personnel, software development, local infrastructure, and standard setting (especially in telecommunications protocols)
3. Political issues: trans-border data flows, protectionism, and hiring practices
4. Problems facing multinational information technology managers: end-users, educating senior management, centralized vs. distributed processing, and data security

5. Information resource management and cost justification
6. Information technology comparative advantage: international information technology arbitrage.

Since little is known about multinational information processing, the course is taught with the use of an extensive bibliography of journal articles and research that has been written about the subject. Another important teaching/learning tool in the course, Dr. Durand has found, has been the practical experiences of his students who have completed their internships in the international business environment. The students are expected to write case studies about their experiences. What better up-to-date learning exercises could there be than the events which are taking place in the "real world"?

Other subjects. The previous discussion has explained some of the applications of international concepts in accounting and information processing. But what about the other subjects comprising the information processing core? One of the primary subject areas left untouched is that dealing with administrative support.

Those holding positions in administrative support usually have as much contact with the international customers and clients as the managers and executives of the corporation. Therefore, education and training must be provided for these workers in such topics as languages, customs, cultural differences, and proper business etiquette. Opportunities exist for business education departments to form alliances with other areas of the school such as the foreign language, history, and geography departments. Close working relationships with these departments will encourage the development of specialized courses for the administrative support students.

In the other areas of the curriculum—electronic communication, records management, and reprographics—units of study can be incorporated into present courses to stress the importance of international regulations. This is an excellent topic for research projects for individuals and groups of students. Added to the written presentation of the students' findings, an oral presentation and discussion could enhance the other students' understanding of the research.

APPLICATIONS IN THE CURRICULUM

Applications in the curriculum can be as unlimited as one's imagination in the development of materials. As mentioned earlier, a concentrated effort must be made to enhance the students' vocabulary with international terms. Students must be made aware that there is *no one right way to do something,* only different ways. The customs and mores of different countries will dictate various ways business situations are handled. Some specific suggestions are discussed in the next few paragraphs to stimulate your thinking in providing applications tailored for your own situation.

Internships. In March 1990, *U.S. News & World Report* ranked the Master of International Business Studies (MIBS) degree at the University of South Carolina as the best in the country. An important component of this program is the student internship. Internships can be divided into three basic categories: U.S.-based corporations with facilities in other countries, foreign-based corporations with facilities in the United States, and foreign corporations in other countries. The category chosen for study is based on the objectives of the program and degree of development of an information processing program.

A six-month internship is required for all students in their second year of the program. Since the program is attracting students from around the world, the internship is coordinated with the language track that the students choose. The work opportunities and assignments are as varied as the companies sponsoring them. For instance, a student working for American Express in Mexico developed a computer analysis of accounts. The analysis program was presented to and accepted by the country manager. Students are placed in corporations such as DuPont, Honeywell, Kraft, Michelin, Price Waterhouse, Sony, and Westinghouse. These students are located in such countries as Argentina, Austria, Spain, Germany, Mexico, Japan, Nigeria, Turkey, and many others.

Ten different departments at the University of South Carolina and more than 100 companies have worked as a team to develop this master's program. W. Robert Clay, vice president of Imaging Systems for E. I. DuPont DeNemours & Co., recently commented, "We need people coming out with an education—an understanding and openmindedness toward other countries —that business isn't done that same way worldwide."

International business study tours. International business study tours are similar in some respects to the internship program just discussed. However, business study tour programs incorporate travel as a primary component in contrast to the work experience of the internship program. The study tour includes visits to foreign service and manufacturing companies, governmental organizations, business, financial, and educational institutions, as well as museums, and scenic and historic areas. The purpose of the program is to focus on the practices and trends of the international business environment.

An example of a program of this type is offered in the Retailing Department at the University of South Carolina. Every year, in May, Dr. June Baker takes a group of undergraduate and graduate students abroad. This experience provides the students the opportunity to identify major international fashion businesses and to investigate emerging trends in the fashion industries. They have the opportunity to analyze marketing and production methods, study contemporary and historical fashion designers and collections, and compare promotional strategies applied in the international/domestic marketing of fashion goods. A course similar to this, with the focus on information processing, is being planned by the Office Administration Department at the University of South Carolina for its students in office information systems. The course will be offered for the first time in May 1991.

Field trips and guest speakers. The focus of this suggestion is to draw upon those international companies and their employees that are U.S.-based to discuss their information processing systems. An on-site visit to one of these companies could provide "real world" and "real time" examples of the efforts which comprise this process. Companies involved in the development and production of information processing goods and services are one example of an industry that might provide an excellent source of information. Another example, which might be more commonplace, is that of a hotel chain with locations around the world.

Foreign language departments. The development of any internationalized program in information processing should include the cooperation of the various foreign language departments. Although most international business is conducted in English, Americans for too long have neglected the opportunities available to those fluent in another language. The personnel in this area of the school curriculum could provide additional resources in the development of an understanding of cultural and language differences.

Written and oral presentations. An innovative suggestion for student research assignments would be to contrast the uses of technology for information processing between the United States and various other developed countries around the world. Some suggestions for topics might include: extent of use of mainframes or microcomputers for information processing among business of various sizes; use of ergonomic considerations in the design of workstations; variations in the consideration of VDT factors such as color, design, and safety; development of electronic cottage (or telecommuting) industries; uses of electronic communication; and the extent of use of voice recognition equipment.

Not only can a written assignment enhance a student's or student group's awareness of similarities and differences, but an oral presentation of the material can also broaden the views and respect for the problems of other cultures. Require the students to add audio or visual aids to make the presentation more interesting and informative for other members of the class. Role playing could be used effectively to illustrate a host of situations involving the electronic office.

International awareness days. One or two days set aside each semester to focus on the customs and traditions of a specific country is another method of broadening the students' awareness of the international influence in business. Several activities could be planned for this type of celebration on the secondary and postsecondary levels. Local guest speakers of international heritage could be invited to talk with the students. Students could also research and demonstrate business dress of the country of the day. Food is another way to bring fun and creativity to the occasion. Often there are local restaurants that specialize in the cuisine of the country under study. Ask the restaurant to provide information about the food of that country and provide samples for the students.

TEACHING STUDENTS WITH LIMITED ENGLISH SKILLS

In many parts of the United States business teachers are confronted with the problem of dealing with students whose primary language is not English. For many years this was only a problem for those who taught in schools in the major cities along the East and West Coasts and those colleges and universities that attracted international students to their specialty programs in certain medicine, engineering, and business curricula. However, in the last few years, this has also become commonplace for teachers in Alabama, Indiana, Kansas, Ohio, Oklahoma, South Carolina, and other states not normally thought of when discussing language barriers in the classroom.

The National Business Education Association is aware of the problems of working with students with these limited skills. In the Policies Commission for Business and Economic Education statement on adult and continuing education and within the 1984 Carl D. Perkins Vocational Education Act, the problem of working with students with limited English skills is recognized. Those educators who have been involved with students who have limited English skills have some innovative suggestions that can be used as a guide to raise students' awareness of some of the problems of internationalizing the curriculum.

The first suggestion—recognizing cultural differences—deals specifically with bringing an international focus into the curriculum. Each culture, the world around, recognizes certain behavior patterns as standard and acceptable within that specific culture. The Mexicans do not place the same value on punctuality and real time as people of the United States. Therefore, if a Mexican student walks into class 10 to 15 minutes late, the tardiness may not have been intentional. Now comes the ethical question—Does the teacher try to "Americanize" the student or is the student allowed to continue to come late to class? Sensitivity on the part of the teacher in helping this student realize the importance of punctuality might be part of an appropriate solution.

Suggestion two is closely associated with the issue of sensitivity just mentioned. Most students respond positively to a teacher who displays a caring attitude. Smiling and employing a relaxed teaching style can relieve some of the students' insecure feelings brought on by the language barrier. To help strengthen the feelings of concern for the student, it is suggested that the teacher become familiar with the language and customs of the students. Occasional use of terms and phrases the students understand strengthens a teacher's rapport with students.

The third suggestion—introducing new material in relation to the background experiences of the student—is really common sense and normally is part of teaching any student new material. Again, the teacher must be responsible for gaining the knowledge to perform such activities. It may take extra time and effort for the teacher to become knowledgeable enough in the culture of the students to feel comfortable with this activity. A way to accomplish this task would be to take the time to get to know the students better. Ask questions. Students would probably be happy to share information.

Any subject will have a set of terms that are central to that subject. Information processing includes such terms and their meanings as RAM, K, disk/hard drives, facsimile, modem, and a host of others not common to students with limited English. A good suggestion for helping these students with such terms is periodically to provide handouts containing new terms and their definitions. A principle of communication is to use simple terms instead of longer words and jargon; however, for these students to become functional workers, consumers, and citizens, they must incorporate these terms into their vocabularies.

For students coming from another culture with educational experiences different from ours, time and effort must be devoted to providing instruction that develops studying and testing skills. Normally, teachers do not focus on every topic covered within a chapter of a given text. If the instructor provides an outline of the most significant reading material in the chapter, the student is able to concentrate his or her efforts in understanding those areas of the chapter that will be the focus of class discussion, problem solving, and testing. Instruction in the development of study skills should include a segment on effective listening skills. Students can be taught to distinguish between important *facts* in the development of concepts and incidental *trivia*. Before testing, provide the students with information on testing procedures. Give a formative test the day before the real thing to help relieve their anxieties.

THE INFORMATION PROCESSING CURRICULUM IN OTHER COUNTRIES

Argentina. Those of us in the United States who continually strive for a better educational system and a better learning environment for our students are not alone in the world. This phenomenon is happening in Argentina as well. Because this country is not as developed as other countries in the Western world and its struggle for adequate resources is a constant battle, the progress of teaching information processing seems to move at a snail's pace.

Money! There seems never to be enough of it. In Argentina, not only is there a struggle for computers, but there is also a struggle for software written in Spanish, a struggle for qualified teachers, a struggle for school buildings, and even, in some locations, a struggle for electricity. In Herminia Azinian's article describing technology education in Argentina, she lists these additional obstacles.

1. The absence of long-range goals in education because of political changes. Many projects have been designed but not implemented because of the lack of continuity in leadership.
2. The lack of information, by school principals, for decision making. There are no visible results of innovation, so there are no available evaluations.
3. The unwillingness on the part of most principals and teachers to alter their roles, preferring to keep the dichotomy between school and the "real world."
4. The rapid obsolesence of equipment and a lack of standardization to allow interchangeability. Thus, there is no justification for commercial publishers to invest in the development of textbooks and courseware.
5. The general lack of funds from the government for research and development of software and innovative teaching methodology.

However, those dedicated educators continue to fight the battle that, to some of us, might seem overwhelming.

Since 1984, the government in Argentina has attempted to address this situation. In that year, the National Committee of Informatics was established to analyze worldwide trends as well as the national environment for teaching information processing in primary and secondary schools. (The term is "informatics" in most other countries.) As an outgrowth of this committee, the Agency for Studies in Informatics and Education was developed. Currently, the activities of this committee are centered around the following four areas:

1. *Research and development.* The Latin-American Center of Research on Computers in Education, in cooperation with the University of Buenos Aires, is developing projects in two secondary schools. A program to produce multi-media instructional packages will be instituted at three universities.
2. *Human resources.* A modular set of courses is offered to educational institutions upon request. The goal is to train supervisors, professionals with leading responsibilities, and educators capable of training others. There are also workshops for disseminating general information about informatics and education.
3. *Technical assistance.* An information system dealing with human resources is being developed and another dealing with Argentinean educational software, containing 175 pieces of courseware and 36 programs for schools and colleges, is complete.
4. *Dissemination.* At a national conference in 1987, a workshop was held to teach educators how to select software. Several papers were presented on the implementation of some of the programs listed in 3 above.

A final concern Ms. Azinian discussed in her article was the importance of developing new teaching techniques. Important to any teacher education program are components in human growth and development, educational psychology, and learning theories. Effective teaching includes the development of good communication skills and thinking and reasoning skills.

India. India, with a growing electronics and computer industry, is a much more developed country than Argentina. It is a significant exporter of software to more developed countries; its colleges and universities, which began instruction in computer science in the late 1960's and early 1970's, attract the best students in the country. India's progress in the teaching of information processing is greatly advanced.

In 1984, a pilot project was begun to bring microcomputers into the schools to help teachers teach computer literacy. The pilot project was limited to 250 of the country's 55,000 secondary schools. This project was sponsored through the collaborative efforts of the Department of Electronics, the Department of Education, the Computer Maintenance Corporation of India, and the British BBC Literacy Project. Entitled Computer Literacy and Studies in Schools (CLASS), the project has the following major objectives:

1. Provide students with a broad understanding of computers and their uses;
2. Familiarize students with the range of computer applications in all walks of human activity and with the computer's potential as an information processing tool;
3. Demystify computers and develop a familiarity with computers that would encourage individuals to be creative in identifying and developing applications relevant to their immediate environments;
4. Encourage teachers to use the technology to improve the effectiveness of their teaching.

The CLASS curriculum focused mainly upon problem-solving activities. Generic packages were used to teach the fundamentals of word processing, spreadsheets, and databases. An interesting point of this curriculum is that the developers believed it was important for the students to learn to use microcomputers in solving the day-to-day problems of life. Unlike most American computer literacy curricula, the Indian curriculum contained no computer programming.

Outcomes since the implementation of the program in 1985 have been overwhelming. The enthusiasm of the students about the studies has been high; the motivation of the teachers has been positive; and the development of new educational software has been tremendous. This last outcome has especially been an inspiration for its developers. Since the country of India has approximately 15 different major languages, there has been a marked increase in the development of educational software for the different native languages. The promoters of the project are pleased with the success of the program.

CONCLUSIONS

Any successful integration of international concepts into the information processing curriculum, or any other of the business disciplines, must be a combined effort of the business unit, humanities unit, and various other areas of the school. To continue to prepare students for the 1990's and beyond, international concepts must be incorporated in all the components of information processing courses. Use some of the ideas mentioned here; but search for and develop other innovative ideas, too.

REFERENCES

Azinian, Herminia. "The Impact of Technology on Argentinean Education." *Technical Horizons in Education Journal* 15:5; December/January 1987/1988.

Baker, June, Ph.D. Personal interview. 5 May 1990.

Bloom, Robert. "Motivating Students in the Introductory Courses with International Accounting Topics." *Journal of Education for Business* 65:4; January 1990.

Durand, Douglas, Ph.D. Personal interview. 30 April 1990.

Loveland, Terry L., Yohannan T. Abraham, and Radie G. Bunn. "International Business Study Tours: Practices and Trends." *Journal of Education for Business* 62:6; March 1987.

Nag, B. "Informatics Education in India: The CLASS Project for Secondary Students." *Technical Horizons in Education Journal* 15:5; December/January 1987/1988.

Scott, James Calvert. "Facilitating the Learning of Limited-English—Proficient Business Students." *Journal of Education for Business* 65:1; October 1989.

CHAPTER 8
Methods of Internationalizing Business Management Courses

CHUCK COLIGAN
New Jersey Department of Education, Trenton

Milton Maskowitz, in the introduction to his book, *The Global Marketplace,* states:

> Most of our lives are touched today by companies whose home base is in another country. At no previous time have goods, money, and people crossed national borders so rapidly and in such high volume . . . but most companies of any size think and act today in international terms, which means (1) they are looking to sell and/or make their products in markets outside their own country and (2) they worry about the competition they face from companies based in other countries . . . As a result people around the world are linked today by brand names as much as anything else.[1]

The concept of nation states becoming less significant than global corporate entities may seem far fetched until we consider IBM with its 1987 global market value at $91 billion against, for instance, Turkey's Gross Domestic Product (GDP) of $59 billion. Or consider Nippon Telegraph & Telephone (NTT) with a $310 billion market value versus Australia's GDP of a mere $161 billion. The significance of these figures is an indication of why we need to teach international business management skills to secondary and post-secondary students.

The purpose of this chapter is to offer educators and their students content outline and methods of teaching that could be included in a unit or course addressing international business management. Due to the diversity of the many different cultures, people, countries, and businesses that exist when considering our world today, only broad concepts will be discussed.

A review of the literature makes it clear that international business management courses or units must touch on the areas of economics, sociology, geography, and political science in addition to basic management content. The basic content of any business management course includes fundamental concepts related to planning, organizing, staffing, directing, controlling, and evaluating. International business management concepts and procedures in these basic areas do not differ greatly. Successfully conducting business internationally is not truly unique. Our study then goes more into international environmental and cultural phenomena and builds on the

---

[1] Moskowitz, Milton. *The Global Market Place—102 of the Most Influential Companies Outside America.* New York: Macmillan Publishing Company, 1987. p. ix.

fundamentals already developed in various affiliated disciplines, such as geography, social sciences, language arts, and business management. When consideration is given to the transfer of goods and services, interaction with new societies and cultures, and conflicts of the national interests of countries, the international flavor of the business management course becomes evident.

The approach to international business management should be one of functional administration and implementation. Take, for example, personnel management. There are similar international characteristics in topics such as mobility and promotion problems, motivating workers, wage and salary administration, benefits, and performance standards, which contain the basics of domestic personnel management.

Identification of patterns in the international business management environment that influence business, and the responses that contribute to a manager's ability to manage a global enterprise must be integrated into the management, business education, and marketing education curricula.

INTERNATIONAL BUSINESS MANAGEMENT CONTENT

The comprehensive outline listed below addresses the fundamental content needed in an international business management course. It was adapted from Rachman, Mescon, Bovee, and Thill's sixth edition of *Business Today*.

Outline:

THE DYNAMICS OF WORLD TRADE
- The development of world trade
  - multinational corporations
  - global corporations
- The basics of foreign trade
  - absolute and comparative advantage
  - importing/exporting and domestic/foreign goods
  - GNP
  - the balance of trade
  - the balance of payments
- Forms of international business activity
  - importing and exporting
  - licensing
  - franchising
  - joint ventures
  - wholly owned facilities

THE REGULATION OF WORLD TRADE
- Free enterprise vs. command economy systems (capitalist, socialist, market socialist, communist, and imperialist economies)
- International organizations
  - free trade
  - the International Monetary Fund and the World Bank
  - economic communities and trade pacts

      -the General Agreement on Tariffs and Trade (GATT)
      -economic summits
  •U.S. foreign trade measures
BARRIERS TO WORLD TRADE
  •Cultural barriers
    -language
    -custom
  •Political and legal barriers
    -protectionist measures
     (tariffs, quotas, embargoes, restrictive standards and subsidies)
U.S. COMPETITION IN THE GLOBAL ECONOMY
  •Fair trading practices
  •Adjustments in currency values
   (exchange rate and foreign exchange)
  •International finance and foreign exchange markets[2]

Generally the topics and subtopics listed above focus on specific aspects of international business management that differ from fundamental domestic management content. However, there are broad areas which deserve additional focus.

Resources. Illustrations of the concepts related to absolute and comparative advantage, economic communities and trade pacts, barriers to world trade, and others tie nicely into comparisons with U.S. business management. For instance, in the domestic marketplace, a common and widely accepted practice to gain market share is to price a product to undercut a local competitor. But when a foreign competitor does the same thing, industry lobbyists in Washington shout foul with accusations of "dumping."

Capital. In the domestic financial market, be it venture capital, Small Business Association loan, or the standard commercial bank loan, terms and rates are generally competitive and seldom significantly different. In contrast, global companies can lower capital costs by establishing plants in countries where interest rates are lower or exchange rates more favorable. As research, development, and manufacturing costs increase so does investment risk. Only global markets can support such large risks.

Labor. In today's knowledge-intensive industries, factors such as a labor force with a regular high school or even postsecondary education represent less of a competitive advantage with modern international competition. Global companies can easily access their labor needs through a global strategy or circumvent them with technology.

Technology and innovation. The technology to operate globally didn't exist ten years ago. Today, global companies with high-tech links can mobilize their resources and respond to market needs. New concepts, "old" ideas revisited, or discovering and utilizing new niches are basic to companies gaining competitive advantage over the competition. When the domestic auto manufacturers were slow to respond to consumer demand for smaller,

---

[2]Rachman, David J., Mescon, Michael H., Bovee, Courtland L., and Thill, John V. *Business Today*. Sixth edition. New York: McGraw-Hill Publishing Company, 1990. p. 111.

compact, fuel-conscious automobiles, German and Japanese companies quickly gained the competitive advantage by exploiting innovations that anticipated both domestic and foreign needs. They just refined existing products and exported what they had already developed for their own domestic markets. In fact, demand in the domestic business environment can hone a company's international competitive edge by giving it an early picture of emerging consumer needs and by forcing it to innovate and create new or improved product versions for a more experienced and sophisticated domestic market.

Entrepreneurial skills. The United States has a practical advantage over most other countries with its unique availability of risk capital and innovation. Given the spirit of Americans to exploit these advantages at every opportunity, entrepreneurship is fostered in the United States by the very nature of our culture and economic system. We celebrate our entrepreneurs and their successes to the point of national superstardom. Consider Trump, Spielberg, Gates, Jobs, Lucas, and Iacocca, to name just a few. With an extensive network of investment capital and a stock exchange for trading the equities of small companies, combined with a marketing system that can bring most products to market quickly, our domestic business environment spurs entrepreneurial activity.

Conversely, neither Europe nor Japan has developed such a mix of risk capital and innovation. In Japan, government, industry, and finance have joined to aid large corporations to develop preferred technological objectives. Employees in large companies who leave to start their own company are unusual. But, these world powers aren't far behind in narrowing our competitive advantages.

Geography. The U.S. transportation system and transportation infrastructure impact on the distribution of goods in our economy. The speed with which the diverse offering of goods can be delivered to consumers from various points of origin in the United States is only matched by the world's most sophisticated societies.

The ability of an economy to get goods to market is influenced by its geography, infrastructure, and a transportation technology dedicated to overcoming its geographical barriers. The significance of this is in part demonstrated by distribution problems related to food or medical goods in central Africa, and to some extent, the Soviet Union. Hawaii and Alaska can be used as good comparative domestic examples of how the transportation of goods is influenced by geographical factors and impacts price and availability.

America's youth have a poor understanding of the world today. Consider this headline: "Quiz Finds High School Seniors Aren't So Worldly on Geography."[3] The article describes how America's high school seniors received generally low marks on the first national geography quiz conducted by the U.S. Department of Education. Results showed that the students' knowledge was "roughly equal" to that of the rest of American society, which

---

[3] "Quiz Finds High School Seniors Aren't so Worldly on Geography." *The Star Ledger.* (New Jersey) February 8, 1990.

was worse than that of people in five other countries—Sweden, West Germany, Japan, France and Canada.

Imports/exports. Considering that four-fifths of the world's GNP is outside of the United States and that 95 percent of our planet's population is in the rest of the world (and growing 70 percent faster than in the United States,) the domestic business environment has an almost unlimited potential for exporting products and services. However, Americans have not taken well to exporting. In 1988, exports represented only about 6 percent of the U.S. GNP compared with about 25 percent of GNP for both West Germany and Canada and about 12 percent for Japan. The U.S. Department of Commerce has indicated that domestic companies are hindered in part by having the greatest marketplace in the world right here at home. In addition, concerns of domestic executives include ignorance of foreign languages and cultures. A summary of the U.S. Department of Commerce's, *Guide to Exporting from the United States,* shows that successful exporting requires knowledge of foreign buyer needs and tastes, as well as different and more complex international channels of distribution.

Of course, foreign businesses have never had much of a problem understanding U.S. buyers' needs, tastes, or distribution channels. Many foreign governments back their own banks and assist international companies wishing to establish markets in the United States. They are starting to make some headway in the traditional U.S.-dominated export industries of aerospace, scientific instruments, pharmaceuticals, chemicals, food, and paper. Even the biggest companies in the biggest countries cannot survive on domestic markets if they are in global industries. To survive and thrive they must be in all major global markets.

As discussed earlier, the fundamental concepts of business management related to the areas of planning, organizing, staffing, directing, controlling, and evaluating are relatively unchanged. However, a study by Ruth Shaeffer on *Developing New Leadership in a Multinational Environment* presents research on how international CEOs make major decisions.[4] It shows significant differences that may be attributed to the culture of the managers. For example, in U.S., European, and Canadian companies, CEOs reported that they tended to listen to their top managers' recommendations about 30 percent of the time before making decisions. However, in Latin American companies this practice was less than 5 percent, and in Asian and Mid-Eastern companies it was almost 45 percent.

The standard hierarchical Japanese management structure is changing due to the international management perspective. Recent changes in management development indicate five related themes when Japanese business executives describe how to keep pace with the global business environment. They are:

1. Greater emphasis on international experience
2. Greater delegation of authority

---

[4]Shaeffer, Ruth. "Top Management: Succession and Development." *Developing New Leadership in a Multinational Environment.* A research report from The Conference Board. 1989. p. 4.

3. Greater emphasis on individual risk taking
4. Greater emphasis on formal management education
5. Greater emphasis on choosing younger business leaders attuned to changing times.[5]

The first item above was considered most important as "chief executives . . . indicated it is important for future executives to learn more about the ways of other countries and about how business is conducted."[6] A cottage industry addressing the training needs of global managers has developed and prospered. For example, firms such as AT&T employ consultants to brief relocating managers on what to expect when living in foreign countries.

The literature shows common themes that justify the need for studying international business concepts and procedures in management courses. Basically, they are:

1. Lack of intercultural communications skills
2. Insensitivity to cultural differences
3. Need for global perspectives related to the environment, energy, and economy, and distribution.

Sensitivity to even subtle cultural differences is important. An Australian chairman of a global company quickly learned that a common language is no insurance against cultural shocks. He complained of getting no respect with his direct Australian manner in England, so he adjusted and learned the ways of the English. He learned that when an English manager reacts to a project by saying, "Perhaps you ought to think about this a little more," he really means "You must be crazy. Forget it." But when he went to the United States he had to unlearn the lesson because when he told a manager, "Perhaps you ought to think about this a little more," the manager took him literally. Later, when he asked the manager why he went ahead with the project, the man replied, "Well, I thought about it, like you said, and the idea got better."

A good illustration of effective management of these kinds of failings was given by Roberto Goizueta, Chairman of the Board of Coca-Cola Company, in his address to the Town Hall of California in February, 1989:

> In the Caribbean, Africa, and the South Pacific [music for the "You Can't Beat the Feeling" advertising campaign] will feature a distinctive reggae beat. In Japan our theme will translate as "I Feel Coke," in Italy, "Unique Sensation," and in Chile, "The Feeling of Life." [However when] we discovered that the literal representation of Coca-Cola in Chinese characters meant "bite the wax tadpole" . . . we engaged an Oriental language specialist.[7]

He goes on to describe the corporate code of "Think globally, but act locally"[8] and how cultural differences affect more than advertising. In product line, the "orange" taste preferred in Germany is tart, but in Italy, it's sweet.

---

[5]Ibid., p. 22.

[6]Ibid.

[7]Goizueta, Roberto C. "Globalization—A Soft Drink Perspective." *Vital Speeches of the Day* (Speech delivered in Los Angeles, California) February 9, 1989. p. 360.

[8]Ibid., p. 361.

So to create a product that appeals to every culture; Coke uses local fruit to make their Fanta orange soft drink.

"Glocalize" is the Japanese term for making global decisions on strategic questions about products, capital, and research but letting local units decide tactical questions about packaging, marketing, and advertising. All successful global companies support this global/local mentality. In Japan the American Express slogan, "Membership has its privileges" translates to "Peace of mind only for members." A good global competitor knows how to assimilate the best aspects of a local practice.

Basically, becoming an effective global manager demands a good mix of multicultural literacy, language skills, global awareness, and fundamental management skills. At the postsecondary level, formal study of world history and geography, foreign peoples, languages and cultures, and comparative social, political, economic, and education systems must be combined with business management content.

Specific competencies have been identified for successful global managers. They are:

1. Know the language (foreign). Be able to speak and write it.

2. Understand the basic geopolitics, economics, social structure and culture.

3. Practice effective human relations.

4. Learn how to negotiate, bargain, and resolve conflicts in a cross-cultural setting.

5. Refine executive skills required to manage financially autonomous units dealing with foreign markets, governments, finances, stockholders, unions, etc.

6. Develop a talent and skill for tolerating ambiguous situations and adapting to new conditions.

7. Develop talent and potential of subordinates.

8. Exercise leadership skills that allow you to use your individual strength and personality to act forcefully but sensitively in an unfamiliar context.

9. Develop an understanding of: time zones, customs, religions, political systems, transportation and travel, international business practices, international business laws, international currency, and international credit systems.

EFFECTIVE METHODS, TEACHING STRATEGIES, AND STUDENT EVALUATION METHODS FOR INTERNATIONAL BUSINESS MANAGEMENT

Business management teachers need to expand their teaching style to include a variety of delivery methods. As language arts and the social sciences are integrated into successful global manager competencies, a team teaching approach to include faculty and students could be most effective.

A foreign language class could meet with the business management class to discuss, simulate, and role play global management situations and concepts. The history or social studies classes could share cultural, political, and geographic information as a "briefing" to the prospective global managers embarking for their foreign duty station.

The Teaching Methodology and Concepts Committee of the Association for Business Communication, 1988, identified a number of proven methods to teach multicultural concepts in a business communications class, which are applicable to international business management.[9] The committee reported poor intercultural communication, differences in languages, beliefs, and values as obstacles to the students planning business careers. Factors contributing to poor management could be one's vocal inflections, gestures, manners, body language, and concepts of time and space. Also, people judge those from other cultures by their own cultural standards, customs, and mores. Effective global managers must demonstrate the qualities of:

1. Patience—when coping with the inevitable ambiguities of intercultural communication
2. Tolerance—when cultural values differ sharply
3. Objectivity—needed because intercultural communication frequently involves different expectations and understandings
4. Empathy—can help to avoid causing unnecessary embarrassment or misunderstanding while remaining alert to differences in cultural perspectives
5. Respect—for the rightful place of all cultures in the world and a watchfulness against racism.

Some effective competency-based teaching materials are available from national consortia (such as MarkED in Ohio), and your local school district child-study team or guidance department may have support materials to address these topics.

Materials should focus on activities that encourage students to examine their own self-concept for trust, open-mindedness, ego strength, and the ability to accept ambiguity and diversity among people. They need to teach the ability to be flexible and adaptable. The committee recommends use of Brent Ruben's *Human Communication Handbook—Simulations and Games* (Vol. 1 & 2)[10], which includes a self-instructional guide to intercultural awareness, structured as a questionnaire.

Additional evidence suggests that role plays and simulations dealing with global markets (and not domestic markets) for the focus of their economic activity would be an effective method. Editorials have called for preparation that leads to competency in the integrated economy that links the United States, Asia, and Europe. The committee recommended John Condon and Fathi Yousef's intercultural cases in *An Introduction to Intercultural Communication.*[11] Role plays, simulations, and cases could be modified to focus on topical management situations that include scripts or roles played by students from a foreign language class in the appropriate language or business students who are learning short-term conversational business-oriented language instruction for "survival" linguistic competence.

Consider activities that involve global ecology issues with regard to international business-management interests, such as Asian whalers, oil spills,

---

[9] Teaching Methodology & Concepts Committee. "How to Teach Intercultural Concepts in a Basic Business Communication Class." *Bulletin of the Association for Business Communication.* v51, n3; September, 1988. p. 2.

[10] Ruben, Brent D., and Budd, Richard W. *Human Communication Handbook—Simulations and Games.* Vol. 1 & 2. Rochelle, New Jersey: Hayden Book Company, Inc. 1978.

[11] Condon, John C., and Yousef, Fathi. *An Introduction to Intercultural Communication.* Indianapolis, Indiana: Bobbs-Merrill Educational Publishing.

or similar newsworthy items like the transfer of technology with competitive nations, international airline security concerns, or issues related to the international exploitation of space for communications satellite placement (your science department may be helpful here).

Games are available from the history/geography department in most schools. Or, you could use commercially available games such as the popular board game, "RISK." And you may modify stock market simulations to confine them to global or multinational corporate stock purchases only. Various popular software games, such as: "Where in Europe is Carmen Sandiego?", "Where in the World is Carmen Sandiego?", "Balance of Power: 1990," and others teach basic geography and international politics. Your local computer store can recommend others.

Of course, travel abroad would be ideal. A supervised program of instruction for credit during a summer or vacation period, which could include a cooperative education component, as a culminating activity related to an international business management course, is supported by most of the research. A foreign business internship could incorporate visits to foreign retail, wholesale, service, and manufacturing companies; government agencies; financial institutions; plus museums and historical areas; and may include travel to several different countries.

Foreign-travel program content could include successful completion of the business management course or units, pre-trip orientation, the requirement of a written paper (which could be written in the host country language and graded by your school foreign language teacher), pre-trip interviews with business managers who have worked abroad, participation in discussions and seminars with foreign company executives, study of foreign company policies and practices, completion of a daily journal of experiences, and staying in the home of a foreign family.

If a relationship can be established with a "sister" foreign school or global corporate sponsor, consideration should be given to faculty exchanges and cooperative education, or apprenticeship students could participate in a job-exchange program with a foreign co-op or apprentice student. Business people, when traveling abroad, could participate in brief exchange or team teaching programs. Local trips to foreign consulates or global corporate headquarters, where available, could also provide students with an intercultural experience. Writing assignments that include reports on foreign trade journals, newsprint/magazine advertisements, or foreign television commercials could be included.

State agencies can also contribute to international business management initiatives by providing state-sponsored international events (such as model United Nations with a business perspective) and international education enrichment programs for teachers and students. Programs, projects, and special events for state/county/district-wide days that focus on world issues, business, and politics could be developed.

Contact local or state world trade centers, governors' offices, state economic development offices, and other affiliated agencies, and offer seminars, conferences and trade shows, and exchange programs.

RECOMMENDATIONS

The ideal method of a foreign internship or exchange does present some financial concerns. However, almost all federal government agencies and many private foundations have international study or exchange programs, with annual financial support of somewhere near $1 billion.

Three major federal sources for funds exist in international studies. They are the Fulbright Scholarship exchange program, the National Education Defense Act of 1958, and the International Education Act of 1966. For a broad range of international educational information, contact the U.S. Small Business Administration, the Agency for International Development, the U.S. Department of Commerce, and the U.S. Department of Agriculture.

Specialty programs, such as the President's International Youth Exchange Initiative and the U.S. Information Agency international (USIA) visitor's program administered through the privately run Institute for International Education in New York City, New York, are excellent sources of information on exchange programs. USIA officials announced a program in September, 1988, that permits the Soviet Union and the U.S. to each exchange 1,500 high school students annually by 1991. Organizations such as Rotary International should also be contacted for exchange programs and potential speakers.

Customized training courses in international business management could be offered to experienced business people who want to improve or expand their capabilities. These courses could be offered to the general public for awareness of diverse cultures, global issues, and business oriented foreign languages.

Another recommendation incorporates a practice that some global managers use—they form a world product (education) group in which group managers have worldwide responsibility for their product lines. The research shows that this works well only when foreign managers are brought into play as group leaders. Consider the formation of advisory councils at national and state levels for international education that could cooperate in joint funding projects with state governments, schools and colleges, and business and industry.

CONCLUSION

To prepare our students for the global marketplace we must teach them about world trade from an economic viewpoint. But we must be sure to instill in our students, at the same time, an awareness of the diversity of the cultures of the world's peoples. The following story depicts how different cultures and societies think. Maurice Van der Kuylen, senior vice president in charge of Asian operations for Alcatel of Belgium, recalls his first contact with the Chinese [in a joint telecommunications venture]. "Mr. Fong," [he] said, "time is money." To which Mr. Fong replied, "Mr. Van der Kuylen, time is eternity."[12]

---

[12] Kupfer, Andrew. "How to be a Global Manager." *Fortune*, March 14, 1988. p. 58.

PART III
INTERNATIONALIZING BUSINESS EDUCATION PROGRAMS: STRATEGIES AND ORGANIZATION

CHAPTER 9

What in the World Is Going On in Toledo, Ohio?

SANDRA KRUZEL and EDWARD CHAVEZ
Toledo Public Schools, Toledo, Ohio

As we approach the 21st century, more and more educational curricula will focus on the happenings of the entire world. Since the world is tied together through international business transactions, business education is an excellent place to develop students' global awareness.

What will become of our country if students in other leading world economies study our customs, culture, and practices but our students know nothing about theirs? Can our business people succeed in small and large businesses if they do not know how to deal with the Japanese? Can businesses in general survive with only Americans as customers, while those same Americans are purchasing more and more foreign products each day?

Our educational leaders must realize that global awareness should begin early in the classroom—in high school, if not before. Some secondary schools that have already included international business concepts and procedures in their curriculum are: Orlando, Florida; Atlanta, Georgia; Toledo, Ohio; and the states of Washington, Oregon, and Alaska. Administrators and teachers should be encouraged to obtain curricula from these pioneers of international business education and use them to create programs and courses to fit the needs of their own students and community.

Glass Capital of the World. As this article pertains to education in Toledo, Ohio, it will interest the reader to know something about this nation's 45th largest city. Toledo is the trading center for 14 counties in Northwest Ohio and Southeast Michigan. Its population, as of 1989, was 461,800 for the metropolitan area. The enrollment in Toledo public schools is approximately 67,000, with another 16,000 students enrolled in parochial schools.

The University of Toledo and nearby Bowling Green State University are the universities attended most often by Toledo students. Toledo has a major port on the Maumee River, which flows into Lake Erie, and its Toledo Express Airport is home to nine airlines.

INTERNATIONAL BUSINESS MANAGER PROGRAM

The International Business Manager program began in Toledo public schools in the fall of 1987. The goal of this outstanding program was to attract interested high school students who wished to pursue a career in the field of international business or explore the possibility. It is a 150-minute vocationally funded program and the first of its kind in the state of Ohio. An article in the *Balance Sheet*, May-June, 1988, entitled "Business Education with an International Flavor," describes all the details of beginning such a program.

Plan of action. The following outline reflects the plan of action taken to begin the International Business program in Toledo public schools:

1. Determine the rationale, goals, and objectives of the program.
2. Survey the business community for support of the program.
3. Get administration approval and vocational funding approval to begin developing the program.
4. Set up an advisory committee.
5. Develop curriculum for the program.
6. Select textbook and other material for the program.
7. Choose a teacher for the program.
8. Establish guidelines for student selection and recruitment.
9. Solicit sponsors for the mentor part of the program.
10. Promote the program.
11. Enroll students into the program.

Rationale

1. Rapid communication, increased travel, and greatly expanded awareness of interdependence by people all over the world have increased the need to know more about the economic, political, and cultural relationships among countries.
2. Today's business functions in a global society. Students need to expand their knowledge of economics, international trade and finance, world politics, and world culture because of the expanding business in our increasingly international world.
3. Toledo has one of the largest ports on the Great Lakes. There are over 2,000 jobs in this area alone that are directly related to foreign trade, from entry-level clerical positions to director of transportation at the Port Authority.
4. There is a need in business and industry for administrative assistants who are fluent in foreign languages and can recognize others' customs and cultures.
5. There is a need to graduate high school students who have a knowledge of international business concepts and procedures and who will obtain entry-level employment in this field and pursue this education at the university level.

Objectives. The objectives of this program include the following:

1. To prepare students for entry-level employment in business in the international trade divisions of large companies or in small businesses dealing solely in international trade operations.
2. To provide a basic background in international business for students who wish to continue their education at the university level in this area.
3. To prepare students with a combination of international business concepts and practices, with emphasis on those countries whose customs and cultures vary greatly from our own.
4. To provide a link between education and business for these international business students by means of a sponsorship/mentor program.

5. To encourage students interested in international business careers to learn a second language, particularly one that will be useful in the business world and in foreign trade, based on information received from advisory committees in the community.

Curriculum. The curriculum for this two-year program includes:

Accounting
Business communications
Business law/regulations
Career opportunities
Economics
Entrepreneurship
General office procedures
Geography
Employment skills
Foreign customs and cultures
Human relations skills
Import/export practices
International finance
Marketing concepts
Keyboarding skills
Metric system
Microcomputer/business applications
Overseas business travel
Trade documentation
Transportation
World trade practices

Students are also required to do reports from such sources as the *Wall Street Journal, Newsweek, Business Week,* and *U.S. News and World Report* and to keep up on current events involving international trade.

Sponsorship. The unique part of this program is that each student has a sponsor who is a business professional in an international company or division in the Toledo area. This person acts as a mentor to the student and provides the student with information about the real world of international trade. The student spends at least two days per month in the sponsor's business office either shadowing or doing actual hands-on duties and tasks. Students report back to their classmates about their companies and the activities with which they became involved. Many of these sponsors also come into the classroom to make presentations on their areas of expertise; for example, an international banker presented a talk about currency exchange. Many sponsors get involved in their students' research projects or put students in contact with someone who can assist them in their topic areas.

Some of these student/sponsor activities include:
1. Discussing the various aspects of international business
2. Explaining how the department functions and its involvement in international trade
3. Touring the company and/or international division
4. Viewing a slide presentation or any other media and/or literature that explains the specifics of the international operations
5. Studying maps of locations around the world where companies trade or have overseas divisions
6. Allowing the student to do hands-on tasks relating to international trade
7. Providing summer employment
8. Acting as a resource person or referring students to other persons in certain areas of expertise (such as the person in charge of international banking or marketing)
9. Learning about the products or services the company provides
10. Helping students prepare reports on the history of the company
11. Coming into the classroom to speak on a specific area of international trade
12. Assisting in research projects
13. Allowing students to attend meetings and/or seminars with division employees
14. Providing students with information on the languages and cultures of countries with which the company does trade (such as arranging a meeting with a person who has just returned from living in Japan for a year).

Companies in Toledo, Ohio, that have been involved in helping to initiate this program or that have served as sponsors over the past three years are:

The Andersons
Dana Corporation
The DeVilbiss Company
Gilbert Mail Service, Inc.
GlassTech
Huntington National Bank
International Projects, Inc.
Libbey Owens Ford
McMillan and Associates, Inc.
Ohio Citizens Bank
Owens-Corning Fiberglass Corporation
Owens-Illinois, Inc.
The Perfect Measuring Tape Company
Sheller Globe
Toledo-Lucas County Port Authority
Trans-World Shipping Service, Inc.

Student prerequisites. Because this area of study is very comprehensive and demanding and because it calls for a relationship with the business community, requirements for students to enter this program are as follows:

1. At least a 2.5 grade average
2. Fluency and/or enrollment in a foreign language course
3. Positive attitude and good human relations skills
4. Interest in pursuing international business as a career
5. Junior or senior class standing
6. Responsibility for their own transportation to and from the sponsoring company

Selecting the teacher. Ideally, the person selected to teach an international business program should have the following qualifications:

1. Certified business education teacher (vocational certification if funded)
2. Additional background or coursework in business administration (especially in the area of economics or marketing)
3. Fluent in and certified to teach a foreign language and appreciation and understanding of foreign cultures
4. Computer literate in business applications—spreadsheet, database, and word processing
5. Motivated to keep up with current events and attend ongoing workshops in the area of international trade.

The instructor is in charge of coordinating the schedules of sponsoring company personnel and the interning student. The instructor also has the responsibility for promoting the program and recruiting students. He or she also updates curriculum periodically and attends workshops and meetings to keep up with current events in the international business world. He or she should also be actively involved in international-trade professional organizations such as the Toledo Area International Trade Association (TAITA) and National Association of Small Business/International Trade Educators (NASBITE).

Foreign language requirement. Students entering this program are required to be fluent in a foreign language or enrolled in a foreign language course. The reason for combining international business education with foreign language competency is very apparent. A knowledge of history of foreign cultures and customs of leading trade partners is pertinent for this career. Students report on the customs of the peoples whose language they are studying and share this information with their classmates.

In addition to European business customs and culture, the program emphasizes Middle East and Eastern cultures which differ greatly from Western cultures with which students are more familiar and find easier to comprehend.

University involvement. Teachers of this program should establish a close relationship with a nearby university offering such a curriculum to encourage articulation and perhaps even scholarships for outstanding candidates. Also, high school students should be introduced to exchange programs and organizations that encourage student travel overseas. The University of

Toledo has an organization called AIESEC (a French acronym that stands for "International Association of Students in Economic and Business Management"). It sponsors an exchange program whereby American students work in businesses in foreign countries and foreign students work in the United States. College students who have participated in such an exchange are brought into the high school classroom to relate their experiences to the international business students.

Although much time and effort is needed to begin a program of this type, it is well worth it for the students, who will gain a strong foundation in business principles and a wealth of knowledge of the world around them. Those who continue their international education in college will already have the "nuts and bolts" needed to facilitate this career path.

Business professionals of America. Students in the International Business Manager program are also encouraged to become members and actively participate in the Business Professionals of America. This youth organization promotes leadership, business ethics, and professional business skills and organization. It creates an environment for students to showcase the skills and aptitude they possess in the various areas of business. It also provides interaction with other students with the same goals and objectives—on the local, state, and national levels.

By participating in events and activities provided by this student organization, students learn responsibility, dependability, friendship, and other human relation skills important to their future in the business community. It creates a learning experience by which students can begin to understand involvement and procedures in adult professional organizations, thereby encouraging professional membership throughout their business careers.

INTERNATIONAL TRADE CONCEPTS AND PROCEDURES

A one-semester course in international trade concepts should be offered as an elective course in all high schools. This course should be offered for business education credit for interested juniors and seniors and should include the following course content:

Careers in international business

Documentation

Foreign business practices

Foreign customs and cultures

History of international trade

Import/export practices

World profiles and current events.

This may be the only course students will ever take in their educational career that will prepare them to live in our international society. Also, this semester course may stir their interest enough to encourage them to pursue one of the international business opportunities.

BUSINESS EDUCATION/SOCIAL STUDIES

College graduates with a degree in geography are often employed by business and industry. The idea of merging course content from business education and social studies creates the ideal course for business students and other interested students to obtain a social studies credit. Together these two departments could create such courses as International Business Geography or Global Economics. While satisfying one of the social studies requirements, this course would give more meaning to a geography course for a business student.

To obtain social studies credit, these courses should be taught by certified economics or social studies teachers. However, the courses should be designed with the help of business teachers. Keep in mind that many business teachers are also certified to teach economics.

INTEGRATING INTERNATIONAL CONCEPTS AND PROCEDURES IN EXISTING BUSINESS EDUCATION PROGRAMS

Secretarial, accounting, data processing, and general office support programs also need to include international concepts and general international trade practices in their curriculum. These business education programs, which prepare students for employment in the business world, need to broaden their awareness beyond dealing with the American business office and U.S. visitors. Office support staffs need to be aware of different cultures as more companies expand and will continue to expand their markets. Their customers may not always be Americans.

If a secretary is asked to make hotel reservations for Chin Ho from Beijing, will the reservation be made under Mr. Chin or Mr. Ho? When asked to set up dinner reservations for executives flying in from India, what restaurants would serve the types of food Indians enjoy? When asked to place a long distance call to Japan, when would be the best time of the day to do so? It takes patience to develop relationships that are necessary to deal with foreign customers and clients, and an office staff dealing often or even occasionally with foreigners needs to be aware of this.

These are just some topics which should be included in the curriculum for preparing students for employment in business occupations. We could go on and on about situations that secretaries, accountants, legal assistants, medical receptionists, or data entry clerks may encounter throughout the next ten years in the business office. Here are some suggested topics to include in these business education programs:

Customs and cultures of major trade partners

Foreign business practices—import/export, documentation

International communications (telex, cable, fax)

International business careers

Overseas business travel.

ENTREPRENEURSHIP

Courses in entrepreneurship must also include global concepts if students are to be prepared to do business in the 21st century. As free enterprise continues to grow throughout the world, it becomes critical to success for a business to have what it takes to succeed in the global arena. Getting into international markets may be an appropriate strategy for small businesses that have an exportable product. A willingness to develop longlasting personal relationships and a different set of values and ethics appeals to many of our foreign customers. These concepts should be included for even small businesses whose continued profits may depend upon overseas trade. Toledo Public Schools hopes to implement this one-semester course beginning in the 1991-92 school year.

As more and more underdeveloped countries and communist countries are entering the free market, students must be taught to think of long-term profits in addition to immediate profits. It may take five or more years to realize a profit from setting up a business in China, India, or Russia; however, it may prove to be well worth the wait.

Going global can provide excellent opportunities for small businesses as well as the large corporations. According to George Rosenfield, owner of Tasco, a family-owned business that has expanded overseas, "Whatever success you've had domestically is available to you in other countries. If you treat those people in the other countries exactly as you do your better accounts in this country, then the opportunity is there."[1]

Because Toledo is second in the state of Ohio in the development of small businesses, Toledo Public Schools hopes to begin a one-semester entrepreneur class soon. This class will also include international trade concepts and practices. Some international trade concepts to incorporate in the entrepreneurship class or small business management program are:

Business ethics

Foreign business practices

Foreign customs and cultures

Foreign market potential

Human relations skills—domestic and foreign

Importing and exporting procedures/documentation.

Help is available to small businesses that would like to know more about exporting their goods or services. Students should be taught where to get this information. A state's commerce department or department of economic development is a place to start. These people would also serve as excellent resource speakers for classes. Students could also contact the International Trade Administration of the United States Commerce Department or the United States Small Business Administration's Office of International Trade, 1141 L Street N.W., Washington, DC 20416 (202) 653-7794.

---

[1] Nelton, Sharon. "Family Firms' Global Reach," Nation's Business February, 1990, p. 51.

CONCLUSION

It is time to begin looking at business education from a global perspective. To do otherwise would be placing business students behind their competition in other countries. As the world is being drawn closer and closer through technology, economics, and democracy, it is important to teach students how others think, how they act, the meaning of their appearance or customs, and how to interact in this international society. Only then can it be said that business students are prepared to enter the 21st century world of business.

CHAPTER 10

Integrating International Business Topics at the Secondary Level

JAMES H. BEISTLE

Unity High School, Balsam Lake, Wisconsin

An early morning telephone call is received by a major distributor of automotive books and periodicals in the United States. A bookstore operator in New Zealand is calling to place an order before leaving for the day. Down the hall in the same U.S. firm the head of foreign accounts checks the clock to see if it is a good time to call a customer in Italy about an overdue account. In another office, about 20 minutes away, management and engineers are discussing with their Swiss owners changes in the design on a new packaging machine. Two blocks up the street a sales department is making preparations for a trade show in Germany while production personnel are meeting representatives of the Peoples' Republic of China about a joint venture to manufacture food stuffs for export to Japan. In a nearby city brewery, officials are anxiously awaiting word from their Australian owner concerning what will be done to solve the current cash-flow problem. Big city, urban, industrial, cosmopolitan America? No! Small town, rural, agricultural, Midwest United States.

Who are the employees in these offices? Most of the administrative support workers are high school graduates with little or no postsecondary training. The production forces are almost entirely workers who ended their formal education with high school graduation. What did these workers learn about international business and trade in high school? Little, if anything, and most likely nothing. Yet they are deeply involved in international business. Do secondary schools have an obligation to teach these international business concepts and understandings? The answer must be a most definite "Yes."

The world has become a global community, and the United States is a major player in it. Students, regardless of where they live, must be offered opportunities to gain and expand their knowledge and understanding of how business operates in an international setting and to develop an insight into how these operations will affect their lives and their future. The following table illustrates changes in the U.S./world economy during the past quarter century:[1]

	Early 1960's	Late 1980's
U.S. exports as a percent of GNP	5.8%	11.0%
U.S. imports as a percent of GNP	4.7%	12.0%
American produced consumer electronics sold in U.S.	95.0%	40.0%
U.S. automobile imports	$1.0 billion	$85.0 billion
U.S. world market in manufactured goods	25.0%	16.0%
U.S. dept foreign owned	4.0%	15.0%
Foreign bank offices operating in U.S.	40.	800.
International banking activities: World income	1.0%	12.0%
International trade: World production	11.0%	17.0%

Politically, economically, and commercially the United States abandoned isolationism with the world wars, but the educational system in America has not yet adjusted to this fact. The school system still operates its programs as if the United States is the only commercial and industrial entity and not part of the total world economy.

RATIONALE FOR SECONDARY INTERNATIONAL BUSINESS EDUCATION

Where and how should the high school, and particularly the business education department, provide students with the necessary concepts, understanding, and skills of international business and trade?

This task can be accomplished by business education through its threefold purpose of imparting knowledge to the students so they can learn to develop their roles as citizen, consumer, and worker.

The business education programs of the past were skill oriented. Typing, shorthand, and bookkeeping were its mainstays, with office practice for the girls and maybe a business-law class for seniors—if an instructor was interested and available. No other department in the vocational education area, or for that matter any curricular area, could challenge the success of the business education department in its preparation of students for their future careers. Business education faculty, however, operated in a self-contained department and made little contact with other departments and academic areas. The advancement of technology has brought about some change, but except for the more progressive schools, the traditional pattern continues.

The business education departments met the goal of preparing students for business, as workers. However, the development of students as consumers and citizens was not aggressively pursued and in many cases is still not given

---

[1] Ankrim, Ernest M. "International Economics: A Path to Understanding the World." *Social Education* 54:90; February 1990.

much consideration. There must be a recognition that whatever the curriculum consists of, it must contribute to developing an understanding by the students of the forces that operate in modern society. The entire school program must focus on helping youth become active, intelligent citizens with a deep commitment to their responsibilities and participation.[2]

What must business education teachers do? A look to the future is crucial. With the presence of computers at the kindergarten level, keyboarding will be taught in the elementary grades, thus losing its past role as the magic drawing card. Increased academic demands mandated by many state legislatures have caused and will continue to cause a decline in enrollments in vocational education areas.

To avoid a drop in student numbers, business teachers have a number of opportunities available. One option is to develop a K-12 business education curriculum. Since business affects all students, who else could serve as a better resource to kindergarten and elementary teachers than business teachers? Cooperation with other departments—both academic and vocational—at the junior high and high school levels through the teaching of joint units and projects could be implemented.

Through these cooperative efforts, business principles and concepts—including those dealing with international business—could be presented. Courses in communications and economics could be added to the business education curriculum and "academic course equivalency credit" granted the students, enabling them to fulfill their mandated requirements in social studies and language arts. Although these are not the typical classes taught by business education teachers, here is an opportunity to open the doors to more students. Many business teachers are better prepared to teach the communications skills needed in today's business-oriented life than those instructors who normally teach these skills. Past research has shown that business education teachers are better prepared to teach economics than are social studies teachers.[3] A review of current college catalogs continues to support this finding.

During the last few years there has been an increased demand for a stronger infusion of international perspectives into the business curriculum, brought about by three factors: (1) the rapid growth in the number of U.S. firms becoming international in both philosophy and scope of operations; (2) the continued multiplication of foreign companies doing business in the U.S.; and (3) the increased interdependency among nations for economic growth.[4] As foreign companies increase their presence in America, an increasing number of Americans will be working for and with these companies in which they must deal daily with different value systems, management practices,

---

[2]Frankel, M. L. "The Emerging Role of the Business Teacher in Economic Education." *The Emerging Content and Structure of Business Education.* Yearbook No. 8. Washington, D.C.: National Business Education Association, 1970. Chapter 21, p. 166.

[3]Hosler, Russell J. and Price, Ray G. "Business Teacher Preparation for Teaching Economic Understandings." *Business Education Forum* 16:8; May 1962.

[4]Chidomere, Rowland C. "A Multi-System Approach to Internationalizing the Basic Business Course." *Journal of Business Education* 61:136; December 1985.

and attitudes.[5] A global perspective must be developed and presented to the students because for American industry to remain competitive in the world market, Americans must become more knowledgeable about the cultural values and practices of other countries.

Should the high school pass on to the postsecondary technical colleges and the universities the task of providing students with knowledge of international business concepts? The answer must be a definite, "No." Less than one-half of high school students continue their education beyond graduation. In some states less than one-half of the students do not graduate from high school. Therefore, topics relating to international business must be presented in the high school program.

REVIEW OF LITERATURE

A review of the literature in business education for the past few years shows a limited number of articles concerning international business education. The 1988 *Business Education Index* listed only 34 articles under International Business; 12 of these were published in the *SIEC Review* and were by European authors.[6] Of the remaining 22 listings, most dealt with internationalizing the business education curriculum at the postsecondary level, offering virtually nothing relative to high school programs.

An examination of current textbooks presents nearly the same picture. Except for a chapter or two in a few textbooks, no mention is made of international business. Textbooks that do include materials are usually in the area of introduction to business, business communication, and marketing.

CURRICULAR APPROACHES

Various approaches can be used to incorporate international business concepts and topics into the secondary school business education program: (1) the establishment of a full curriculum with a number of courses covering a number of years in the secondary program, (2) the designing of just one or maybe two courses, and (3) the integration of units within already existing courses. The particular approach used will vary with each situation.

Core-curriculum model. A joint vocational education project, funded through the Carl Perkins Act, was used by the states of Alaska, Oregon, and Washington to design a four-course international trade curriculum and was built on the skills and knowledge gained in other business education courses and general education courses taught at the high school level.

---

[5]Varner, Iris I. and Alexander, Wilma Jean. "Internationalizing the Basic Business Course." *Business Education Forum* 38:15-17; February 1984.

[6]Blockhus, Wanda. "Research in International Business Education." *Business Education Forum* 44:35-38; February 1990.

SCOPE OF INTERNATIONAL TRADE

Background for International Trade Core

Basic Math Skills	Keyboarding
Metric System	Computer Skills
History	Foreign/World Language
Government	English/Communications
Geography	Employability Skills
Cultural Awareness	Marketing
Economics	General Office Procedures

International Trade Core

State/Regional Profiles	Import and Export Basics
World Profile	Laws and Regulations
International Economics	Communications
International Finance	Entrepreneurship
International Marketing and Transportation	Trade Documentation
	Employability Skills

Specialized or Advanced Courses

Trade Documentation
- Telephone Usage
- Telecommunications
- Written Communications
- Office Procedures
- Computer Skills
- Business Meetings
- Flow of Documentation
- Documentation Preparation

Entrepreneurship
- Evaluation of Personal Opportunities
- Business Plan Development and Implementation

Advanced International Trade
- Distribution Systems
- Sales Strategies
- Pricing
- Import/Export Plan
- Overseas Business Travel
- Finance
- Laws and Regulations
- Economics

SOURCE: Oregon Department of Education. *International Trade Curriculum*, p. 8.

The goal of the international trade curriculum is to provide students with a foundation in international business that will serve as a basis for further training and development in international trade careers. Competencies were identified for specialized training as well as advanced-level international trade education.[7]

---

[7] Oregon Department of Education. *International Trade Curriculum*. Salem: Oregon Department of Education, 1989, p. i.

COURSE: INTERNATIONAL TRADE. Length: one semester of year. Grades: 9-12.

This course provides introductory knowledge and basic skills in international trade. State/regional profiles, world profiles, exporting and importing basics, international economics and finance, international marketing and transportation, laws and regulations, communications, entrepreneurship, trade documentation, and employability skills are covered. Students must successfully complete this course before they can participate in more advanced courses leading to international trade employment.

COURSE: INTERNATIONAL TRADE DOCUMENTATION. Length: One semester. Grades: 12th grade or postsecondary.

This course provides specialized training in skills necessary for employment opportunities in international trade. Procedures, processes, technology, and the preparation of the highly specialized documents used in international trade are covered.

COURSE: ENTREPRENEURSHIP. Length: One semester or year. Grades: 9-12 or postsecondary.

This course provides specialized training for students interested in learning how to start a business. It covers evaluating business opportunities, developing a comprehensive business plan, and establishing a business.

COURSE: ADVANCED INTERNATIONAL TRADE. Length: One semester or year. Grades: 12th grade or postsecondary.

Students will acquire advanced competencies in international trade including international marketing and transportation, overseas business travel, business planning, laws and regulations, international economics, and finance.[8]

The St. Paul, Minnesota, school systems at its Humboldt Secondary Complex approached international business from a different angle. At the six-year junior high/senior high school, the eight-course program in "International Studies and Careers" is designed to fulfill the social studies requirements of the students. All of the courses are offered with an international perspective. In addition to four to six years of a world language, students take the remainder of their courses in either college preparatory classes or career-related courses, primarily in business education and home economics and focus on international careers. The goal of the program is to provide students with a strong preparation to enter the international arena, particularly meeting the needs of international business and organizations for employees who are competent in more than one language. Students work toward proficiency in a foreign language, awareness of cultural differences, competencies in communications, and attainment of basic skills to work cooperatively in multicultural settings.[9] Career opportunities, available both in the United States and overseas for graduates of the program, are international office careers, tourism and airlines, international sales, language translation, international hotel services, international food services, import/export business, international communications, international law, teaching, the United Nations, and the Peace Corps. The employability skills for these careers are taught primarily in the business education department.

---

[8] Ibid., p. 11.

[9] St. Paul (Minnesota) Public Schools. "International Studies and Careers." Brochure.

Courses in the International Studies and Careers program are:[10]

7th grade	American History—ISCP	One year
8th grade	World Geography	One year
9th grade	Comparative Governments—ISCP	One semester
9th grade	International Careers Exploration	One semester

Students will assess career interests and research to develop a personal career direction. Special attention will be given careers where international understandings and language training are important factors. Procedures will involve some on-the-job experiences. Students will build practical thinking skills in investigating careers and setting up a high school study plan.

10th grade	World History/Citizenship	One year
11th grade	American History—ISCP	One year
12th grade	International Relations/Communications	One semester

Problems of interpersonal contact with people of other cultural and national backgrounds will be studied to guide students to understanding the importance of cultural knowledge in effective international relations.

12th grade	International Economics and Trade	One semester

An introduction to basic economic theories will be followed by an examination of multi-national trade. The reasons for, the importance of, and the procedures used in international trade will be presented and evaluated. Students will develop an understanding of international trade and analyze its influence on our local economy.

Course model. Another approach to internationalizing the curriculum is to offer a course in international business or international trade. A number of these have already been designed; an example is in the Joint Council on Economic Education's Teaching Strategies: "International Trade."

Some states have developed a course or are in the process of doing so. Alabama, in its business organization/business management module, lists six of the eight topics and identifies 60 percent of the student outcomes in the international area as presented below.[11]

TOPICS	STUDENT OUTCOMES
	Students will
Basic Concepts	(1. - 6.)
Management	(7. - 18.)
International Trade	19. Describe the effects of competition and the profit motive in our economic system.
	20. Contrast the American enterprise system with other economic systems, and explain how national economics are measured.

---

[10]St. Paul (Minnesota) Public Schools. "International Studies and Careers." Curriculum draft paper; Fall 1989.

[11]Alabama Department of Education. "Business Education: Business Organization/Business Management Module." p. 27-31.

	21. Discuss ways exchange rates are set and the role they play in foreign trade.
22. Differentiate between real and apparent standards of living among peoples of different countries.
23. Generalize reasons for business investments in foreign industry.
International Banking	24. Illustrate methods of payments for international transactions.
25. List services provided by the banking industry to foreign trade.
26. Describe how banks transact business with overseas counterparts.
International Transportation	27. Give examples of how international shipments are transported from one country to another.
28. Determine the required arrangements and paperwork for international transportation.
29. Develop an understanding of how title and risk pass from seller to buyer in foreign trade.
American Business Office	30. Give examples of how the computer affects foreign trade.
31. Compare the American business office with the foreign business office.
32. Identify the types and uses of equipment in international business.
Government's Role in Foreign Trade	33. Outline the role of trade in the United States' foreign policy.
34. Explain ways governments protect their local industry from foreign competition.
35. Identify federal government agencies that monitor imports.
36. Recognize ways in which the federal government restricts access to American know-how and selected products.
37. Describe uses of federal and state government assistance in exporting American products.
International Business Careers	38. Explore various career paths available in international business.
39. Determine ways to change international perceptions, stereotypes, and prejudices affecting international trade.
40. Compare customs and cultures of major trade countries that affect cultural interactions on an international basis.

41. Discuss the impact of foreign holidays on international trade.
42. Recognize the importance of knowing a foreign language.
43. Examine the effects of terrorism on international trade.
44. Explain how and where disputes between citizens of different countries are settled.
45. Explain the importance of protecting intellectual property (patents, copyrights, trademarks) in foreign trade.

Fairfax County, Virginia, public schools have designed a one-year senior elective course in international trade and marketing. Taught in the marketing department, the course's purpose is to acquaint students with the vast opportunities in the world economy, including international finance and banking, import and export trade, and international marketing. Course content blends macro- and micro-economic theory with a study of international culture, economic concepts, practices, and applications. Domestic and foreign internships provide students with additional opportunities for actual experiences in an international business environment. The course consists of nine units:[12]

INTRODUCTION TO INTERNATIONAL TRADE & MARKETING: an overview.

BASICS OF ECONOMICS: Micro and macro economics.

INTERNATIONAL MARKETING TRANSACTIONS: Importance of international trade vs. isolationism.

INTERNATIONAL TRADE: History, present day perceptions and practices, world political economy.

THE U.S.A. AND INTERNATIONAL TRADE: Balance of trade, regional differences.

TRADE TRANSACTIONS: Financing and structuring a trade transaction.

INTERNATIONAL MARKET ASSESSMENT AND DEVELOPMENT: Contracts, implementation of sale, understanding foreign cultures.

MARKETING PENETRATION: U.S. pentration into foreign markets, foreign penetration into U.S. market.

MARKETING A PRODUCT: Market/product research, Target Marketing.

An important consideration that should be kept in mind when developing an international business course is to design it so it can be used to fulfill the academic and/or graduation requirements of the general education classes—the use of course equivalency credit.

Unit-integration model. The third approach to internationalizing the business education curriculum is the unit-integration method—limited only by the imagination of the teacher. Many of the textbooks in basic business, marketing, and communications have a unit, chapter, or topics within a chapter covering a variety of topics in this area. Currently, one publisher

---

[12]Fairfax County (Virginia) Public Schools. "International Trade & Marketing." Brochure.

is planning a series of unit-type publications concerning international trade studies that will include topics such as culture, careers, communications, and economics.

Joint projects with other departments in the school, particularly foreign language and social studies, could be undertaken. Involvement in the "sister school" program where a U.S. school is paired with a similar school in a foreign country is another possibility. Team teaching with other departments should be explored. Little add-ons such as typing of foreign addresses, using the international date and time formats, or figuring the exchange rate of money could enhance a regular unit.

STRATEGIES AND SUGGESTIONS

There are many ways a teacher can incorporate international business concepts into the classes now taught or proposed for addition to the curriculum in the future. Space does not permit a total list nor could one person come up with a complete listing. But one method that could be used in all classes is to use the school's foreign students or students who have lived overseas as resources. Listed below are a few suggestions that may be used in the various curricular areas.

Basic business. The business law class could focus on the purchasing of goods from a foreign country and how breach of contract and warranties are handled. Also, the passing of title, the risk of loss, and the preparation of necessary documents for import could be covered. The impact of religious influence on both trade and law, something unknown in the United States, could be discussed. Almost all of the topics listed above could be woven into the different economic and general business classes whether as a unit or just as an enhancement of some chapter or subunit. Materials from the Joint Council on Economic Education are excellent resources. Students could prepare bulletin boards showing imports and exports with the various countries, including balance of trade figures. Newspaper and magazine articles relating to international trade might be another source for classroom discussion. An employee from a local company involved in international business could be invited to give a presentation on how foreign trade affects his or her job and the economy of the local community.

Communications. This is probably the area that allows for the most imaginative ways of infusing international topics into the classroom activities. The computer and electronic communications have opened up a whole new set of skills needed by students entering the labor market after high school graduation. Placing an international telephone call, converting the American units of weights and measures into the metric system used in most other countries, applying for a passport and visa, and calculating the exchange rate of money are but a few of the activities that might be assigned. Letter writing styles including the proper form of address could be presented. Student projects might include the figuring of postage and telephone rates to other countries and the researching of limitations on kind and type of items that may be mailed and the reasons for such restrictions. The use of a fax as a means of international communications should be explored. The impact of non-verbal communication on individuals of a foreign nation should be discussed, stressing what message certain actions convey. Cooperation with the foreign language teacher could result in letter transcription from notes in shorthand or another system in one language into another language. Gregg materials are available in both English and Spanish editions. Cultural differences need to be stressed when dealing with citizens of other countries—even if it is an English-speaking nation.

Finance. Currency exchange rates, credit card use in a foreign country, banking facilities, and methods of international communications are some items that would interest students going fishing in Canada or taking a winter vacation in Cancun. A discussion of the whole area of tourism could include tariffs, import duties, and limitations. Advanced classes could study the balance of trade and balance of payments along with the impact of U.S. investments in foreign countries and the impact of foreign investments in the United States.

Marketing. The curricular area having the greatest potential for expanding into international business is marketing education. Not only could an international trade course be established incorporating these concepts and topics, almost every course in this area could be enriched by the addition of these items. Joint projects with agriculture, home economics, social studies, and foreign language departments should be explored. Here again use of materials from the Joint Council on Economic Education might be beneficial. Analysis of magazine advertisements could be made and the preparation of advertising materials for use in a foreign country might be assigned. How best to market a product when television and radio is not available, as in some foreign countries, should be discussed.

In incorporating any of these activities and projects in any class, the level of ability of the students should be a major consideration. It may be necessary to modify the activity or project. The advantage of this approach is the infusion of international business concepts into the various courses and an explanation of American practices relative to foreign and developing countries.[13]

CONCLUSION

International business concepts and topics do have a place in the secondary school curriculum. It is imperative that all persons involved—business education teachers, teacher educators, state and local supervisors and consultants, and publishers—work cooperatively to accomplish this goal.

To achieve the goal of incorporating international business concepts into the business curriculum, the following recommendations should be pursued:

- Business education teachers need to become more aggressive in designing new programs and courses for the high school curriculum.

---

[13]Chidomere, p. 138.

- Colleges and universities should provide high school teachers inservice workshops and summer courses on how to internationalize the curriculum.
- Undergraduate programs in business teacher education should allow students to acquire an economics minor as part of the regular course of study so they may teach courses that fulfill some of the social-studies credit requirements.
- State business education directors, supervisors, and consultants should have courses or units on international business added to state curriculum guides, involving state departments of trade and economic development for suggested topics most meaningful to that state.

The importance of students' understanding international business was summarized in comments made by Scott McCallum, Lieutenant Governor of Wisconsin, on his return from a 1990 trade mission to China:

> With the rapid increase in telecommunications and transportation systems, the world is becoming more of a global community. We must not isolate ourselves. The more students prepare themselves to face the international marketplace, the better off we will all be. We have entered a new age, with democracies emerging in all corners of the globe. With those democracies will come more "open door" policies. The states and businesses that become involved in international trade early, will be poised to reap the benefits of their investments in later years.

CHAPTER 11

The International Business Education Program at Central Piedmont Community College

RICHARD K. ZOLLINGER and JUDITH F. PATTERSON
Central Piedmont Community College, Charlotte, North Carolina

Central Piedmont Community College is responding to the new era of the global economic market across the curriculum, with innovative programs in response to industry's needs, and through its international business education and assistance programs. By providing students with the knowledge and skills needed in an increasingly competitive job market, the college is also assisting the local economy by creating a valuable, competent workforce for its international business community.

CHARLOTTE AREA

Central Piedmont Community College is located in Charlotte, North Carolina, the southern piedmont region of the state. Served by an international airport and a strong ground-transport industry, the area is a magnet for business.

Charlotte is one of the fastest growing cities in the South. Since 1970, the population of Charlotte has grown from 241,420 (1970 census) to 315,473 (1980 census) to 389,650 (1989 census update estimate). This represents a net growth of 62 percent in a twenty year period. Charlotte is the geographical center of the nation's fifth largest urban region, and more than half the nation lives within a 650-mile radius. More people live within this radius than live within 650 miles of Atlanta or New York.

Furthermore, Charlotte has more banking resources than any other city between Philadelphia and Los Angeles. Its banking resources total $57 billion compared to Atlanta with $48 billion and Miami with $13 billion. This financial power enables the city to attract business and industry to the area. Twenty-three hundred firms have relocated to Charlotte within the last 10 years, bringing a total of 380,000 jobs and $2.5 billion in investment.

INTERNATIONAL BUSINESS COMMUNITY

Not only growing as a center for American business, Charlotte is becoming a center for international business as well. A Foreign Trade Zone was established in September of 1980, and an inland port was opened in 1984. Over half of North Carolina's firms and nearly one-third of the nation's top 100 foreign firms are represented in the Charlotte-Mecklenburg area. By 1989

Charlotte had attracted a total of 251 foreign-owned firms representing 20 countries, with West Germany leading, followed by Great Britain, Japan, and Switzerland.

North Carolina as a whole is one of the few states in the nation to have a favorable balance of trade. Because of the diversity of its industry, exports have exceeded imports for the last two years. First Wachovia Bank's North Carolina World Trade Index released in the fourth quarter of 1989 indicated the following statistics: International trade activity rose 18.4 percent in the fourth quarter of 1989 compared to 1988. The 1989 fourth-quarter trade figure was $12.2 billion, of which $6.6 billion was in exports and $5.6 was in imports, and the trade surplus was $990.1 million in merchandise for the year.

CENTRAL PIEDMONT COMMUNITY COLLEGE

Such dynamic population growth and economic expansion has challenged Central Piedmont Community College to change and grow to meet the needs of its constituency. The college has worked to meet this challenge.

Central Piedmont Community College is the largest community college of North Carolina's 58 technical and community colleges and is ranked in the top five community colleges nationwide. Founded in 1963, it has grown from a college initially serving 2,000 students annually to one serving 50,000 students each year. In addition to its main campus, Central Piedmont Community College has many other teaching facilities including four learning centers around the city, and over 200 satellite locations dispersed throughout Mecklenburg County. Within the last few years, the college has implemented a system of delivering courses via cable and microwave television broadcasts to the learning centers, enabling students around the viewing area to take the same courses, at the same time, from the same instructor. In addition, the college has further developed instructional telecommunications to offer educational opportunities through nontraditional modes of education such as TV, radio, and computers. These courses differ from traditional courses in that students view and hear lectures at home and take tests in testing centers on campus or in off-campus learning centers.

THE INTERNATIONAL BUSINESS EDUCATION PROGRAM

With the growing interest in international business in its service area, the college's leadership in 1984 recognized the need to establish international business information, training, and assistance programs to serve both students and the business community. A survey of the business community was conducted to identify the services, information, and training that business leaders found lacking locally. Based on the analysis of survey results, a program was designed and a grant was solicited from the U.S. Department of Education through its Business and International Education Program. The first of three matching grants under HEA Title VI-B, was received in 1985 to establish the International Business Center at the college, to activate and to maintain the International Trade Education Network, and to develop an associate degree and a certificate in international business.

The staffing of the International Business Center reflects the three main focuses of the program:

(1) *The International Business Program,* which comprises the degree and certificate tracks, the curriculum or credit side of the overall international business education program, is under the charge of the International Business Program director;

(2) *Information delivery,* including the International Trade Resource Library and the International Trade Education Network, is the responsibility of the Information Services/International Trade Education Network coordinator;

(3) *Community outreach,* which includes non-credit international business courses and seminars, one-on-one business counseling, and other services, is directed by the International Business coordinators. The Center's director is the administrative head.

Objectives of the International Business Program. The continuing growth in the number of international companies choosing Charlotte as their U.S. base of operations, the growing interest on the part of North Carolina companies in engaging in international trade, and the increase in international competition for domestic markets requires a labor force able to function within an international business environment. The International Business Program was developed to meet this need by providing trained and educated personnel. In addition, the program provides the knowledge and skills needed to be a valuable resource in the areas of international banking, freight forwarding, customs brokerage, import/export transportation, and international sales and marketing.

The program is also influencing other curricula at the college. For example, the International Business Program supports guest lectures on international business topics and offers an introductory international business course as a free elective for twelve targeted programs. The programs were selected according to the potential involvement of each program's graduates in international trade or international business. The programs are accounting, banking and finance, business administration, business computer programing, general office technology, insurance, marketing and retailing, paralegal technology, real estate, secretary legal, secretary executive, and traffic and transportation management.

Associate degree. Graduates of the international business curriculum earn the associate in applied science-international business degree. This degree program is made up of 115 total quarter credit hours of which twelve courses, or 36 quarter credit hours, are directly linked to international business and make up the core courses of the International Business Program. These core courses are

Introduction to International Business

International Business Practices

Business Foreign Language

Export Transportation Management

Import Transportation Management

International Marketing
Economics of International Trade
International Business Law
International Banking
International Accounting and Taxation
Cooperative Work Experience I
Cooperative Work Experience II.

In addition to the core courses, other important courses were incorporated that are essential to an education in international business but taught under other departments. An example is introduction to world geography.

In order to receive the associate degree, a foreign language is also required. The college offers language classes in Spanish, German, French, and Russian. A student with no prior foreign language education experience must typically complete 24 credit hours to obtain a usable communication level. Requiring students to be fluent in a foreign language is not only a valuable asset for the international business community, but also serves as an avenue for gaining exposure to different cultures represented globally.

The International Business Program serves a broad range of customers. The program is composed of students who are continuing their education after graduation from high school and students from the business community who want to change or advance their careers by studying the field of international business. To meet the unique needs of each of our students, each course is offered as a day course and as a night course.

Cooperative education. After students satisfactorily complete four required courses (Introduction to Business, Introduction to International Business, International Business Practices, Introduction to World Geography), three elective core courses, and if they have a 3.0 grade point average, they are eligible for a two-term or six-month cooperative education placement. Through the Cooperative Education Program students can apply their skills under the guidance of a company actively involved in international business.

The International Business Program is working with the Cooperative Education Department to recruit firms in the international business community that are interested in offering students a minimum of 110 or 220 hours of employment per quarter depending on course credit assigned. The program director and the supervisor of the firm will closely assist the student in developing and evaluating measurable learning objectives that are related to the student's academic studies. These objectives have been generated by the students and approved by the Cooperative Education Office and the International Business Program director.

Presently, students are placed in the following specific business areas: international banking, freight forwarders, custom house brokers, customs, international business sales, and international marketing.

International Business Certificate. The program also offers a certificate track consisting of 36 credit hours of core courses in international business. These are the same core courses offered in the degree program, excluding the cooperative education courses.

The typical certificate student differs from the degree student in that many already have ample experience in business and/or international business, have a bachelor's or even a master's degree, and want to specialize in international business.

Information delivery. A second needs assessment of the international business community, conducted in the spring of 1988, showed clearly that of all direct services provided, the companies surveyed found the International Trade Resource Library the most useful. Though small in terms of space and number of volumes, the library has both background and current materials directly related to international trade, marketing, and culture that small to medium sized companies could not justify purchasing, but that are invaluable to them in making sound business decisions. Of course, Central Piedmont students and faculty use the library for research as well.

The International Trade Education Network is a computerized bulletin board and file system that provides for the efficient exchange of information related to international trade and international business education. Colleges and universities beginning or expanding such programs are often frustrated by being unable to find a central reliable resource for gaining a comprehensive view of available materials in the field. The International Trade Education Network addresses this problem.

Information includes abstracts of Title VI-B funded projects from 1983 to the present, lists of publications and videos on international trade topics, news of upcoming events of interest to international trade educators, and the like. All files may be downloaded from the host computer to the user's. It is not simply a database maintained in a central location; participation implies a responsibility to enrich the available information by uploading information as well. Electronic mail and teleconferencing are two other services available through the network.

Community outreach. Maintaining a close and cooperative relationship between the college's international programs and those businesses, government agencies, and private organizations having an international focus is the responsibility of the Office of International Coordination. This is achieved through service on Chamber committees, participation in the local chapter of the World Trade Association, arranging for cosponsorship of seminars and other such projects, and similar activities.

Recent seminars that have been conducted have included several related to trade with Canada, a particular emphasis for the Center because of the U.S.-Canada Free Trade Agreement and because of the vigorous trade relationship North Carolina has with Canada. North Carolina exported over $1 billion worth of goods to Canada and imported around $552 million in 1987, so there is a great deal of interest in the business community in topics related to the nation's largest trading partner. The Center has also sponsored seminars on doing business with Japan, on the implications of Europe 1992, and on marketing opportunities in Mexico.

In addition, the responsibilities of the International Business coordinators are to develop and supervise all international-business continuing-education courses. The college currently offers five noncredit courses on a regular basis:

Fundamentals of International Trade, a 27-hour course featuring a series of guest lecturers in all aspects of international business; Letters of Credit; Principles and Documentation; International Marketing; and two transportation management courses (export and import).

One-on-one counseling for new entrants to international business is a popular service of the Center. Not only is this service utilized by local businesses, but referrals are received from small-business centers across the state, from the Small Business Administration's regional office, from the regional office of the International Trade Administration, and from the North Carolina Department of Economic and Community Development (formerly Department of Commerce). Because many of these offices are understaffed for the volume of requests they get for counseling, Central Piedmont's ability to provide this service has helped define its niche in the international business resource network in the state.

All of these aspects of the program work together to create and maintain international awareness in the community as a whole and to serve the international informational needs of the community. This in turn both creates and serves the demand for international business education.

LOCAL RESOURCES AND PROGRAM DEVELOPMENT

The subject matter that is taught in the International Business Program in itself determines the special need of planning and development. World events affecting international business have increased so dramatically that course content must be reassessed almost daily. The nature of a community college also requires delivering a combination of academic and applied knowledge. This is especially true in international business where specific information could affect import and export directly on a daily basis.

Information accessibility. Many resources are brought to bear on this ongoing requirement for accurate, current information. Foremost among these resources is the International Trade Resource Library. Here such periodicals as *The Journal of Commerce, The Wall Street Journal, The Economist, 1992: The External Impact of European Unification,* and *The Week in Germany,* as well as annually updated volumes like Dun and Bradstreet's *Exporter's Encyclopedia,* are available to faculty, students, and the public. Some 458 books are housed here on all aspects of international business and culture.

Other resources available in the library include videotapes on international business and culture, games useful in illustrating the need for cultural sensitivity, and interactive software offering in-depth information on Europe 1992 and other subjects. The International Trade Education Network is available online for national contacts in international education, for information on international education programs around the country, and for bibliographies of publications and videotapes on international subjects.

Often the best information in a rapidly-changing environment comes from those who are conducting business abroad, so direct contact with the business community is vital to the success of international programs. The Business and International Education Advisory Board maintains such links for Central

Piedmont Community College. Composed of 21 leaders from both the public and private sectors, board members give advice and counsel to the college on the relevancy of its services to the community's needs as well as provide requested information in their areas of expertise. Since board members are selected from a broad cross section of the business community, there is a multiplier effect in contacts available to the international programs.

Another valuable resource for international business contacts is the Metrolina World Trade Association (MWTA), the Charlotte-area chapter of the North Carolina World Trade Association. With over 500 members, this is the largest local chapter of one of the most active state WTA organizations in the country. The director of the college's Small Business Center is also the executive director of the MWTA, and the director of the International Business Center serves on the directing boards at both the local and state levels. Thus, association members are both aware of Central Piedmont's international programs and are willing to assist the college in various ways, including serving as guest lecturers or seminar panelists, providing information, and cosponsoring seminars on international topics.

The same sort of cooperative relationship exists with other local entities with an international focus. For example, International Business Center staff have served on the Mayor's Sister Cities Committees, with the result that the college has had two visiting professors from the People's Republic of China, and there is a possibility of a faculty exchange with schools in Krefeld, West Germany. Also, Central Piedmont cooperates with International House, a privately-funded organization providing services to international newcomers to the area, in arranging appropriate itineraries for international leaders in business, government, and education who are brought to Charlotte under the International Visitors Program of the United States Information Agency. Meetings with these visitors provide opportunities for college faculty and staff to share knowledge with their international colleagues as well as to learn more about other cultures. Such opportunities are invaluable, since international education of students must begin with the "internationalization" of their teachers.

THE FUTURE OF INTERNATIONAL EDUCATION AT CENTRAL PIEDMONT COMMUNITY COLLEGE

As regional awareness of the new global economy increases, Central Piedmont's role is ever changing to meet the growing international sophistication of the community's needs. The International Business Program, a fledgling in 1988, is now a solid, successful part of the International Education Program, attracting many new students each year. Continuing education courses in international business and languages are seen as high-quality, cost-effective training by the business community. The International Trade Resource Library is recognized as a valuable node of the statewide international resource network.

In the spring of 1990 Central Piedmont began an informal feasibility study to determine strategies for upgrading and expanding its foreign language curriculum and for adding an international dimension to all its curricula.

Recognizing that globalization has implications for every discipline, the college had "Internationalizing the College Curriculum" as the theme for its annual faculty/staff symposium on international awareness in 1990.

Central Piedmont Community College works with its sister community colleges across North Carolina to develop international education programs in their service areas. A statewide education initiative bringing together private industry and public education was proposed in 1990 to foster economic growth and jobs by preparing citizens of North Carolina for successful participation in a global economy; the proposal was taken under advisement.

SUMMARY

Central Piedmont Community College clearly sees its mission for the future to include bringing an international perspective to the education of all its students in all aspects of its programs. Central Piedmont's President Ruth Shaw, in her inauguration speech in January of 1987, defined six educational priorities for the college. Among the six, she listed this one:

> We will build connections with each other, with our community, with our world. We will help Charlotte-Mecklenburg expand its role in the global community. It is a paradox; communication and transportation have made our collective world smaller, but have made our individual worlds larger. Central Piedmont Community College will bring an international focus to our curricula. We will recognize the increased importance of foreign language and culture, and we will continue as a catalyst for expanded business horizons.

With such support and commitment from the leadership of the college, international education will continue to expand and thrive at Central Piedmont Community College.

CHAPTER 12

The International Trade Education Program at Waukesha County Technical College

BARBARA MOEBIUS

Waukesha County Technical College, Pewaukee, Wisconsin

The obvious importance of global markets to local, regional, and national economies and the staggering trade deficit are the impetus for international trade education at Waukesha County Technical College (WCTC), in metropolitan Milwaukee, Wisconsin. The program includes an associate degree and certificate of specialization in international trade, continuing education seminars and workshops, customized training and research, and a comprehensive trade resource library. An advanced technical certificate in importing is also being added to the program.

NEED

The program developed during the early 1980's when there was little emphasis on exports. Our vast domestic market had allowed us to become complacent. We barely noticed foreign competition until it was almost too late. According to the U.S. Department of Commerce, the United States saw its balance of trade move from a surplus in 1981 to a deficit of $160 billion in 1987. By 1986, the value of manufactured goods exported by the United States trailed West Germany and Japan by sizable margins. As a percentage of the gross national product, U.S. exports declined 20 percent from 1979 to 1983, far exceeding any other industrialized nation. The U.S. Small Business Administration estimates that only 10 percent—30,000 out of 300,000—United States firms export. Less than 250 domestic companies account for 75 percent of all exports. This alarming situation alerted the nation that a crisis was at hand. Portions of the discussion that follows appeared previously in an article by this author entitled "Helping Small Business Compete with the World: A New Community Service," in the *Community, Technical, & Junior College Journal*, December/January 1989.

Rust Belt. Nowhere was the crisis more obvious than in the Rust Belt of the Midwest. Old manufacturing cities with smokestack industries, once flagships of the region, were hit hard by foreign competition, from automobile to machine tool manufacturers. Plant closings and related layoffs were common. The U.S. Department of Commerce has concluded that for every $1 billion lost in exports, 25,000 jobs disappear. Headlines in the March 14, 1982, *Milwaukee Journal* reported that 2,000 people lined up for 40 jobs being created by a new supermarket in Milwaukee, once the machine tool capital of the world.

Industry survival. The surviving industries and entrepreneurial efforts, in order to compete in the global marketplace, required workers with practical training in international trade. Nonexporters needed to know that:

1. Exports create additional sales and increase total profit. The extra sales can reduce fixed costs by increasing plant capacity.
2. Exports balance seasonal production schedules because the end of summer in the United States foretells the beginning of spring in another part of the globe.
3. Exports flatten business cycles if one region of the world is in recession and another area is booming.
4. Exports extend product life because obsolete technology in the developed world may be state of the art in the newly industrialized nations.
5. Exports diversify risks, identify new investment and financing opportunities, and discover ways to adapt products for new uses.

Some of the businesses affected by the changing economy are of sufficient size to develop their own international training divisions. The majority, however, are small businesses. The health of these small businesses is critical to the economy because they are responsible for the creation of two-thirds of the new jobs in the country. Yet they are too small to have their own international resource and training facilities. Smaller businesses are also hesitant to enter foreign markets because they lack knowledge of how to export, are unfamiliar with foreign business practices, and find export financing difficult to obtain.

THE ASSOCIATE DEGREE PROGRAM

Development. In 1984, WCTC began a three-pronged approach to address the issues just described. A forward-looking board of directors and president provided the important first step by adopting an international/intercultural education policy to guide the college efforts. The board and administration believed students and staff should be provided with an opportunity to increase their understanding of customs and cultures different from their own. Local employers with the potential for exporting or importing needed to be served and employees needed to be trained for them to hire.

In direct response to requests from area employers and on the basis of a market survey that assessed the level of employment opportunities for graduates, the associate degree in international trade was initiated in 1985. Enrollment grew steadily from 38 the first semester to 85 some five years later. Course offerings in international business principles, export documentation, cultural awareness, business Spanish, and international courses in marketing, transportation, and finance have been developed to provide the practical skills necessary to conduct trade.

Job skills. To determine the typical job skills and tasks involved in entry-level jobs in international trade, a DACUM (Developing a Curriculum) analysis was conducted by the program advisory board composed of experienced exporters from small and medium-sized business, government, education, freight forwarders, international bankers and lawyers, consultants, and export management firms.

This day-long process identified the actual skills a graduate of the program should possess. Course objectives could then address these skills and be used to guide course development.

Target markets. Contrary to original expectation, the target market has not proved to be the recent high school graduate seeking an associate degree to prepare for a career in the global marketplace. Perhaps this is because the job market is new and varied, not clearly understood by the high school graduate or the counselling staff. Job opportunities for those persons without prior experience exist mainly in the area of export documentation clerk, with a starting salary of $14,000-$16,000.

The international-trade program is most popular among evening school students, many of whom are already employed by firms exporting to some degree. Some of these students already have undergraduate or graduate degrees in another field and are taking the international core courses to increase their knowledge and promotability. Other students include skilled technical and clerical employees who have found their domestic responsibilities suddenly expanded to include some aspect of international trade. Still others benefiting from the program include those making career transitions or already possessing foreign language skills.

Since 1987, 20 students have completed the associate degree. They have found employment in areas as varied as freight forwarding, international banking, customs clearance, and export coordination, or have developed their own export-import businesses.

Certificate of specialization. Students who choose not to complete the 68 credits for an associate degree, either because they already have an advanced degree or desire only the international core courses directly applicable to their work, may obtain a certificate of specialization in international trade. This certificate identifies that they have completed the 19 credits in the international trade core curriculum and allows both the student and the college to consider them completers, rather than program leavers or drop outs.

SEMINARS AND WORKSHOPS

The second component of the international trade education thrust at WCTC is the continuing-education training seminars. Not everyone can afford the luxury of semester-long directed study. Employees with more immediate training needs and greater time pressure prefer one-day seminars. The program advisory board works closely with business and industry to offer the types of seminars needed for effective participation in the global marketplace and is careful not to duplicate other services and seminars offered in the metropolitan Milwaukee area.

Target markets. Prior to the WCTC program, available training at universities and through private consultants focused on the needs of top management personnel in Fortune 500 companies. The target market of the technical college is the smaller firm whose prosperity depends on extending their market into other nations. Since many of these firms are managed by self-made entrepreneurs with narrowly focused technical educations, they may lack the research skills necessary to expand their markets. In fact, according to a survey completed by the National Association of State Development Agencies, the main reason preventing smaller businesses from exporting is lack of knowledge of how to export. This lack of knowledge includes unfamiliarity with export mechanisms and a sense of being overwhelmed with the complexities of nation-specific regulations for exporting. The first workshop offered by WCTC, "Developing an Export Program," was targeted to address this concern.

A follow-up seminar addressed how to penetrate a foreign market by conducting research, developing an international marketing plan, and selecting and managing overseas agents and distributors.

The needs of the technical and clerical level employees are met through two of WCTC's most successful workshops, "Export Documentation and Payment Methods" and "Moving Cargo Internationally." These workshops focus on providing hands-on practical experience in preparing documents related to the flow of goods and money internationally and present an overview of air and ocean transportation and the shipment of hazardous cargo. A tour of a cargo-loading vessel helps participants see how their products are handled.

Food distributors, agribusiness, and the hardwood-forest products industry form a target group needing to diversify products and markets. "Opportunities in Asia," designed for this group, focuses on understanding market potential and special export requirements for the Pacific Rim.

Small exporters also express concern about unfamiliar foreign business practices. "Communicating Internationally" addresses language barriers and promotion techniques for the six world regions, as well as potential product adaptations and trademark patent protection.

Perhaps the most unique seminar focuses on the opportunities, preparations, pitfalls, and advantages of being a woman in international business. Experienced businesswomen share their secrets for selling to Asia, Europe, Latin America, and the Middle East. A panel of businessmen discuss their perceptions of a woman's chance for success in various international markets.

All of these seminars, as well as the associate degree classes, provide information and skills directly transferable to the workplace, with little emphasis on theory. Seminar participants and students ask questions about situations that have arisen in their daily work life. All seminar presenters and classroom instructors are from the business community and can give immediate, relevant answers. The process integrates the information students are learning with the work setting in which it will be used. Students in the associate degree program can attend the seminars at no charge, enhancing their interaction with the practitioners in the field. The seminars average 40 participants, with a range of 25-75 depending on the topic.

Videotapes. The potential audience of the WCTC workshops and seminars has been greatly extended with the assistance of a grant from the Fund for the Improvement of Post-Secondary Education (FIPSE) for developing export-training videotapes. Every skill covered in the seminars has been taped, edited, and packaged as stand-alone instruction, complete with learning guides.

The 40 export-training videotapes have been widely sold throughout the United States and Canada. The tapes are especially effective in nonurban areas with no access to frequent export development training or on campuses without extensive international business offerings. The tapes can be duplicated for use at outreach centers located some distance from the main campus. By joining the Export Video Membership Club at WCTC, local businesses can rent the videotapes to conduct in-house training programs for employees newly hired or given expanded responsibilities in the export department. This process has proved to be a desirable option for small companies and has generated revenue for the school.

Funding organizations are attracted to projects with potential for reaching the widest possible audience and for continuing once project funds have been expended. The WCTC program had both of those possibilities. Today, some five years after the inception of the FIPSE grant, the export videos are a unique and varied source of training with wide national appeal. The sales of the tapes produce revenue that is channeled back into the program to update and produce new videos.

Colleges are unlikely to discontinue activities that approach self-support. Furthermore, the college made a significant commitment to continuation through providing matching funds to develop an extensive resource and reference facility.

THE INTERNATIONAL TRADE TECHNICAL CENTER

WCTC also began development of the International Trade Technical Center in 1985. This reference and resource center, funded through matching funds in the FIPSE grant, contains extensive information on all aspects of international trade. Trained personnel are available at the center to help businesses find needed information and provide answers to questions over the phone or by FAX.

The references include directories to assist in finding distributors and sales leads; guides to information on foreign firms, worldwide marketing, statistical and media guides; handbooks on how to get started; country and regional information, foreign periodicals and newspapers; government publications and forms; and audio-visual materials.

This reference library is the most extensive in Wisconsin, representing a $60,000 investment in materials and requiring $14,000 to keep it up to date. In order to best serve the business community, the center lends materials statewide. Student status and/or residency in Waukesha County are not requirements. This liberal lending policy has in turn attracted monetary donations from the trade community. More than 1,200 clients have used the center since it opened.

Commonly sought information. Clients frequently seek additional information about a company from which they have received an inquiry. They want to determine how large and well established the company is, with whom they do their banking, and who are the officers of the company. KOMPASS directories have proved invaluable in providing this information as well as information about potential agents and distributors, sales leads, and offshore purchasing opportunities. Published by Croner Publications, the directories are somewhat expensive and, unfortunately, are available mainly for European and Southeast Asian countries.

The explosion of FAX communication has made the *Jaeger & Waldmann Telefax International* directory more important than the *Telex & Teletex International* directory, but it will be some years before the listings will reflect the true extent of FAX proliferation. The Telex directory is a good way to locate addresses for companies all over the world.

Current country and area specific information can be obtained from Business International Publications, Inc., consulates and trade offices, as well as various Departments of State and Commerce publications. The *Export Shipping Manual*, published by the Bureau of National Affairs, is a wealth of information on trading procedures for exporting to particular countries.

Customized training. The International Trade Technical Center also conducts customized training at the request of business and industry. This may include export documentation workshops for a specific company, using their forms and analyzing real blunders that have cost the company money. The programs may involve conducting cultural and business protocol training for the Governor's trade missions or for a company planning business in a new world market or entertaining overseas clients. Rapid response time in initiating the training program, usually a week or less, reflects the flexibility and innovation that small and medium-sized companies appreciate from the educational sector. These same characteristics enable smaller businesses to respond more quickly than Fortune 500 firms to rapidly changing international markets.

LESSON LEARNED

Top level support. One of the most important factors in the success of international trade programs is the support of the college president. Information sources to support the requisite training are two to three times more costly than usual library acquisitions. Recognizing that data are frequently collected in one language and then translated into Spanish, French, German and English, makes the cost of materials more understandable. It takes at least a full year to develop recognition and support from state and local agencies that can assist the program. Without high level support in the institutions, educators will find it difficult to offer quality programming, especially since the number of full-time equivalent students generated by the programs may not be large. The same axiom applies to businesses seeking to establish export markets: The sales or marketing manager cannot do it without the support of the CEO.

Variety of resources. The scope of information sought by clients does not lend itself to easy classification. As soon as the decision is made not to renew an unused but expensive resource, then clients will suddenly begin asking for that information.

In 1985, business was interested in the Pacific Rim and our Asian collection reflects that. The approach of 1992 signaled an increased interest in Europe.

These requests were not too difficult to satisfy, since a wealth of information and statistics on Europe is available. But the stunning changes in the global economic and political arena that began with the dismantling of the Berlin Wall unleashed requests for information about the Soviet Union and Central Europe for which we were unprepared and for which few resources were available.

American business now realizes that Japanese business practices are significantly different from our own and usually understands the necessity of cultural protocol training for Asia. The necessity of cultural preparation for European ventures and those in English-speaking countries is a much harder sell.

Perhaps the most frustrating lesson to be learned in building an international trade program from the ground floor is patience and perseverance. Careful planning of what needs to be done and how to go about it invariably underestimates the amount of time required. Program planners need to listen to the same advice they will be giving exporters: this is a long-term commitment, and it may take a couple of years to get the program off the ground.

FORMING PARTNERSHIPS

Building support. Redirecting the nation's focus to an international orientation is a monumental task. Daily articles in newspapers and world events viewed on television have increased awareness and spawned the development of many programs. A needs assessment survey of the business community and input from an advisory board will help avoid duplication of effort and develop a niche to fulfill unmet training needs. The market is thin enough and the needs diverse enough to warrant careful attention to existing services.

Working with community groups. Visibility within the business community can be achieved through working with established connections to commerce including chambers of commerce, world trade organizations, and state and federal development agencies. These agencies can provide mailing lists for a targeted needs-assessment survey. As valuable members of an advisory committee, they can provide much guidance in early stages. They can be important cheerleaders, spreading information about programs through their networks.

It is important to unceasingly pursue the public eye. Volunteering to speak at community or service groups' monthly meetings, joining small business organizations that are possible candidates for exporting and volunteering to work on the education committee of world trade organizations or start one if there is none in the area are effective ways to gain visibility.

In 1987, the programs at WCTC received the Wisconsin Governor's Export Achievement Award for service to the business community. This was the first time an educational institution had ever received this award. Success increases recognition and visibility with other organizations, encouraging them to seek out the program.

Working with other colleges. In a desire to expand export education throughout the 16 technical colleges in Wisconsin, WCTC offered to co-sponsor export seminars at the other college campuses. With little investment, since WCTC did all the marketing and program development, colleges could test the market for training within their service areas. "Export Documentation & Payment Methods," a consistently well-attended seminar, convinced most colleges to consider additional programs, and in some cases, to dedicate staff to international trade.

The Committee for International Trade Education (CITE) was formed in 1990, consisting of representatives from 12 of the 16 technical colleges, to further export/import education in Wisconsin. One of the important goals of this committee is to attract grant funds to the state for internationalizing or infusing global awareness throughout the curriculum. The competition for federal, state, and private funds is extremely competitive; however, CITE believes the potential of internationalizing 16 college curriculums at once will be an attractive funding package. These colleges have chosen a cooperative, rather than competitive, mode for access to limited funds.

NASBITE. The National Association for International Trade Education (NASBITE) is an outgrowth of the first International Trade Education for Small Business Conference held in Portland, Oregon, in May 1988. NASBITE's annual conference showcases successful trade education programs throughout North America. Members enthusiastically share materials on how to develop and implement programs that work. Participation in NASBITE activities is the single most effective way for small business throughout the nation to keep informed about innovative trade education.

NEW DIRECTIONS

Until recently, the WCTC programs and most available training in the country focused on exporting. The reality of our $109 billion trade deficit indicates that more products are being imported than exported. The United States has not had a trade surplus since 1981. Although the situation has improved during the past two years, no one expects a trade surplus in the foreseeable future. (Wisconsin is one of 28 states with a surplus; however, removal of agricultural exports from the equation highlights the significance of manufactured imports.)

Competition, both from foreign products and from domestic companies that buy overseas, demands that purchasing departments consider low cost/high quality sources worldwide. Offshore buying presents problems not encountered in domestic purchasing. Yet, no associate degree courses or programs in Wisconsin that focus on the important skills and information required for cost effective importation of goods are offered.

While it is immediately apparent that the United States needs to increase its exports, it is also true that many manufactured products eventually exported include components that were first imported from an off-shore source. *The Journal of Commerce* (November 29, 1989) reports that as much as $3 billion in refunds are due exporters through duty drawback for customs paid on imported components, yet only a small portion of exporters ever apply for the refunds due to ignorance or fear of the necessary paperwork.

Import certificate. To address the realities of the global market, WCTC has developed a certificate program in importing. This certificate will consist of courses in the Fundamentals of Importing, Off-Shore Purchasing, Import Transportation and Finance, and Cultural Awareness. These courses resulted from a DACUM analysis to determine the skills needed and tasks performed by an import coordinator.

Job market. The job market for those with importing skills will be in distribution, purchasing, and import brokering. Currently, importers are unsure of how to handle the transportation, import documentation and financing used by import merchants and commission houses. This certificate program will make the middle people less necessary.

Recent shifts in policy have placed greater emphasis on the enforcement of customs law and regulations. Importers now face detailed audits by Customs Service personnel as part of their enforcement program. In particular, companies whose sources exist in Hong Kong, Korea, Taiwan, and Singapore face increased exposure to audits because of loss of duty-free status for goods covered by the Generalized System of Preferences.

The Canadian-U.S. Free Trade Agreement and the Harmonized Tariff System changed established practices, resulting in problems of interpretation. Computerization has begun to enter the transportation field, improving efficiency and accelerating communication, yet the skills to evaluate, select, and use this new software are not widespread. All of these directions indicate increased employment opportunities for import coordinators.

OUTCOMES

There is a growing awareness in the business and education sectors of the global nature of the nation's economy. Small businesses are developing the necessary skills for export activities. These skills include access to information resources and increased sensitivity to cultural differences affecting business practices.

Students in the degree and certificate programs are gaining an ability to compete in the international arena with marketable skills. The WCTC videotapes allow business and other postsecondary institutions to improve and extend their educational programs.

If an "export mentality" is not communicated across the curriculum through an internationalization of all courses and a renewed emphasis on foreign language, cultural awareness, and geography, colleges nationwide are doing their constituencies a disservice. A need exists for training a new generation of highly qualified exporters, aware of global relationships and ready for the 1990's—the decade of trade.

CHAPTER 13
International Business Education Programs At Ball State University

RODNEY E. DAVIS, J. LEE DYE, and ROBERT A. UNDERWOOD
Ball State University, Muncie, Indiana

Intense competition, increasing global markets, and rapid technological changes are problems that will continue to intensify as American businesses enter the 21st century. Will America's future business executives be prepared to succeed in the approaching international environment? This is a question that has to be addressed by the nation's colleges and universities, because few would disagree that we live in an era in which the international competitiveness of America's businesses could become the key to their survival.

Rapid technological advances in transportation and electronics have made the concept of a global society a reality in the 20th century. Americans have been purchasing foreign-made goods and engaging in international business at an increasing rate each year. This foreign competition has caused problems as well as provided benefits for American consumers; but foreign manufacturers have helped raise the standard of living for the typical American by providing high-quality goods at reasonable prices.

With these concepts in mind, the authors will describe what is being done at Ball State University regarding international education in general, and how the concept of international business education is being addressed in the College of Business and in the Department of Business Education and Office Administration at BSU.

INTERNATIONAL PROGRAMS AT BALL STATE UNIVERSITY

Ball State University is organized into six academic units (Applied Sciences and Technology, Architecture and Planning, Business, Fine Arts, Sciences and Humanities, and Teachers College) and offers degree programs ranging from the associate to the doctoral level. There is a strong commitment to international education. Approximately twenty-five hundred inquiries from overseas concerning study at BSU were received in 1989.

As compared to 1988, there was a 16 percent increase in the admission of foreign students and a 17 percent increase in actual new enrollments in 1989. The five largest nationality groups in 1989 were from China, Korea, Indonesia, Thailand, and Japan. Computer science had the largest number of foreign enrollees, followed by English, physical education, architecture, and music.

In the following paragraphs, excerpted from a pamphlet entitled "Come to Ball State . . . And Study Abroad," the international education programs at Ball State University are described.

London Centre. In the largest of the University's "study-abroad" programs, approximately fifty students yearly are given the opportunity to study regular Ball State classes at Regent's College in London with Ball State faculty members or with British instructors. Students normally spend 18 weeks abroad and are provided the opportunity to travel on the European Continent.

Vienna Center. Operated jointly by Ball State and other Midwestern universities, BSU students are offered opportunities for study at the Vienna Center, which are similar to those available at the London Centre.

China/Korea Exchange. Each summer, approximately 15 to 20 BSU students and faculty visit selected locations in China, Korea, and the Far East, and exchange ideas at Ball State's sister institutions in those countries.

Westminster College. Each year, approximately 10 BSU Honors College students study in the Oxford, England, area and are given the opportunity to travel extensively in Great Britain.

Polyark and Architecture Abroad. The BSU College of Architecture and Planning has a strong emphasis on experience abroad for its students. In this program, selected students and faculty members study architectural styles found in various countries.

EDEL-Overseas. Selected students with majors in elementary or secondary education can work with teachers in British schools for a term and earn credit at BSU.

Community Health Nursing in London. In this program, nursing students spend a five-week summer term gaining clinical experience in the British health-care system.

Ethnography in Jamaica. This program is geared primarily to give BSU anthropology majors (students with other majors often participate) the chance to perform field research in Negril, Jamaica.

International Student Exchange Program (ISEP). In this program, which normally requires one entire year abroad, BSU students trade places with students from other participating universities.

Ball State direct exchanges. In addition to the China/Korea exchanges, BSU has agreements with universities in other countries where students and faculty are given the opportunity to study abroad.

Foreign language exchanges. The BSU Department of Foreign Languages has agreements with universities in West Germany and France whereby qualified students are given the opportunity to exchange places with students in sister institutions during the academic year.

Fulbright Fellowships. BSU seniors and faculty members can apply for these grants, which make it possible for them to study in foreign countries.

Study abroad through other universities. Many opportunities to study abroad and to transfer the international credit are available to BSU students each year.

Internships and Summer Work. Opportunities are abundant for BSU students to serve either internships abroad or to work in foreign countries.

International travel courses in global studies. In this program, faculty members can create new travel experiences for students, using existing courses, and have these international travel course sections count toward the general studies requirements at Ball State University.

Canada Year. In an effort to raise the awareness of the university community about a nation that has a tremendous impact on Indiana, the entire 1989-90 Ball State University school term was declared "Canada Year." Canadian individuals gave lectures on campus, and various events were organized by administrators, faculty members, and students. This culminated with the establishment of a Canadian Studies Program, in which Ball State students will be given the opportunity to take elective classes that deal with Canadian topics. A similar program, "Europe Year," will be undertaken during the 1991-92 school year.

The following section describes international education activities in the College of Business. Background information about the College of Business is provided first, followed by explanations of international involvement through the curriculum, faculty, and special programs.

INTERNATIONAL EDUCATION IN THE COLLEGE OF BUSINESS

The College of Business consists of six academic departments with 120 full-time faculty members. It is the second-largest college on the Ball State Campus; approximately thirty percent of all baccalaureate students at Ball State graduate with degrees in business. Majors with several options are available in accounting, office systems administration, business and marketing teacher education, economics, finance, management, marketing, and business administration.

Ball State's College of Business is among the 20 percent of business schools nationwide accredited by the American Assembly of Collegiate Schools of Business (AACSB). The accreditation is for both the undergraduate and master's levels. The AACSB prompted accredited schools to internationalize their programs. Consequently, the accrediting body has accepted the challenge of the 1985 President's Commission on Industrial Competitiveness to "reflect the increasing internationalization of our markets."

The College of Business has long recognized the significance of international education. In addition to the active participation in AACSB programs and the university-wide programs previously mentioned, the College of Business has moved forward on several fronts relating to international business education. These efforts include internationalizing the curriculum, encouraging faculty involvement, and sponsoring special programs.

Internationalizing the curriculum. Like other accredited schools, the College of Business must meet AACSB Standard IV, Curriculum. Item D requires world wide dimension for each major or degree program. At Ball State, this requirement is met through the integration of international units into the Common Body of Knowledge courses. For example, in microeconomics, students study international trade and comparative advantage, in business law it is foreign legal systems, and in principles of marketing it is marketing strategy planning for international markets. Undergraduate business majors may also choose from among several other international business courses offered in each department in the College of Business, with the exception of Accounting.

Furthermore, a new international business major was approved by the Indiana Higher Education Commission in 1989-90. The development of this major was partially funded through a U.S. Department of Education grant in 1987. During the spring semester 1990, 40 students were majoring in international business. Besides the College of Business Common Body of Knowledge courses, this program incorporates nine international business courses. Seven required courses are business communication, business law, economics, finance, business competitiveness, management, and marketing. Majors elect two other international business courses. This major requires a 15-semester hour foreign language minor in Chinese, French, German, Japanese, or Spanish. The objective of this program is to produce international businesspersons with a comprehensive business degree who are attuned to the cultural differences of other countries and the impact of those differences on business. These individuals must be able to communicate in at least one foreign language and be able to learn additional languages quickly, if necessary.

Encouraging faculty involvement. During the fall semester of 1989, a faculty task force was convened to make recommendations to the dean of the College of Business regarding internationalizing activities. Based upon the results of a survey of faculty interests and background conducted by the task force, the dean established a new standing committee for international activities consisting of 14 members, to include students, representing each department. The International Committee is divided into five subcommittees investigating the following areas: exchange programs; international resources; curriculum and student affairs; grant proposals; and outreach programs and faculty development.

The results of the survey previously mentioned provided insight into the interests, experience, and aspirations of the College of Business faculty related to international education. Twenty faculty members responded to the questionnaire. Faculty indicated a proficiency in the reading and writing of 11 languages. Eight faculty members have taught in foreign universities in the past five years. The respondents reported 46 research projects and/or publications were undertaken dealing with international business since 1984. Numerous other service activities, consulting assignments, and travel experiences were also reported. The whetted appetite of the faculty for further international involvement was clearly demonstrated by 32 items listed for future international pursuits.

Sponsoring special programs. For many years, the College of Business has sponsored the Institute of Transnational Business. The ITB provides services to Indiana businesses by conducting workshops, seminars, and conferences related to international trade. Informative publications, brochures, and other documents have been developed to promote international business.

The College of Business is also in various stages of developing four faculty and/or student exchange programs. These programs involve universities in Japan, Turkey, England, and Korea.

Building upon the programs, activities, and direction of the university and the College of Business, the Department of Business Education and Office Administration is also committed to international education. The following section describes the BEOA Department's efforts to incorporate the international element into its programs and courses and ensure that its students and faculty experience global awareness.

INTERNATIONAL EDUCATION IN THE DEPARTMENT OF BUSINESS EDUCATION AND OFFICE ADMINISTRATION

The Department of Business Education and Office Administration founded the College of Business in 1965. Traditionally, as its title implies, the department has provided academic programs in office administration and business teacher education. Within the College of Business, the BEOA Department plays a major service role, providing courses in business information systems, microcomputer applications, information processing, and communications.

International involvement through the faculty. Many of the faculty of the Department of Business Education and Office Administration have traveled extensively not only in the neighboring countries of Canada and Mexico, but also in England, France, Austria, Belgium, Switzerland, Germany, Spain, Greece, Italy, Crete, Czechoslovakia, and the Netherlands. One faculty member has traveled extensively in Korea while teaching at Yeungnam University. During the summer of 1990, he also was part of a Ball State delegation that toured South Korea, China, Hong Kong, and Japan for five weeks.

Two faculty members from the Department are involved on the College of Business International Committee, which addresses student and faculty exchange programs, international curriculum and student affairs, outreach programs to alumni, faculty, and businesses, and grant procurement for international scholars and for establishing a Center for International Business Alliances. The department is also represented on the University International Committee.

The Department of Business Education and Office Administration has had two faculty members teach overseas. One taught in the Ball State Executive Administration master's degree program during two different years in Europe. He has taught one quarter in the Netherlands, one quarter in Crete, and two quarters in Germany. The program was a joint arrangement between Ball State and the United States Air Force. The classes were all taught on Air Force bases and, for the most part, served the military personnel, but a few nationals were also enrolled.

The second faculty member taught for three months in South Korea at Yeungnam University near Daegu, Korea, as a Ball State exchange faculty member. He taught English Communications to the Foreign Trade students, and his wife taught English Communications and Composition to English-as-a-second-language majors.

Research/publications and consulting. A third faculty member has served as a visiting lecturer at Chichester College in Chichester, England, and was also involved in the development of an exchange program for faculty and students there. While in England, she was able to attend several international conferences on information technology and on the European single market. She was also able to visit the Mid-Kent College of Technology and the faculty from the Cambridge College of Technology.

Two faculty members have been involved in research on the status of international-business communication training in the 100 largest multinational United States corporations. Their study involved firms that conduct a large volume of international business and have formal training programs to prepare their employees for overseas assignments. The purpose of the study was to determine what topics were included in the training programs and to determine the qualifications of the training directors responsible for these programs. They found that only 7 of 43 respondents' firms had formal programs to train employees for overseas assignments, that the training programs lasted most commonly only two or three days, that "family relocation," "cultural differences," and "cultural sensitivity" were the topics receiving the greatest emphasis.

Based on the study, one of the faculty members undertook another study to determine what problems would be encountered and what content should be included in an international-business communications course. The following are the understandings that he found needed to be developed:

- Understanding one's own background
- Understanding different cultural backgrounds
- Developing openness to new learning concerning the culture of others
- Developing tolerance of cultural differences
- Developing empathy for the specific needs of cultures that are much different from ours
- Developing global awareness
- Developing the ability to cope in stressful cultural situations
- Developing the ability to function in multicultural environments.

International involvement through the curriculum. Some of the courses in the department include topics related to the multinational aspects of business. Furthermore, the department teaches International Business Communications, which is one of the core courses in the International Business Major. International Business Communication explores the norms and values that executives face while working in different cultures, organizational structures, management styles, and external task environments and how these variables impact written, oral, and nonverbal communication in an international business culture. An emphasis is placed on sensitizing the student to important intercultural impersonal, personal, group, and organizational issues that facilitate or frustrate international business transactions. The course has a cross-cultural prospective including Europe, India, Canada, South

America, and South Africa. Special attention, however, is given to the Far East (Japan and Hong Kong) and Latin America.

The classes in the Business Education and Office Administration Department, as well as most departments in the college, contain students of varying ethnic backgrounds. A number of foreign students also serve as graduate assistants and student assistants.

Special program—agreement with Sanno Institute of Management of Japan. In April, 1989, Dr. Keith Montgomery, a Ball State graduate who works with the Education Exchange Center, approached the Center for International Programs at Ball State concerning the possibility of developing a student exchange program with Sanno Institute of Management, Tokyo, Japan. Sanno, founded in 1950, consists of two accredited colleges and the Sanno Research Center, which is a broad mixture of in-company management consulting and training at all levels. The undergraduate divisions of Sanno College are located at Isehara Campus (30 miles from Tokyo) and Sanno Junior College at Todoroki Campus, where Sanno's headquarters are also situated. Sanno is known for its diverse management, socioindustrial, and international training/consulting programs, as well as for vocational activities through either public or in-company seminars, consulting services, and extension courses.

The programs are developed and conducted by a corps of expert trainer/consultants in several specialized research groups and centers. Their services are offered and arranged through a nation-wide network of client services, including overseas assignments.

Sanno has several affiliated businesses, including two computer software research firms and a college press that edits and produces books and texts on management and business. Sanno can be seen as a complex of schools for student education combined with a wide-scope management training, consulting, information service, and publishing house.

Because of the development of Japanese companies in the United States, the professional secretaries who have studied abroad and who have an understanding of international concepts are in great demand. Sanno desired to establish a foreign student exchange program to provide relevant cultural and technical experiences and advance the exchange of knowledge between students and faculty of the two institutions as culture partners—a program in which one American student becomes a partner for one international student and helps him/her to understand the American culture and college life. In addition to a partnership arrangement, Sanno wanted a program that would provide the international student with an opportunity to study with other international students and to travel while in the United States.

Sanno desired an exchange program in which its students would become more fluent in English and in secretarial skills. The Business Education and Office Administration Department worked with the Center for International Programs at Ball State to set up a program for students of Sanno to study in the secretarial area at Ball State. Sanno sent several delegations to visit the campus, and a contract was agreed upon whereby Sanno would send between 15 and 30 students to study at Ball State.

The students began their study in April 1990 at Sanno in their general and core requirements, with emphasis on introductory secretarial and office automation courses. A course is offered in English in office automation. They will also take courses in English as a second language to prepare for the TOEFL (Teaching of English as a Foreign Language) examination.

The Japanese students came to Ball State in July 1990 to begin special orientation sessions. For the first three months, the students met individually with the coordinator/counselor at least once a month. On-going orientation sessions were provided throughout the year. In August, Ball State provided a special mandatory intensive three-week English-as-a-Second-Language (ESL) American Culture/Orientation course.

During the fall and spring semesters, the Sanno students were enrolled in Principles of Business Correspondence, Beginning Keyboarding, Intermediate Keyboarding, Introduction to Word Processing, Microcomputer Applications in Business, Secretarial Administration and Procedures, and other secretarial studies as English proficiency permits.

The faculty became involved in cross-culture learning through the International Office at BSU and planned departmental interactions with the Sanno students. The International Office presented a number of sessions in which the faculty became familiar with Japan, its history, its people, and its culture. Social gatherings between the students and the faculty provided better interaction between the cultures.

The students also worked extensively with English while studying in the secretarial area. The faculty in the Business Education and Office Administration Department and the faculty in the English Department worked together to coordinate the learning of the business vocabulary used in their classes.

INTERNATIONAL EDUCATION FOR BUSINESS TEACHER EDUCATION MAJORS

The significance of international business mandates that teachers be equipped to integrate appropriate learning in the curriculum. Therefore, the preparation of business teachers must include a thorough understanding of international business. The question becomes: "What should a business teacher know about international business?" A perusal of the certification regulations is not helpful. In Indiana, the certification rules are more than 10 years old; consequently, international business is conspicuously absent. Therefore, at Ball State University it has been determined that prospective business teachers must meet the same international education requirements as those students preparing to enter the business world.

For a business education major at Ball State, the minimum exposure to international education includes a three-hour general studies requirement in international/global studies, the various units integrated in the College of Business common body of knowledge courses, and assignments in methods class covering basic business subjects. On the other hand, business-teaching majors have a variety of further international education learning opportunities from which to choose. As previously described in this chapter, these opportunities include foreign travel, internships and summer work, interaction with foreign students on campus, and elective classes like International Business Communications.

Integration of international education in the methods class covering basic business subjects was investigated by students taking the economic literacy test provided by the Joint Council on Economic Education. Since this test incorporates international business items, students see its significance. Furthermore, the methods class instructor emphasizes the importance of teaching today's secondary students about international business, foreign trade, and balance of payments.

SUMMARY

Central to the mission of Ball State University is the premise that life in a contemporary world requires a global perspective not called for in any other era. With this in mind, the authors have described what is being done across the BSU campus and in the College of Business to prepare students for life in the 20th and 21st centuries. Only time will tell if international business education should have an even-greater emphasis in the future.

CHAPTER 14

The International Business Education Program at Illinois State University

JEAN GREVER and IRIS VARNER
Illinois State University, Normal, Illinois

Today, international business links America with many countries of the world, and, indeed, has forged a global network that brings all countries, institutions, and individuals much closer than ever before. Exportation of products is very important to the U.S. balance of trade and the U.S. economy. For example, one out of every 15 jobs in the United States depends on exports. On average, $1 billion of exports creates 25,800 jobs.[1] The foreign investments of the U.S. multinational companies are extensive. In 1988, the foreign operations of America's 100 largest multinational companies booked sales of $506 billion, which represents a 15 percent increase over the previous year.[2]

While the U.S. volume of business in foreign countries continues to expand, the U.S. participation in world trade measured as a portion of the world market share has declined. Countries whose businesses have a more global perspective, like Japan, for example, are aggressively increasing their share of the world market, while other countries are beginning to enter the international market. Clearly, America's competition in the world of international trade is already tough, and getting tougher. As U.S. businesses work to meet this increased competition in world trade, they will be looking for college graduates who already have international skills.

At the same time, the business environment within the United States is exhibiting an expanding foreign flavor. Increasingly, foreign countries are investing in American companies. In 1988, direct foreign investment in American companies and real estate reached $390 billion.[3] An example is Diamond Star Motors, a car manufacturing plant located in Bloomington-Normal, Illinois, which is a joint business venture between Chrysler and Japan. Similar joint foreign-American business ventures are evident throughout this country.

Foreign student enrollment in schools throughout the country also shows an international dimension. Leading the influx of foreign students is China, with 40,000 students, followed by Taiwan, with 26,660 students. Other countries in order of student numbers are India, South Korea, Malaysia,

---

[1] U.S. Department of Commerce, Office of Trade and Investment Analysis, "Contribution of Exports to U.S. Employment," Staff Report by Lester A. Davis, March 1986, p. 2 and p. 9.

[2] "The 100 Largest U.S. Multinationals," *Forbes*, July 24, 1989, p. 320.

[3] "Foreign Investments in U.S. Increase," *The (Bloomington IL) Pantagraph*, March 18, 1990, E1.

Japan, Canada, Hong Kong, Iran, and Indonesia.[4] These foreign students and others who have immigrated to this country add different cultural views to the schools they attend and to the neighborhoods in which they live and work.

To market U.S. products in foreign countries, to work effectively with foreign investors in business in this country, and to deal with foreign students and immigrants, American business personnel need international skills. To meet this demand, American business schools are modifying their curricula to prepare graduates capable of coping with rapid change, global marketing, intensified competition, and new ethical and political concerns. One of the new priorities is to give students a global perspective, beginning with a knowledge of a foreign language and culture.[5]

OBJECTIVES

As a member of the American Academy of the Collegiate Schools of Business (AACSB), the Illinois College of Business recognizes the importance of an internationalized curriculum. All AACSB schools must have a curriculum that will provide a broad education and prepare students for imaginative and responsible citizenship and leadership roles in business and society—domestic and world-wide.[6] In keeping with this policy, the Illinois State University College of Business, in 1983, developed a major in international business. The primary objective of this major is to prepare students with an international language and the necessary business skills so that they can become productive workers in international and multinational business firms.

International business courses are available to all students in the College of Business, and all students are required to take at least one international business course. Specifically, one of the objectives of the College of Business is to expose all students to an international dimension so that:

1. Graduates are better prepared to work in a multicultural society.
2. Business teachers are better prepared to work with foreign students in the classroom.
3. All students and graduates are better prepared to live with the cultural differences of others.
4. Graduates in training roles are better prepared to work in multinational businesses.
5. Students can communicate better with people of other cultures.
6. Students become sensitive to the cultural differences of people from foreign countries.

---

[4]"Monday Memos," *The (Bloomington IL) Pantagraph*, October 16, 1989, A2.

[5]Main, Jeremy. "B-Schools Get a Global Vision." *Fortune*. July 17, 1989, p. 78 and p. 80.

[6]American Assembly of Collegiate Schools of Business. *Accreditation Council Policies Procedures and Standards 1989-90*. St. Louis: AACSB, 1989, p. 30 and p. 31.

STUDENTS BEING SERVED

The major in international business prepares students for multinational careers. The internationalization of other courses is beneficial to all other business majors in the College of Business. Students majoring in accounting or marketing, for example, can take the international accounting or the international marketing course. As a result, students acquire an added dimension of global awareness and the skill to work with international accounts in a business firm. By selecting other internationalized courses, students broaden their multicultural understandings and expand their career choices.

Foreign students are also served by the international business courses. They may select courses in the area of their expertise or perhaps choose to major in international business, selecting an appropriate sequence other than their own nationality.

Students who are preparing to teach business courses or work with administrative systems and office technology in business will also find internationalized courses beneficial to them. With the increasing number of immigrants in the educational system and workplace, sensitivity to the cultural differences of others will create a better working atmosphere for every one concerned.

Students with majors in other colleges may also take the international courses. They must, however, have 60 hours of credit to enroll in courses which are at the 200 level, and they must also fulfill any prerequisite requirements.

DEVELOPMENT OF THE INTERNATIONAL CURRICULUM

Internationalization of the core courses. All business majors must complete a core of business courses. AACSB requires that all business majors be exposed to international business issues. Some schools fulfill that goal by requiring an international course for all majors, but the College of Business at Illinois State University, rather than offer one required course, elected to internationalize the core courses wherever appropriate and cover international dimensions in these courses. Some courses, such as statistics, for example, by the very nature of the subject matter, do not lend themselves to internationalization.

Internationalization is a more comprehensive undertaking than a specific international requirement. It requires the cooperation of all faculty, the necessary international background for faculty, and careful monitoring so that courses are actually internationalized. The beginning was somewhat slow, but during recent years, faculty have become much more positive. To a great extent the internationalization has been given impetus by foreign students in the class, and particularly by partner institutions in France and Germany.

As a result of the international philosophy and the input from foreign students, an increasing number of instructors are getting involved in international research and international travel. In the beginning, faculty from each field put on some workshops and developed materials for the internationalization of key courses.

Internationalization of other business courses. The following discussion gives a picture of the internationalization of representative courses in the College of Business.

Business And Its Environment. This course is a freshman-level course required for business education majors. Numerous topics and issues explored in this course lend themselves to international perspectives. For example, the economic system of the United States is studied and compared to that of two or three other countries—sometimes socialist countries or Third World countries. Their market systems, in particular, are studied and compared to those of the United States and other countries. Their social services and health systems are also discussed.

Students also examine various monetary systems and learn how to determine each system's value in terms of the dollar. They study the currency in terms of personal income, its purchasing power for consumer goods, and the resultant effects on the standard of living. Also studied are the monetary systems, money black markets, and recent fluctuations in the value of the currency.

Students explore case studies on foreign economies, and for each case study identify its major problem and then prepare a suggested solution. They then give class presentations on their solutions.

Issues in marketing provide a good base for studying many international concepts. Students look at the success of foreign countries marketing goods in the United States and then examine the aspects that need to be considered when marketing U.S. products in foreign countries. These include foreign regulations, language requirements, and types of international advertising. Cultural aspects that might affect international marketing are also emphasized.

Also studied are the trade deficits and balance of payments and the reason some foreign countries are major investors in the United States. European and Japanese management styles are examined and compared to American management styles.

Business Communications, and Report Writing. The business communications course is an elective at the freshman/sophomore level. The report writing course is required for all business majors. Because as more and more business people will be dealing with people from other countries and other cultures, it was considered important to internationalize both courses.

The communication process today is so fast and efficient that an increasing number of business people are in direct contact with business people from other countries and other cultures. Communication conventions are different in different cultures. American business communication, compared to that of many other countries, is very direct and factual. What is considered good communication in the United States may not be considered good communication in Japan or Germany. For example, the Japanese are much more indirect. Even in modern business communication, the Japanese attempt to create a personal atmosphere. They want to do business with someone they know and trust. As a result, Japanese letters tend to start and close with personal references and statements about the weather and the health of the receiver of the letter. Both the Japanese and the Germans are more formal than the Americans. Business people in these two countries simply do not use first names in their business dealings.

The two courses introduce students to cultural differences, different ways of organizing materials, and to various formats of reports and business letters. They study examples of letters and reports from several countries and practice writing to different international audiences. Most business communication and report-writing classes have several students from abroad. These students are used as resource persons in the discussion of international practices.

Typewriting/Word Processing I and II. Typewriting/word processing I is a freshman/sophomore course required of administrative systems and office technology majors and of business education majors desiring to teach typewriting/keyboarding skills. Typewriting/word processing II is a junior course required of business education majors.

The number of American organizations sending and receiving correspondence from business people in foreign countries is increasing rapidly, and office personnel as well as teachers preparing students for careers in business need to be aware of and have practice in formatting various types of business letters used in various foreign firms.

For example, in China the letterhead stationery upon which the letter is written contains only the name of the business organization. It does not contain the address and telephone number. No inside address is used, and after the salutation and the body, the closing is followed by the printed name and the date (year, month, and day).

On the envelope, the receiver's address and name are placed in the center of the envelope, and the sender's address and name are placed in the lower right-hand corner. The name of the country (China) is typed on the first line followed by the province, city, street, and name. The sender's name is also followed by the telephone or telex number.

Foreign students enrolled in the course are an added source of information for studying different international format styles for communications.

Students also type itineraries for traveling from the United States to foreign countries. Departure times and dates are given along with the time-length of the trip. Students then must determine the arrival time at the foreign destination as well as the arrival time back in the United States keeping in mind the international date and time zone changes. Travel expenses for hotels and other necessary accommodations in foreign countries must be converted to U.S. dollars using foreign exchange rates so that total expenses can be determined in U.S. dollars. When students do a similar project later in the semester and must again determine expenses in the same currency, they quickly become aware of the fact that the value of the dollar often fluctuates.

Problems of Office Management. This course is an elective for seniors and graduate students and lends itself to studying problems that might evolve in the office because of differences in culture and in ways office work is done in a foreign country. In some countries, for example, the cost of labor is cheaper than the cost of carbon paper, and in managing work time, one would have to allow for this. Therefore, it is cheaper to type a letter several times than it is to make a carbon copy of the letter. In Thailand, family relationships are very important. Therefore, future plans might be changed as family matters considered more important arise.

The International Business major. The International Business major at Illinois State University, established in 1983, grew out of a series of individually designed contract majors. Today we have over 240 international business majors. The major requires work in the following areas: the business core, international business courses, a foreign language, and area studies (geography, history, politics). The major is based on the philosophy that nobody can be an expert in all areas of the world. Therefore students must choose one of the following sequences: German, French, British, Chinese, Russian, Japanese, or Spanish. The availability of the sequences was based on existing course offerings and the importance of an area to American business.

The college offers international business courses in all areas: accounting, business law, finance, management, marketing, international economics and includes a study of cultural influences on international business. These courses are open to all business majors, and many take advantage of the courses to gain a more formal international background.

International business majors take a minimum of four semesters of a foreign language and 12 hours (four courses) in area studies.

BUSINESS STUDIES OVERSEAS

Summer programs open to all business majors. In 1983 the College of Business sent nine students to its partner institution, the Ecole Superieure des Sciences Commerciales d'Angers (ESSCA). Today there are three summer programs in three countries (France, Germany, and Great Britain) involving a total of 95 students. These programs are intended for international business majors and regular business majors. The percentage of noninternational business majors who take part in the summer programs has increased dramatically. Students have found that the overseas experience has a very positive impact on their job search.

The summer programs have three parts:

(1) A preparatory course during the spring before students go overseas. This preparation is crucial. It informs students about the historical-political-economic environment of the country where they will be studying. Because the students are well prepared, the program overseas can be conducted at a much higher level.

(2) The overseas program, lasting four weeks. During these four weeks students attend lectures given by foreign business people and professors from the partner institution. They also visit a variety of firms and go on field trips. For example, the France group visited one of the largest advertising agencies in France.

(3) Individual travel. While this part is voluntary, most students travel for several weeks after the program has ended. This experience helps consolidate their academic experience. Students can, for example, observe marketing and advertising practices first hand.

Semester programs. Business students can study business at a foreign university in the foreign language. The College of Business has a program with ESSCA in France. Programs with Germany and Mexico are in the developmental stages. While these programs are available to all business majors, because of the language requirements it is mostly international business majors who enroll. Illinois State University tries to run all these programs on an exchange basis because students who do not have the opportunity to study overseas can benefit from the presence of foreign students in their business classes.

University-wide programs. Illinois State University has an Office of International Studies which organizes and administers a variety of overseas programs, most notably language programs and general education programs. These programs are open to all students at the university. A number of international business majors enroll in a program with the Office of International Studies during their freshman or sophomore year and then enroll in a College of Business program during their junior or senior year.

FOREIGN STUDENTS ON CAMPUS

Illinois State University has students from all continents. European students and Japanese students are here with exchange programs. Students from Hong Kong, Taiwan, and India come on an individual basis. With the growth of the International Business major, the number of foreign students in business classes has increased consistently.

The international students live in International House. All of them have an American roommate. International House organizes a number of events throughout the year, with the International Fair the most visible. Groups of students from each country also prepare a "cultural night" program open to the public, in which they dress in native costumes, prepare native food, show films about their country, and present entertainment. International students also have American host families to make them feel more welcome in the community. Foreign student enrollments have remained fairly steady since 1984, generally fluxuating between approximately 310 and 350 students.

ADMINISTRATION OF THE INTERNATIONAL BUSINESS PROGRAM

The International Business Committee. In the beginning the international business major was administered out of the dean's office. An international business committee with representatives from all departments in the college acted as an advisory committee to the dean and made curriculum decisions. A long debate transpired on whether the international business major should be independent or housed in an existing academic department. The decision was made to keep the major independent and create the position of international business director.

The director of International Business. The director is administrator of the program and reports directly to the dean of the College of Business. Since no personnel lines go with the new office, the director must coordinate all international offerings with the chairs of the academic departments.

INTERNATIONAL BUSINESS CLUB

The International Business Club provides another opportunity for international involvement for students. The club was founded in 1982 with just a handful of students. Today the club has over 160 active members. Most of the members are international business majors, but the club has attracted a number of students from other majors, mostly business majors and foreign language majors.

The club arranges for speakers from academia and industry and it hosts a number of social events. The faculty Round Table, which brings together the international business majors and instructors in all areas of international studies, is the social highlight of the year.

The International Business Club keeps track of alumni and has put together an alumni directory. The club also acts as host for the foreign students from partner institutions.

EVALUATION OF INTERNATIONAL PROGRAM

Recruiting of students. The international business major attracts some of the best students in the university. Well-planned recruiting efforts could bring even better students to campus but recruiting will require coordination with other departments. The goal is to recruit outstanding high school students who have had four years of mathematics and four years of a foreign language. Many of the students who have this type of background are not aware of the International Business program at Illinois State University. The international business majors themselves are eager to recruit at high schools with solid language and mathematics programs.

Job placement. In the past, job placement was the weakest link in the program; however, this year great strides have been made towards improvement. One problem has been that business executives talk to the press about the need of a broad and international education, but then these same executives send recruiters to campus who look primarily at how many accounting or computer courses a student has had. Another problem has been that many business people do not know what an international business major is. Most of them think that it is essentially a foreign language major without any business background. A third problem involved the placement office at the university. The problem evolved primarily because of lack of familiarity with the international skills obtained by the majors and with business' need of these majors and their potential for job placement. Some thought that international business graduates were only interested in overseas travel. This situation is gradually changing as awareness increases and more of the program's graduates enter international jobs right after graduation. The college is marketing the program and educating the business world. Whenever the major is explained, the response from business is very positive.

The college is also working at educating the students in the job search for international positions. Most of the majors have a second major or a minor in a functional area or in a language. They know that they will not start out as presidents of the international division. They are also aware that international business is not synonymous with an assignment in Singapore, Hong Kong, or Paris. They know that many business people, active in international business, spend most of their working lives in the United States.

Overall, the program's graduates have been very successful. Graduates of the international business major work in international business in all parts of the world. International business graduates continue to invest time and resources into their continuing education to function better in international business.

Informal feedback. Business students who are not international business majors but who participate in one of the summer programs or who take at least one international elective report that employers look very favorably at the international experience. A number of finance and accounting graduates, for example, who had some international background, received job offers from major firms because of their international exposure. This experience set them apart from other students. Business people interpreted the international component as willingness to work hard, to accept uncertainty, to go the "extra mile." As students talk about the impact of the international experience in the job search, more business majors are interested in going overseas.

International research. One sign of the quality of the international program is the quality of international research by the faculty. Over the past decade several professors who were hostile and at best neutral to international business have started to be interested in international research opportunities. They have published international articles, presented papers overseas, and taught seminars in other countries. As a result, the international atmosphere has increased. Today, international endeavors are encouraged by a substantial majority in the College of Business. The international orientation has also improved interdisciplinary work with faculty from other colleges.

Overseas teaching/learning experiences. Overseas teaching experiences have developed out of the overseas exchange programs. Several of the professors who have accompanied students on the overseas programs have gone back to the partner institutions to teach short seminars and courses. In the future there will be more of these opportunities.

The Societe Internationale pour l'Enseignement Commercial (SIEC), better known in this country as ISBE (International Society for Business Education), also offers the opportunity for business-teacher educators to enhance their professional insights and gain competence in providing richer business education programs. Seventeen member countries have national chapters, and each year this international organization holds a week-long conference in one of the member countries. Some professors are actively involved in the organization and attend international conferences. During this time the participants attend lectures and pedagogical sessions, visit business firms and schools, and study the political, economic, educational, and cultural aspects of the country hosting the conference.

As a result of these exchanges and learning experiences, professors have gained a greater appreciation of the importance of international business. They also see that international business does not take place in a vacuum but is the result of societal, historical, and political forces.

BENEFITS

The most obvious benefit is the advantage the students have in the job market. International experience sells. However, there are also many long-range benefits which may not be quite so obvious.

For example, people who have had international courses and who have studied overseas are more familiar and comfortable with the realization that different cultures do things differently. They get away from a narrowly focused ethnocentric view and reach a more global view.

In classes, American students work together with students from other countries—an experience very similar to working with business people from other countries. The emphasis on international business throughout the curriculum has heightened the awareness toward differences and similarities. Students talk about the differences and explore the "whys" behind the differences.

CONCLUSION

As a result of the internationalization of the core, the availability of international courses, the international business major, and overseas study opportunities, business students at Illinois State University have developed a greater respect and understanding of other cultures which, in turn, has lead to a greater capacity for cooperation.

PART IV

SELECTED FOREIGN BUSINESS EDUCATION PROGRAMS

CHAPTER 15

Business Education Programs in the United Kingdom

JAMES CALVERT SCOTT
Visiting Fellow, Bristol Business School, Bristol, England,
Utah State University, Logan

Over a period that will culminate on December 31, 1992, the Single European Act has committed the member countries of the European Community (EC) to the establishment of a single common market, an area in which the free movement of goods, services, capital, and people will be ensured. Significant progress has been made toward the achievement of that market, and the dismantling of the remaining barriers, which exist in such forms as technical barriers and national restrictions and policies, will open up substantial new business opportunities. With a domestic market of about 323 million people, the single European market is nearly as large as that of the United States and Japan combined. Its influence on the global economy will be significant. Will the potential of this single market be realized? What stumbling blocks lie ahead to slow or stop its success?

One stumbling block could be the incompatibility of the European educational systems. Different educational structures and curricula exist in each of the EC countries—Belgium, Denmark, Eire (Ireland), France, Greece, Italy, Luxembourg, the Netherlands, Portugal, Spain, United Kingdom, and West Germany—because education has been perceived primarily as a national, not EC, matter. Since educational practices within the individual countries do not reflect current economic realities, major changes in European education are on the horizon.

In European countries vocational training is generally perceived as a major aspect of education. Vocational training is being standardized and integrated into regular education, especially in secondary schools, in hopes of reducing high levels of unemployment. All European countries do not invest to the same degree in education and training. For example, the United Kingdom of Great Britain and Northern Ireland (UK) is now spending less of its wealth on education and training than it did 10 years ago. Ironically, this low expenditure comes at a time when business involvement with the other EC members is at record high levels, accounting for about 50 percent of all UK exports and 52 percent of all UK imports. This places the UK in a very difficult competitive position compared to that of its increasingly important EC trading partners. It is also causing far-reaching upheaval throughout British society, and education for business has not escaped the effects.

This chapter focuses on the British system of education for business at various educational stages while briefly describing the overall British system of education. The chapter also provides information about British business education curricula, preparation of business studies teachers, and linkages with the business community. The chapter concludes with an assessment of the British system of education for business.

OVERVIEW OF THE BRITISH SYSTEM OF EDUCATION

Statutory responsibility for the provision of education in the United Kingdom is divided among a number of different national and local governmental units in England, Wales, Scotland, and Northern Ireland. As a result, the educational systems in each of the four constituencies have evolved somewhat independently and differently. This chapter spotlights education for business in England and Wales, the two most similar constituencies in terms of educational systems.

In the United Kingdom education is divided into three stages: Primary education is for pupils from age 5 through about age 11 in England, Wales, and Northern Ireland or about age 12 in Scotland. Secondary education is for pupils from about age 11 or 12 through age 16, the termination point for compulsory education, or older if the pupils remain in what is known as sixth form to work toward additional qualifications. Further and higher education for pupils ages 16 to 18 upwards, includes such institutions as universities, colleges of technology, and commerce, as well as evening institutes and polytechnics.

The government's aims in education are to raise standards, to obtain the best possible value for money, to increase parental choice in educational matters, and to widen access to further and higher education while linking education more closely to the needs of the economy. National policy stipulates that no pupil shall be excluded from education by lack of means, and various funding schemes are available to provide needed financial assistance.

EDUCATION FOR BUSINESS IN THE PRIMARY AND SECONDARY SCHOOL STAGES

This section of the chapter is divided into two major parts that discuss education for business at both the primary and secondary school stages.

Primary and secondary school stages. The National Curriculum, consisting of the three core subjects of English, mathematics, and science, and the seven other foundation subjects of history, geography, design and technology, music, art, physical education, and modern foreign language, is in the process of being implemented for pupils of compulsory school age who attend maintained (government-funded) schools in England and Wales. The National Curriculum has specified attainment targets, programs of study, and assessment arrangements. It also includes some important cross-curricular themes such as personal and social education, including health education, career education and guidance, environmental education, and economic awareness, which do not necessarily fit into the subjects of the National Curriculum.

The discipline of business studies contributes to the foundation subject of design and technology in the National Curriculum by providing relevant business and economics and information technology subject matter as specified in the programs of study at each of the 10 progressively higher levels of attainment. Exhibit 1 suggests a few of the ways in which business and economics and information technology are to be integrated into the design and technology foundation subject and thus be incorporated into the National Curriculum.

Since, under the National Curriculum, business studies content will be integrated with content from the other disciplines that contribute to the foundation subject of design and technology, business studies teachers will most likely function primarily as members of design and technology teaching teams rather than as independent teachers as they have in the past. While it is likely that primary teachers will continue to deliver the business and economics and information technology instruction in the primary schools, business studies teachers will deliver it in the secondary schools.

Exhibit 1.

Business and Economics and Information Technology in the Design and Technology Foundation Subject of the National Curriculum

Key Stages	Attainment Levels	Ages	Representative Items from Programs of Study
1	1-3	5-7	To recognize that goods and services are bought and sold.
			To recognize that information can be held in a variety of forms.
2	2-5	7-11	To recognize the importance of consumer choice and, hence, the importance of product quality.
			To understand how to collect and organize information in a form suitable for entry on a database.
3	3-7	11-14	To calculate and relate costs and revenues in order to make decisions on price and volume (break-even analysis).
			To understand how to combine graphical and numerical information, images, and text in an appropriate way for a variety of audiences.
4	4-10	14-16	To develop an effective product pricing, promotion, and distribution strategy.
			To analyze real systems that are to be modeled using information technology, to make appropriate choices in designing, implementing, and testing the model, and to justify the methods used.

Secondary school stage. In England, Wales, and Scotland secondary education has largely been reorganized along comprehensive school lines, with most schools maintained by the government, and accepting pupils with a wide range of abilities without any selection by examination. In Northern Ireland secondary education is still predominantly based on selection by examination, with most secondary schools maintained by the government. Approximately five to six percent of secondary school pupils in the United Kingdom attend exclusive, highly selective, and often expensive fee-charging "public" schools, which are in fact private, independent schools that still wield disproportionate prestige and influence in British society.

GENERAL CERTIFICATE OF SECONDARY EDUCATION. During the final two years of compulsory secondary school education in England and Wales, most pupils study for external examinations, which are set by several examining boards, among which schools have a choice. The most important of these examinations, formerly called O-level for General Certificate of Education Ordinary level and now called General Certificate of Secondary Education (GCSE), are taken at about age 16 in up to 10 different subjects. These examinations mark the end of formal education for the majority of pupils.

To prepare pupils for the GCSE in business studies, business studies teachers over a period of two years carefully teach the core content that is specified in the business studies syllabus developed by an examination board. That core content is grouped under these five broad headings: external environment of business, business structure and organization, business behavior, people in business, and aiding and controlling business activity. Business studies teachers devise a wide variety of approaches that allow pupils to develop their understanding of business activity, to apply their knowledge to business problems, and to come to their own conclusions. Often the active student-centered learning is community based, problem or decision oriented, and reported back to other pupils. Although the structure of the GCSE examination in business studies varies somewhat from examination board to examination board, it covers the core content using a variety of types of assessment, including short answer questions, essay questions, case problems, and coursework assignments.

TECHNICAL AND VOCATIONAL EDUCATION INITIATIVE. Within the framework of general education, the Technical and Vocational Education Initiative aims to give pupils between the ages of 14 and 18 in maintained schools and colleges a curriculum that is more relevant to adult life and work. The Certificate of Pre-Vocational Education is primarily for those pupils who want to determine what type of work they might do well and to prepare for adult work, but who are not yet committed to a specific occupation. This certificate is a one-year full-time or two-year part-time course for a wide range of pupils who do not intend to pursue A-level examinations but who would like to continue their education after completing secondary schooling. Under guidelines laid down by the Board for Pre-Vocational Education, schools and colleges design their own courses, which often incorporate examination board schemes that yield certificates or diplomas.

NATIONAL VOCATIONAL QUALIFICATION FRAMEWORK. In the United Kingdom the tasks of establishing a coherent national framework for vocational qualifications and of making qualifications relate to the standards required for competent performance in employment have been given to the National Council for Vocational Qualifications. It aims for a multi-level nationwide system that is comprehensible and that shows clearly the routes available to vocational qualifications. To be accredited as a National Vocational Qualification (NVQ), there must be an industry-provided statement of competence, composed of a number of elements of competence accompanied by performance criteria, which has to be achieved to the given standards before a candidate can receive an award. Because NVQ's are expressed in terms of outcomes, they do not specify the content or length of education and training programs that enable individuals to gain NVQ's. Since the implementation of NVQ framework, it is bringing about a number of changes in the design and delivery of vocational education and training, including that in business-related subjects. But it is too early to know if the NVQ framework will achieve its aims in the perplexing world of British vocational qualifications.

SIXTH FORM EDUCATION AND RELATED EXAMINATIONS. Those fortunate enough to remain in sixth form education after age 16 prepare for some form of higher education by studying for A-level examinations. Those remaining to improve their qualifications and skills study for other examinations.

Traditionally, pupils working toward A-level examinations have specialized in up to three subjects for two years by studying content prescribed by syllabi prepared by examination boards. But now pupils have the option of studying additional subjects for two years, but with not less than half the instruction required for an A-level syllabus, and then taking AS-level examinations.

In general, the two-year process used by business studies teachers to prepare pupils for an A-level examination in business studies is similar to that for an O-level examination in business studies, but the syllabus covers more detailed content and does so at a higher level of sophistication. Through a variety of short answer and essay questions, an A-level examination in business studies probes mastery of these four broad topics: basic business organizations and their objectives; internal factors affecting businesses in pursuit of their objectives, including finance, marketing, and manpower; external factors affecting the attainment of business objectives; and the integrated nature of business decisions and objectives.

Those schools that choose the Cambridge A-level business studies examination, for example, must also have their students complete a major project in the business community that counts 25 percent of their final A-level marks. That project might, for instance, be a feasibility study of whether a local business should buy a particular piece of equipment. The project would be assessed regarding the skill with which the problem has been put into context, defined, and considered; the skill with which the objectives have been set; the information gathered; the theoretical base of the project; the analysis provided; the conclusion reached; the effectiveness of the pupil's communication; and the viva, the related one-on-one interview regarding the project.

Those wishing to improve their qualifications and skills for practically any conceivable business-related career, but who choose not to study for an A-level examination in business studies, receive instruction that follows a relevant syllabus provided by an examining body, such as the RSA Examinations Board (RSA), or by a validating body, such as the Business and Technician Education Council (BTEC). While pupils studying such subjects as accounting, communication in business, and word processing may work toward RSA examinations at the advanced diploma and higher diploma levels during sixth form education, others studying such subjects as business and finance, distribution studies, and public administration may work toward BTEC National certificates and diplomas during sixth form education.

At about age 18, pupils take the A-level or General Certificate of Education Advanced level examinations in specialization subjects and the AS-level or Advanced Supplementary level examinations in optional supplementary subjects, or other examinations relevant to their study. Pupils with two A-level passes meet the minimum formal entry requirements for a degree course, although some polytechnics and universities require three A-level passes for admission to their courses. Those who pass the other types of examinations often enter the labor force on a full-time basis, although some enter an institution of further education to continue their preparation for the world of work.

EDUCATION FOR BUSINESS AT THE FURTHER AND HIGHER EDUCATION STAGE

This section is divided into three major parts that discuss further, higher, and continuing education for business.

Further education sub-stage. In the United Kingdom the term *further education* refers to any less-than-degree-status education that occurs after pupils leave secondary schools. Further education is provided by a wide variety of colleges, institutes, and other establishments throughout the nation. Often the business-related instruction essentially duplicates that which is provided in secondary schools and sixth form, but higher and different qualifications are also available. Further education students may study business-related subjects fulltime or parttime on a non-advanced (less than A-level) or an advanced (higher than A-level) basis in the following broad occupational areas: reception, clerical, secretarial, and administrative; business and financial; retail distribution; and warehousing, storage, and distribution. Certificates in such specific subjects as audio-typewriting in French, core text processing skills, languages for international trade, and cost accounting are available through various examining boards.

Higher education sub-stage. Under the binary system in the United Kingdom, higher or degree-level education is offered by two types of institutions, polytechnics and universities, which are equal but different. Polytechnic education focuses on the world of work. Most polytechnics offer a wide range of courses from the less-than-degree level through the doctor's degree level and confer their degrees through the Council for National Academic Awards. Education for business plays a major role in almost all polytechnics. On the other hand, university education focuses on the pursuit of knowledge for its own sake. Universities offer courses from the bachelor's degree level through the doctor's degree level and confer their degrees directly. Education for business plays a less important role and sometimes a minor role in the universities. Although about three times as much education for business is delivered by polytechnics as is delivered by universities, both polytechnics and universities deliver about equal amounts of management education. Polytechnics and universities generally offer similar degree-level education for business and, consequently, are sometimes in direct competition with each other.

In the polytechnics, education for business at the less-than-degree level may include, among other things, foundation courses in accountancy and the BTEC Higher National certificate and diploma courses in business and finance with specializations in such areas as business information systems, financial services, marketing, and tourism. In both polytechnics and universities, at the bachelor's degree level, education for business may include such courses as accounting and finance, business studies, European business studies, and financial services, as well as others. Most bachelor's degrees in the United Kingdom require three years of full-time study unless they are sandwich degrees, which require another year for the work experience that is sandwiched between the blocks of academic work. At the postgraduate level, which is equivalent to the graduate level in the United States, such one-year full-time or two-year part-time courses that confer diplomas in management studies, marketing, personnel management, and European business management with information technology are available along with the one-year or two-year full-time or three-year part-time master of business administration degrees, the two-year full-time master of philosophy degrees, and the three-year full-time doctor of philosophy degrees, and others.

Continuing education sub-stage. Many of those who pursue further and higher education continue on to become members of the many professional bodies that exist in the United Kingdom. Individuals may obtain partial or total exemption from the examinations of professions by virtue of successfully completing certain widely available courses; however, some professional qualifications are obtained only by completion of special courses of direct preparation, which are usually offered by further and higher education institutions at the behest of various professional bodies. For most professions, including business-related ones, individuals are required to study additional subjects beyond those that are needed for entry into the world of work and to obtain responsible related work experience before they can become members of the profession. A number of the professional bodies have several classifications of membership, and further study and work experience may be required to advance to the higher membership classifications.

The Management Charter Initiative is a recent attempt to establish a clear and comprehensive system of management qualifications in the United Kingdom. After developing and promoting a code of practice, the Council for Management Education and Development has recently unveiled its certificate aimed at all of those entering management for the first time. The prime objective is the development of an understanding of the nature of management, the issues involved, the language and techniques in general use, and the competencies required within the first two years in management. The issues of when and how to deliver the related education and training are now being debated; it is likely that several types of educational institutions will have roles in the implementation process.

Education for business in the United Kingdom also occurs in the business community, either within a specific business or within a group of similar or related businesses. This type of education and training for business, which is growing in importance, is delivered in four basic ways: tailor-made courses provided by polytechnic or university staff on the premises of the educational institution or at the business; tailor-made courses provided by private training or consultancy companies on the premises of the company or the business; in-house courses organized and staffed by trainers employed by the business; and public courses offered by polytechnics or universities, by private training or consultancy companies, or by governmental agencies.

PREPARATION OF BUSINESS STUDIES TEACHERS

This section of the chapter is divided into two major parts that discuss the preparation of business studies teachers for both the secondary education and further and higher education stages.

Secondary education stage. About 20 educational institutions, primarily polytechnics, prepare business studies teachers for the secondary schools in the United Kingdom. While there are three basic types of courses that yield initial teacher certification for business studies upon successful completion and the recommendation of the educational institution, the majority of educational institutions that train business studies teachers do not offer all three types.

The four-year full-time bachelor of education degree with honors is designed for prospective business studies teachers who have A-level qualifications in business studies or, in the case of mature candidates, equivalent qualifications with relevant business-related work experience. Those without the normal entry qualifications may take access courses at technical colleges to gain the necessary entrance qualifications. This course, like the other two, is designed to equip individuals to teach such subjects as commerce, economics, business studies, accounting, and, in some cases, office technology and information processing in both single-discipline and, increasingly likely, multi-discipline courses. The first two years of this course are devoted primarily to business studies in all major functional areas with a small amount of education and teaching studies. During the last two years, the emphasis is reversed. A period of placement in a business and a minimum of 15 weeks of full-time supervised teaching practice is typically spent in three block periods at three different schools.

The two-year full-time unclassified bachelor of education degree is designed for prospective business studies teachers at the secondary stage who have already completed a two-year BTEC Higher National diploma in business studies or a similar post A-level qualification in business studies and have business-related experience. This course emphasizes education and teaching studies with academic enrichment in the functional business areas. School experiences in the first year and two block periods of supervised teaching practice, including one in each year of the course, form an integrating focus throughout this course.

The one-year full-time postgraduate certificate in education is designed for prospective business studies teachers at the secondary stage who have already completed a bachelor's degree in business studies, economics, or a joint degree in which economics features as a major element. Since those enrolled in this course already have basic subject mastery, their course places heavy emphasis on education and teaching studies. The course enrollees are regularly involved in activities in schools, including periods of block teaching practice amounting to at least 10 weeks.

Two other routes exist to teaching in the secondary schools. In special cases those without qualified teacher status, including teachers trained overseas, can become licensed teachers by participating in a two-year paid on-the-job individualized training program. An experimental articled teacher scheme is being tested; under this scheme individuals earn partial pay for two years while not only working four-fifths time in schools under the supervision of a tutor from a teacher training institution and a teacher-mentor but also studying one-fifth time at a teacher training institution.

Limited opportunities exist for secondary school business studies teachers to pursue higher degree-level qualifications although there are opportunities for in-service courses and a variety of Open University offerings. Since the school year extends into July, lengthy summer school sessions for teachers are not available. Furthermore, the few relevant subject-area courses available at the master's degree level are usually full-time courses, which exclude practicing teachers.

Since the demand for qualified business studies teachers exceeds the supply, the Department of Education and Science through its Teaching as a Career scheme actively recruits prospective teachers, especially mature persons, via traveling roadshows and short taste-of-teaching courses.

Further and higher education stage. Those teaching business studies at the further and higher education stage usually do not follow one of the initial teacher-certification routes. Instead, they pursue an appropriate certificate, diploma, or degree in a business-related discipline and relevant business-related employment.

For a variety of reasons, including historically limited course offerings in business-related areas, the majority of business studies teachers possess lower academic degree-level qualifications in the United Kingdom than do their counterparts at equivalent educational institutions in the United States.

LINKAGES BETWEEN EDUCATION FOR BUSINESS AND THE BUSINESS COMMUNITY

Although there have been a number of promising developments in terms of linkages between education for business and the business community in recent years, three culturally-based impediments to these linkages exist in the United Kingdom: business studies teachers' tradition of academic independence, businesspersons' perceptions that they are unable to devote time and money to education and training, and businesspersons' giving insufficient recognition to the importance of education and training. Nevertheless, these obstacles are being overcome.

The government has mounted a campaign to increase the level of involvement of businesses in schools, and the Confederation of British Industry has added its support for such linkages. For the business community especially, the linkages are critical; given the dramatic decrease in the number of school leavers in the years ahead, the need for more highly skilled workers, and the increased competition for the more able school leavers from both higher education and the public sector, the business community will miss vital recruitment opportunities unless it has strong ties to educational institutions.

Linkages between education for business and the business community vary according to the target audience, the objective, and the degree of penetration into the educational process. When pupils are the target, these types of linkages may develop: work shadowing; work simulation; work experience; school enterprises; industrial site visits; use of industrial resources; use of industrial advisors; special events such as competitions; joint business education-business community curriculum development projects; and joint business education-business community training activities such as mock interviews. When business studies teachers are the target, these types of linkages may develop: attachments to businesses; attendance at business-sponsored training courses; attendance at courses with business contributions; research into external learning resources; development of new learning opportunities involving external resources; development of personal contacts; and provision of services for businesses. When businesspersons are the targets, these types of linkages may develop: contributions to activities of pupils and business studies teachers; consultantships in school-related matters; designations as businessperson in residence; assistance with student project work; advisorships to pupils; development of business-related learning materials; service on business education committees; and service as school governor or member of the school board.

ASSESSMENT OF THE BRITISH SYSTEM OF EDUCATION FOR BUSINESS

This section of the chapter is divided into two major parts that provide general comments and concluding remarks.

General comments. Through no fault of its own, education for business in the United Kingdom is handicapped by its status. The historic disdain that Britons have for both practical and vocational education plus their class-system hierarchy that gives business occupations low to moderate status make it difficult for education for business to be highly valued. Nevertheless, there is a growing realization that the economic security of the nation depends on a business community that is competitive at home and abroad. The days of the gifted amatuer, upon whom the British business community has relied for so long, are over; highly educated and trained British businesspersons are needed to compete against the professionals from other countries. There will be British business professionals in sufficient numbers for the challenges ahead only when education for business receives its proper recognition and the adequate resources to do what must be done—catch up with the international competitors. National campaigns to upgrade the images of both the business community and education for business are needed, since both are seriously undervalued in contemporary British society.

Adequate funding to support education for business is necessary if the business community in the United Kingdom is to be competitive. The efforts during recent years to get value for money have created considerable disarray. While some economies have been achieved, overall the process has been destructive rather than constructive. Now teachers of business subjects do not always have the necessary physical facilities, equipment, and other educational resources to do their jobs well; the quality of education for business is in jeopardy in some locations. Low salaries, low status, and poor working conditions are demoralizing teachers of business subjects. Nevertheless, many dedicated business educators are laboring diligently to deliver better business education, and their efforts have been successful. Yet there are unfulfilled needs for additional education and training in business-related subjects at all stages, especially at the MBA level where tomorrow's top business leaders are being prepared today and where the enrollments are disproportionately low. Teachers of business-related subjects themselves also need more education and training opportunities. With a fair share of resources, business education institutions can provide the necessary types and amounts of education for business that will help the economy to prosper again.

The system that delivers education for business needs refinement at all stages, although some improvements have been made in recent years. As long as there is lack of consensus about what business education means, especially at the secondary school stage, it will be difficult to devise a system that delivers it effectively. The existing system seems overly complicated and confusing with essentially the same education and training for business offered at several consecutive levels by sometimes competing educational institutions. At the same time the majority of pupils, those who leave school at age 16, have inadequate opportunities to develop the increasingly sophisticated business-related vocational skills that are needed. Subsequently, this valuable but largely neglected human resource is swelling the ranks of the unemployed and underemployed, which does not bode well for the future. The jungle of examination boards, with their different and sometimes competing examinations, further fragments the system of education for business and contributes to the narrowness of focus that characterizes much of the education for business. To remedy these concerns, some single entity needs overall responsibility for developing a more cohesive and efficient system of business education within cultural and other constraints. Insofar as is feasible, the system should be designed to be inclusionary rather than exclusionary, allowing all persons full access to whatever business-related education and training they need in order to rise to their potential.

The business-related curricula that are offered need to be scrutinized to ensure that they have appropriate emphases. Both the needs of the educational institutions for academic rigor and the needs of the business community for practicality must be reconciled if education for business is to thrive. Most of the business-related curricula are examination-board led, and this may lead to premature and excessive specialization that may not be in the long-term interest of either the person who attempts to advance to higher positions or to the business community, because it may limit the potential of its most valuable resource, people. What is needed is business education and training with a broad foundation and enough specialization to do the immediate work while retaining the flexibility to function later at higher and broader levels of responsibility. Although some efforts have been made in recent years to internationalize education for business, much more work needs to be done at all stages. Insular attitudes, which are ingrained in the British culture, must be overcome. Business foreign language skills must be promoted, perhaps building on the modern foreign language foundation in the National Curriculum. More truly international content, not just Western European content, must be systematically added to courses at all educational stages. More overseas education and training opportunities in both the educational and business communities must be cultivated if Britons are to reach fruition as international businesspersons.

Concluding remarks. The articulation of concerns and shortcomings within the United Kingdom education-for-business system is not the problem; the problem is taking concerted action to overcome the concerns and shortcomings where prior attempts have been less than entirely satisfactory. Pressures are mounting on the providers of education and training to serve better the needs of the business community. Progress is being achieved toward that goal, but additional actions are necessary. The time has come for all of those concerned with education for business in the United Kingdom to accept the challenge fully and to build a new future for a once-great nation, based upon a highly educated and trained work force that produces and sells high quality goods and services around the world.

CHAPTER 16

Comparative Business Education Programs in the European Community Countries

ALBERT G. GIORDANO
Monterey Peninsula College (Retired), Monterey, California

As 1992 approaches and the European Community (EC) grows closer to becoming a reality, the need for additional international business programs in United States colleges and universities will increase. Those working in the European society will need a deeper appreciation of the major evolving commercial and economic forces. Business management will require mobility between the EC countries; therefore foreign language fluency will become an added asset. Another requirement will be ability to adapt to other cultures and a personality that is flexible, understanding, and cooperative.

One of the primary purposes of this chapter is to show the similarities and differences of business education on the post-high school levels in the EC countries. Whenever possible, unique and outstanding programs will be highlighted. As the EC emerges in 1992, we can expect changes in business education programs in member countries. International trade and international investment between European countries will be enhanced. Greater mobility of employees, management and, of course, their products and services will exist. The import and export of products and services will not only increase but will also become a daily routine. International business transactions may become as commonplace as transactions that are conducted between states in the United States.

Business education programs will not only have to include many traditional courses such as accounting, finance, purchasing, marketing, production, management, human resources/personnel administration, research and services but also specialized international trade courses that deal with the daily trade functions among the EC countries.

EUROPEAN ECONOMIC COMMUNITY

The EC was established to promote economic and political integration among its member nations. Another goal was to eliminate all trade and investment restrictions among the member nations. The plan included the establishment of a common currency for all EC countries, often referred to as ECU—Economic Community Unit. This new ECU threatens to challenge the economic dominance of the present leaders. As 1992 approaches, additional countries may become members of the EC. International trade and investment among member countries have already increased and further increases can be expected. In addition there has been a surge of foreign investments into the EC by United States firms and other outside countries.

International business will continue to be influenced by substantial changes in international competitiveness. Institutions that offer education for business will have to become more competitive as well. There is already a strong movement among many colleges and universities in the United States to offer not just one or two courses, but programs in international business.

In undergraduate programs, the development of foreign language ability will become more important. The exchange of students between colleges and universities will become more commonplace. Exchange opportunities are extremely valuable preparation for a career in international business. Often, business programs will have multi-disciplinary majors with an international orientation.

In the United States an increasing number of colleges and universities are now offering undergraduate and graduate degree programs in international business. International programs will move upward into MBA programs and even into doctoral programs.

SPECIALIZED INTERNATIONAL BUSINESS DEGREE PROGRAMS

There are four universities that have programs that have required their students to combine business course work with foreign language training and international studies courses: The American Graduate School of International Management in Glendale, Arizona; The Monterey Institute of International Studies in Monterey, California, with an MBA in International Management; The Wharton School of Business's Lauder Institute Program at the University of Pennsylvania in Philadelphia; and the University of South Carolina, Columbia, South Carolina, which offers the Master of International Business Studies. These university programs require overseas language and cultural training, and a corporate internship abroad as part of their degree requirements.

DOCTORAL PROGRAMS IN INTERNATIONAL BUSINESS

Doctoral programs offering a specialization in international business that require international business majors to develop a proficiency in at least one foreign language and complete courses in international business include: the University of Michigan, New York University, Columbia University, Indiana University, the University of Washington, and the University of California, Los Angeles.

UNDERGRADUATE SPECIALIZED DEGREE PROGRAMS

Michigan has shown leadership in undergraduate specialized degree programs in international business with programs at Eastern Michigan University, Ypsilanti, and Michigan State University, East Lansing. Clemson University, Southern Illinois University, Auburn University, and California State University, are among those that have established recent international business programs. Programs are being developed at many other universities. In fact, many community colleges are also developing international programs.

COMPARATIVE BUSINESS EDUCATION

Business education finds itself operating on ever-broadening horizons, not only in the United States but also within the nations that make up the European Community (EC). As the global economy continues to develop and the mobility of people, products, and ideas increase, the impact on business education programs will be significant. The remainder of this chapter focuses on the similarities and differences that exist in business programs offered in selected European countries. Special attention is given to describing those programs that are considered unique or outstanding.

UNITED KINGDOM

The distinctive feature of the British system is its highly selective process, the comparatively short and intensive nature of courses, very low failure and drop-out rates, and the fact that most students prefer to study away from their home. Although there are differences between the Scottish and Northern Irish educational systems and the United Kingdom, in general, the system throughout the United Kingdom is fairly homogenous.

The United Kingdom does not guarantee right of entry to higher education for those with minimal formal qualifications in contrast to most of the continental European countries. Most courses last only three years; however, in certain subjects, courses may last for four or more years. Teaching is very intensive and syllabi are specialized with comparatively little choice for the students. Therefore, the program enables the student to reach a very high level in a very short time even though there is a restriction in the range of subjects studied. Examination failure is kept comparatively low. Most institutions permit retaking of failed examinations. Most students, therefore, complete their studies at an early age of twenty-two or twenty-three. About one-fourth of those students completing their first degree will continue with further education. The remainder enter the job market at an early age or continue with part-time training for further professional qualification.

Because of the comparatively short and specialized nature of first degree courses in the United Kingdom, there is a greater need for professional education and training at a postgraduate level than there is in those countries with longer courses.

A feature of some continental European systems, which is not well developed in the United Kingdom, is that of being able to transfer between institutions while studying for a particular major. Requirements of the educational system and differences in syllabi have created the obstacle. In the United Kingdom most degrees are considered a general qualification, thus enabling students to enter a wide variety of careers. Finance, management, and other non-technical areas recruit graduates from any discipline. Arts graduates, therefore, are not limited to careers in teaching or other specialized fields for which their degree may be relevant. These graduates commonly work in the financial field—banking, accounting, insurance, marketing, sales, and finance. This situation was made possible because of the long tradition of general education, rather than vocational education. Further business training, therefore, has been the responsibility of business and industry. Smaller businesses prefer to recruit graduates with relevant degrees in business and management.

Approximately a quarter of those students graduating from universities continue with master's and doctoral programs with an emphasis more on the research aspect. A number of universities have developed postgraduate business schools that offer MBA courses similar to the American system. As the English language becomes more prevalent among EC countries, the mobility of students among the countries will become more common.

LUXEMBOURG

Higher education is limited in Luxembourg, the smallest of the EC member states, with a population of only slightly more than a third of a million people. The official language for education is French, but the press generally uses German. Luxembourg is considered a major financial center.

The university center offers one-year courses in the faculties of law and economics, arts and humanities, and science. In their second year, students enter programs at universities in neighboring countries, mostly Belgium, France, and Germany; but some go to Austria, Switzerland, and the United Kingdom. The university center also offers a short two-year course in law, economic science, computer systems, business, commerce, banking, and business control.

The mobility expected to come with the establishment of the EC in 1992 is already taking place in Luxembourg. There is a European Institute for Information Management which offers a postgraduate course in computer science. Students are not required to even begin their first-year studies in Luxembourg.

THE NETHERLANDS

Radical changes have taken place in the programs at the Dutch institutions of higher education. The Ministry of Education has forced the universities to cut the length of their courses, to reduce staff, and to concentrate the teaching of certain subjects in a limited number of institutions.

Dutch universities are characterized by a mixture of centralization and independence. Academic freedom is strongly held in the Netherlands and its universities. The two universities in Amsterdam work closely together to avoid duplication, and the three universities in the southwest part of the country do likewise. In recent years more courses are being taught in English. Among the universities in the Netherlands, there are three engineering institutions known as technical universities. They were formerly called Technishe Hogescholen and have always been considered universities but should not be confused with the Higher Vocational Schools which promote non-university higher vocational education. The former Netherlands Business School at Nijenrode has become a degree-awarding institution.

Although most Dutch universities are state financed, there are three denominational universities also financed by the state; religious factors do not seem as important as in Belgium. The Netherlands also has a system of high schools that provide vocational education in a number of practical fields including business.

Most university courses, including higher level vocational education, continue for four years. Business education takes place principally at two universities, Groningen and Rotterdam. The new system graduates will have less background in research elements, but this should not affect the knowledge gained from their other studies. Like many other continental countries, the Netherlands has an open access system similar to Germany's. The right of entry is the right to study any subject, although it may become necessary for students to make up deficiencies in other subject areas.

In some schools there may be a requirement for students to spend some time in appropriate work experience during their program of studies. More and more students in the Netherlands are expected to take their degrees in relevant subjects and employers expect the same of graduates. Economics is very much geared to applied economics and management studies. Only two full-time MBA programs in postgraduate business education are offered—Nijenrode and Rotterdam. Universities in the Netherlands are actively recruiting foreign students since there is a shortage of students from their own country.

The Netherlands will have increased opportunities to attract students from other EC countries after 1992. Differences between cultures may become less important, with greater mobility of students and workers becoming a reality.

IRELAND

After Luxembourg, Ireland has the smallest population of the EC countries, with a population of less than four million. Ireland also has the youngest population in the EC with about fifty percent of its citizens being under the age of twenty-five. Therefore, Ireland's student population is much larger than its small population might suggest.

The Irish educational system is much like the Scottish and the Anglo-Saxon system. One of the major differences is that the age of completion certificate is only seventeen and one-half rather than eighteen and one-half years. The number of courses provides a broadly-based secondary education and more students in Ireland study at local universities than abroad. Many students help finance their studies through employment during vacation periods.

Ireland only has two major universities—the National University of Ireland and the University of Dublin. Each has a number of recognized colleges. In addition, there are two national institutes for higher education, one at Limerick, the other in Dublin, that provide degree-level education oriented towards technology, applied sciences, and business.

A number of technical schools providing sub-degree level education are funded through the local vocational education committee. Nine regional technical colleges are spread throughout the country. The National Council for Education Awards governs the awards of these institutions as well. There are no separate business schools in Ireland. The institutions of higher education teach business studies. Courses in commerce and business studies, as well as law and engineering, are very popular.

The length of courses for degrees varies from institution to institution but four years is most common. Beyond the graduate diploma there is also a national diploma. There is a strong preference for relevant courses in commerce. Thus, faculties of commerce and business studies are strong in Ireland.

Irish employers in accounting and banking prefer relevant candidates although some other candidates are hired. At least three-fourths have relevant degrees in business. This is almost a complete reversal of what is found in England and Wales. The preference for relevant degrees partially reflects the preferences of students. It is often vocational courses that are the most difficult to enter and that, therefore, attract the highest caliber of applicants. As a result, employers tend to find better caliber graduates from the vocationally-oriented faculties.

The system of postgraduate study in Ireland is very similar to that in the United Kingdom. Master's degrees may be taken either by instruction or research or a combination of the two. Many are available through part-time study such as those run by the Irish Management Institute in conjunction with Trinity College, Dublin.

In the future, more students from Ireland can be expected to enroll in EC universities. It is expected that more Irish nationals will be available for work in Europe. Ireland should continue to attract a limited number of foreign students.

GREECE

Greece, with a population of about ten million, has a strong sense of its own individuality in history. Although heavily influenced in origin by the German and French tradition, this southern Mediterranean country differs greatly from the Germans and French by having a selective system with a highly centralized method of allocating students. The system, administered by the Ministry of National Education and Religion, does not allow the universities much discretion in matters such as subject syllabi.

A unique feature of the country is that many people of Greek origin living outside the country retain strong cultural links, and many return home for study. Few non-Greek students study in Greece due to the language. Most of the foreign students in Greece come from Africa and the Middle East. Many native Greeks choose to study abroad, the United States, Italy, United Kingdom, France, and Germany being the most popular choices. More Greek students may be found in EC countries in the future.

The only recognized institutions of higher education in Greece are the universities and the nonuniversity level institutions, the TEIs (technical educational institutions). The universities consist of schools of faculties that are divided into departments. These are further divided into sectors. The oldest university in Greece is the University of Athens. A technical university was created in Crete in 1977. The law of 1982 set up several new universities, some of which are still being developed. Several important university-level institutions are teaching economics and business studies; notably, the Industrial School of Piraeus, the Industrial School of Thessaloniki, the Athens School of Economic and Commercial Studies, and the Panteios School of Political Sciences. Most university-level business education is carried out in the Athens School of Economic and Commercial Studies and the Industrial School. Contrary to the selective procedures at institutions in Ireland, the United Kingdom, or France, Greek institutions have no power of selection but must accept those students allocated to them by the Ministry of Education and Religion. Similar to most continental Europeans, Greeks take a fairly restrictive view of the relationship between subjects studied in higher education and career possibilities.

BELGIUM

In most of Europe, many of the differences in education are more by language groups than by majors or disciplines. Universities in Belgium are both French- and Dutch-speaking, but Vesalius College in Brussels teaches bachelor-degree courses in English. The University of Antwerp is especially strong in applied economics and commercial subjects. One specialization that is available in Belgium is commercial engineering, a mixture of business studies and scientific subjects. This program is designed to prepare people by giving them business training and a technical background. Since it is a scientific degree, the syllabus varies from institution to institution.

High schools offer two types of courses—a short course and a long course. The short course is for two or three years while the long course is for four or five years. These courses prepare people for careers in industry and commerce as well as teaching and selected highly specialized areas.

Belgium, similar to other continental European countries, has a strong traditional belief that degree subjects should be directly related to future careers. The job market for graduates in the arts has deteriorated; more students must seek employment outside of their subject areas. Therefore, the second part of their degree program finds them studying more vocational subjects.

MBA programs, not the equivalent of the American-type MBA programs, prepare students with appropriate business qualifications. Some universities also offer part-time MBA programs. Many Belgian universities focus their attention on programs to attract overseas students, especially to their postgraduate courses.

DENMARK

Although Denmark is a member of the EC, it also has very close ties with other Scandinavian countries. The higher education system in Denmark is modeled after the German model. There has been an attempt to get universities away from a teaching mode and to make instruction more relevant to the business community.

In addition to three major universities, there are two new university centers in Denmark. There is also a new technical university near Copenhagen. There are business schools within the University of Odense and the University Centre at Alborg and three separate schools of business administration.

Students are selected on criteria laid down by the Ministry. Manpower requirements as well as resources and student demand are also considered. Expansion of subject areas is based upon demand.

The Danes, like the Dutch, consider the basic degree to be the equivalent of a master's degree rather than a bachelor's degree. This basic degree has two subjects, a major and a minor, and generally takes up to six years to complete; most students take even longer. This basic degree is referred to as the Candidatus and has been reduced to five years of study. The system of business education in Denmark operates at two levels: (1) The Universities of Copenhagen and Arhus offer degrees in business studies. (2) The University of Odense and Alborg University Centre jointly with the business high schools produce graduates in business studies. A high school curriculum offers full-time courses enabling students to achieve university level. The Ministry of Education controls the syllabi; therefore, courses tend to be similar in both content and status in all universities. Examinations are held twice a year. In subjects like economics, business studies, and engineering, there is a system where a final grade is computed. The best students seldom fail examinations, but there is a high dropout rate primarily due to the fact that financing courses is difficult. Danish students often take a long time to complete their degree requirements.

Computer science graduates are in great demand. Most of the computer scientists going into industry graduate from the Technical University and not from the traditional schools. Available grants limit the number of people taking licenciates. Denmark does not offer MBA programs as we know them in the United States.

FRANCE

The educational system in France is different from that found in most other European countries. An important feature unique to France is the distinction between universities and écoles. Écoles are highly prestigious institutions offering three-year courses in a variety of subjects with an emphasis on applied or vocational aspects. Therefore, business education is carried out in the écoles. Majors in law and computer science are, however, found in universities.

French commercial and industrial employers fill their vacancies almost without exception from students completing courses in the écoles. Students in France, many highly educated, are unwilling to speak foreign languages, a major contrast to other European students, especially in Northern Europe.

The university system in France is entirely state run and is the responsibility of the National Ministry of Education. The écoles are a mixture of state and private institutions. Some are the responsibility of the National Ministry of

Education while others are run by a variety of organizations such as the chambers of commerce.

High grades in the baccalaureate courses are necessary for admission to the university. Admission to the écoles is highly competitive and usually requires a period of preparation in special classes of one to three years, that leads to an entry examination. The écoles are well regarded as national institutions, and the more prestigious schools attract students from all over France. Contrary to other countries, the students in France are mobile and do not confine themselves to local institutions.

Business schools in France have an undergraduate studies program, a diploma course, and a postgraduate MBA type course. The time spent in intensive preparatory study plus the time to get a higher education (a diploma from one of the écoles), is usually five years.

Vocationally-oriented majors are in technical subjects, such as management and business computing. More recently, universities have been introducing vocational conversion courses, either in the second or third cycle, to combat the problems of unemployed graduates. An important feature of many programs is the built-in practical experience. This requirement is traditional in the écoles and is found in vocational courses in the universities as well. A diploma from an école is generally regarded as sufficient professional preparation. Therefore, écoles do not offer postgraduate studies.

French employers prefer the relevant degree requirements and are more familiar with the graduates of the écoles. Some universities have developed close links with industry and commerce in certain majors. The University of Paris, for example, has developed its link in both economics and business studies.

There are a number of MBA courses available in France that also attract foreign students. INSEAD at Fontainebleau is a business school, not part of a university or école, and offers a one-year MBA program. Four of the better known commercial écoles in France offer two-year MBA programs. The École des Affaires de Paris offers an MBA that includes one year of study in France and a second year in each of two overseas branches in Germany, the United Kingdom, or Spain.

ITALY

The Italian higher education system originated during the unification of Italy in the late nineteenth century. It was modeled after the German system, and it still retains many similarities. The Italian higher education system has undergone a series of reforms, most recently within the last 10 years. It is essentially an open access system; all those who have the appropriate school-leaving qualifications are entitled to enter. The most recent reforms are perhaps more closely related to the American system. Although individual institutions have considerable freedom, the Italian educational system is controlled by the National Ministry of Education.

Higher education in Italy is confined to the state-run universities. There are a number of private universities that are still largely state funded and operate similar to state universities. Two well-respected private universities are the Bocconi University in Milan, a commercial university, and the Libera Universita Internazionali degli Studi Sociali in Rome. Prestigious Catholic universities are located in both Rome and Milan and their standard qualifications required for entry may, therefore, be higher than the state universities.

Education outside of the universities is done either in special vocational colleges or in high schools with courses two or three years in length. The European Business School has recently established a branch in Rome. Two other international institutions are the European University Institute at Florence and the Johns Hopkins Centre at Bologna.

Recent reforms have given greater flexibility in the structure of courses themselves. It now is possible for students to devise personal programs of study. Graduates from the same program and the same university often have completely different backgrounds due to this freedom of choice.

As in Germany, students can sit for their exams at different times of the year and, therefore, can graduate almost any time of the year. The laurea is the only official title awarded by Italian universities. Master's and doctoral degrees are now being developed with the reforms of the 1980's. Italian universities have not been involved in joint courses with other countries to any degree, but recent agreement between the Italian and French Ministries of Education has established courses involving study in these two countries.

In the commercial field the degree in economics and commerce meets the normal qualifications for employment. Arts graduates are occasionally recruited into areas such as marketing, especially if they have a strong personality or personal contacts. In Italy, personal or family contacts are more important than in most other European countries.

A recent development in certain Italian universities has been master's degrees in business studies modeled after the American system. These have been developed at existing universities in economics or business and also in specialist business schools such as the Scuola di Direzione Aziendale, Bocconi University in Milan. Other master's degrees in business administration exist at the universities of Ancona, Bari, Genoa, Padua, and Turin. Italy does not have a large number of foreign students. There is a limit on foreign students with the exception of those from Greece. With the advent of the European Community in 1992, no doubt there will be greater mobility of students to Italy.

Business education and vocational education are generally offered at the secondary school level. The trend has been to offer most courses at the secondary school level II, which is a total of five years. (Level I is two years and level II is three years.) These last two years would be similar to post-high school or pre-university level. Level II is where vocational training and technical schools offer programs. Liberalization of university admissions has increased the number of students attending these schools.

In 1990 Cesare Guasco of the Ministry of Education, Italy, reported, "The structures of the technical institutes have changed radically. They are now divided into a system of nine types of institutes with 47 branches of specialization. Today, almost 50 percent of upper secondary school students attend this type of school."

The technical institutes for commerce are commercial schools that have specializations in business administration, trade, data processing, industrial management, and accounting. Business administration is the most popular specialization. Among these 47 institutions, specialization has evolved. For example, there are technical institutes for tourism, personnel business management specialists, and foreign language secretaries. The Italian educational system has not responded appropriately to today's young people, society, and the job market.

In Italy most of the vocational schools and institutes focus primarily on local community needs. For example, at the Instituto Europeo di Design, Professor Joseph Manca reports that one program prepares young people to manage small to medium-sized business firms. The course lasts three years with about 300 hours of instruction per year. In addition, there are seminars and conferences off campus that include a one-month job-training program with a local firm. The class offerings for each year are extensive and compare favorably to those offered at private business schools and community colleges in the United States.

New programs in schools of technology include administrative secretary, accountancy analyst, and commercial operator. This last program is similar to small business management programs in the United States. Vocational education has shifted from the age of compulsory education to that of post-compulsory education. The outdated idea of training as pure acquisition of manual ability has been transformed to the affirmation of the new concept of formation.

Changes in legislation regarding tax reform, economic operations in customs, banking and currency matters, innovations in commercial law and business economics in general, and automated data processing procedures have developed new programs to meet these qualifications. Finally, the need to measure up to the requirements of the EC will have its effect on business education programs. Standardization as well as specialization will change to meet the needs of the EC community.

THE FEDERAL REPUBLIC OF GERMANY—WEST GERMANY

West Germany is a federal republic with 11 constituent states (landers). Responsibility for higher education is divided among the various federal ministries and the individual governments of the states. Variations do exist among the different landers; however, responsibility and powers of the different levels of government are regulated closely.

Although the major responsibility rests with the lander governments, the federal government has two important functions. First, it is responsible for drawing up a Framework Act that sets out certain guidelines for higher education. In addition, the Federal Ministry for Education and Science is involved in the financing of university buildings and in legislating with the state parliaments about systems of financial support for students.

Most institutions of higher education are the responsibility of their local parliament. The institutions of higher education do have some independence and propose their budgets, a structure of courses, and recommendations of appointments to the teaching posts. An important philosophy of higher education in Germany is that students have a right to study whatever they wish. Basically, any German students who have the necessary qualifications in the school-leaving examination can enroll at a university to study a subject of their choice.

The large number of students currently passing through the university system has created difficulties—the number of available places is being expanded. Also, graduates being produced at a time when the economy is having difficulty in absorbing them has created problems for foreign graduates who wish to work in West Germany.

There are basically two groups of higher education institutions in West Germany: (1) The first group of institutions have university status. Since some of these institutions grew out of nonuniversity institutions of technology, some have retained their original names as "technical university" or "technical high school." Today, most of these technical schools teach the whole range of subjects and have been given a high status in educational circles. (2) The second group of institutions consists of seven model institutions. Perhaps these are best described as "comprehensive universities" whose purpose is to integrate the two types of educational programs—those offered in the universities and those offered in the technical universities.

While business studies are very common in universities, there are no separate schools of business as in America. The European Business School has branches located in Germany.

The structure of course offerings and qualifications in German universities is complicated. The basic degree program that leads to a *diplom* does not apply to all subjects. Often they structure their teaching for what is really a professional qualification awarded by the state. Another program qualifies people to teach who had studied the arts but did not originally plan to teach. They earn the MA (Magister Artium), which is considered equal to the *diplom* degree.

The German academic year is divided into two semesters. All courses are not available when students wish to take them, requiring them to wait until the following semester. The present average length of study of university graduates is almost seven years. Their freedom to choose subjects of study as well as changes of courses and universities often extends the time of study. Therefore, students are generally older when they graduate, often in their late twenties.

Students are often required to have periods of practical experience during the course of their studies. This is true in the areas of both economics and business.

The Federal Republic of Germany is typical of most continental European countries where employers seek graduates with relevant degrees. Arts graduates are normally regarded as being qualified only for teaching; these graduates are only considered for employment if they possess outstanding personal characteristics.

German universities normally offer two programs that are considered relevant to commercial jobs. One program is oriented toward economic policy and economic theory. The second program generally is described as business studies and is primarily geared toward careers in management. As in a number of other continental European countries, a law degree is regarded as being directly relevant to business and commercial careers, as well as to the legal profession.

A number of short postgraduate courses leading to a certificate of study have been developed in recent years. The university degree in business studies and especially in accountancy is regarded as sufficient.

There are a large number of foreign students enrolled in German universities —about 25 percent of the total student population are from EC countries. Since Germany has a large population of immigrant workers, many of the nationals and their children study in Germany. Germany may therefore be a productive source for employers seeking their own nationals.

PORTUGAL AND SPAIN

Education in Portugal and Spain is similar to the pattern of education in the southern European and Mediterranean countries. The free movement of labor will not apply to Portugal and Spain until 1993, making it more difficult for Portuguese and Spanish-trained business students to migrate to the European continent. Also, job applicants from other countries will need special permits to work in Portugal and Spain.

Much of the business training in Spain is done by specialized programs on the post-high school level. The universities, although general education in nature, have provided some excellent specialized education in business. For example, the business school at Barcelona has an excellent reputation. Also, the European Business School has branches in Spain. While the graduates of schools in Portugal have been less mobile, the emerging EC will bring changes to both of these countries.

Administrative technicians are prepared with a broad business background and a global perspective for entry-level positions in the professional field of business administration. They are trained to resolve the majority of administrative questions that arise and carry out management functions in businesses effectively. The training program strives to develop initiative and is the beginning preparation for future company managers.

To enter higher levels of administrative vocational training, students are required to have the title of Bachelor. Specific subjects may be required at the baccalaureate level to coincide with the professional studies that students wish to take.

Students who complete a higher level and a more specific vocational training program receive the title of Higher Technician in the corresponding profession. The title of Higher Technician allows direct access to certain university studies when there is a close relationship with the corresponding vocational training studies.

Relevant business courses have become more popular as international trade expands. The emerging EC will provide greater opportunities for students to work in other countries. French students often spend the second year of their MBA program in Spain.

NON-ALIGNED EUROPEAN COUNTRIES

No doubt, in the near future, other European countries will join the EC. Some of the Scandinavian countries—Finland, Norway, and Sweden—are prime candidates. Switzerland, with the spirit and history of neutrality, may remain an outsider, yet retain its role as the banking and financial center in Europe. Austria may find it essential to become more directly involved in the European economic community, especially with the political and social changes of its Eastern European Bloc neighbors. The International Society for Business Education and business educators in Western nations should take the leadership in providing curriculum materials, syllabi, textbooks, programs of study, as well as new methods and strategies of teaching to the new Eastern Democracies. Dynamic, constant changes in all areas will become the rule rather than the exception.

SUMMARY AND CONCLUSIONS

Just as many Europeans have enrolled in many educational programs at United States universities, Europeans will increasingly be attending and traveling to specialized international business programs in closer European countries. More textbooks will need to be published in the European languages to meet these students' needs in developing business programs. For example, business magazines are published regarding international business such as: *The L'Expansion* in France, *Wirtschaftswoche* in Germany, and *El Mondo* in Italy. The exchange of concepts, ideas, and procedures between countries will be enhanced as more and more students from a given EC country study in adjoining countries.

The EC integration will make mobility within the community easier and more routine. In addition to linguistic and cultural differences, the total system of higher education in Europe varies from country to country. The United Kingdom and Ireland has what is referred to as an "Anglo-Saxon" educational system. A characteristic of this system is a highly selective entry procedure.

The European continent, although there are major variations between countries, has a different approach to higher education. Students in most of the continental European countries have a broad educational base for entry to higher education. The right to study any subject is the students' choice. The higher education courses may be less specialized with large classes and a high drop-out rate. European students often study at local universities and live at home. Most students, for economic reasons, have to work part time. Therefore, European graduates are also older than students who study in the British Isles.

Placement services for employment are common at universities in the British Isles but are not common on the European continent. With the development of the EC, this is one aspect that universities will have to develop to assist companies in recruiting the best trained business students.

Employers will be forced to look to other member states of the EC to supply some of their needs for new graduates. An increasing interchange of students and workers between member states should benefit the entire European Economic community.

Many educational institutions in European countries conduct university education on a series of cycles or phases—generally, there are three similar phases. The first is a broad introductory phase and may qualify the student for employment. However, most students would enter the second phase to complete their program of studies. At the end of this second phase most university trained people qualify for an undergraduate or master's degree. The third phase is for further research and specialization, generally leading to a doctoral degree. A comparison of business programs is difficult because the length of programs varies considerably between institutions and countries.

On the entry level, the course content, as well as the teaching emphasis are found to be considerably different from country to country. Some institutions will have small specialized classes while others have extremely large classes. The first phase of university education generally has an academic emphasis; the second phase may deal with applied subjects that often include economics or business studies. The third phase may include nonuniversity higher education including technical education and vocational training in a variety of institutions. Generally, these nonuniversity institutions differ from universities in having shorter term courses and different qualifications for entry students.

International business will continue to increase in importance as will the demand for international business experts. A specialization in international business, whether it be global in nature or European continent in orientation, offers significant challenges and opportunities for employment.

Editor's Note: During October, 1990, the unification of the two Germanys —East and West—became official. Political and economic changes in the former Eastern Bloc countries are occurring daily as witnessed in Hungary and Poland. More changes are inevitable.

CHAPTER 17
Business Education Program in the U.S.S.R.

RAY D. BERNARDI
Morehead State University, Morehead, Kentucky

To some extent the educational problems in the U.S.S.R. and in the United States are the same. Both nations are committed to the principle of universal education; both have many differing racial and cultural groups within their borders; both have large land masses with great diversity in climate and topography, crops and industries; and both have courses and programs to educate and train millions of people.

But the U.S. citizen who visits the U.S.S.R. is struck by the sharp contrast between the two nations. In general, authoritarian theory and authoritarian practices characterize the Soviet educational system. In contrast, we generally see education in the United States as dedicated to freedom and democracy, with a goal of the individual development of human beings with the freedom and opportunity to choose their own life's work.

The way in which a nation raises its children and the kind of educational activities it provides its citizens reflect the thinking in that country. A study of the education of a people can be a clue to what a given culture considers important, what its expectations are, and in what direction it is heading.

HISTORY AND BACKGROUND

When the Bolsheviks seized power in Russia in 1917 approximately 60 percent of the population of the country was illiterate, and elementary schooling was available for only about half of the children between 8 and 12 years old. Access to secondary higher education was strongly biased against the lower classes (peasants and workers).[1]

Prior to 1917, Marxists (the forerunner of the Communists) considered education as a weapon of the bourgeoisie through which they (the bourgeoisie) educated themselves and their own children in order to ensure their continuing rule. But the Marxists saw any attempt by the capitalists to educate the masses as only a means of raising labor productivity in order that the capitalists could make more profits. They denounced popular education as being in the selfish interests of the capitalists. The Marxists maintained that genuine education was available only to members of the ruling class, which further used their intellectual superiority to maintain the status quo. When they came into power, the Communists promised themselves that they would make

---
[1] Kuebard, Fredrich. "Union of Soviet Socialist Republics," Kurian, George T. *World Education Encyclopedia*, III New York, NY: Facts on File, 1988. p. 1,294.

education open to all and that they would replace other ideologies and religion with Communism.

From Tsarist Russia, the Soviet regime inherited an intellectual tradition, a respect for learning, and academic and scientific excellence. The typical European pattern of education was predominant in the early days of Communist rule, with factual learning receiving the most attention and with little attempt to integrate the pupil with his environment.

Lenin believed in education as a political weapon for setting up the dictatorship of the proletariat and the eventual triumph of Communism in the Soviet Union. In 1920, Lenin wrote:

> We would not believe in teaching and education if they were confined only to the school and were divorced from the story of life . . . Our school must impart to the youth the fundamentals of knowledge and the ability to work; it must make educated people of them. In the time during which people attend school, it must train them to be participants in the struggle for emancipation from the exploiters.[2]

The revolutionary period, 1917-31. Soon after the October Revolution, all church authority over the schools was abolished and the entire educational system was placed under the control of the state, the administration of education being transferred to the individual republics. According to the Party program adopted in 1919, the Communists regarded the school as a "tool of the Communist transformation of society."[3]

During this period, the schools had two primary goals, to create a revolutionary awareness among the masses and to impart the knowledge so urgently needed for industrialization and modernization of the nation.[4] These two goals also inspired the attempts to overcome illiteracy among the adult population, especially among the peasants.

The reform years, 1931-84. This period was characterized by several changes in the goals of Soviet education as well as in the organization of the school system. Social research was encouraged as a basis for decision-making, and policies were aimed at raising the quality and efficiency of education. In 1966, compulsory vocational training in general education schools was abolished, and subsequently, on November 10, a decree was adopted outlining a new policy in the field of general secondary education. The U.S.S.R. Ministry of Public Education, as an agency for supervising and coordinating the countrywide implementation of educational policies, was established in the same year.[5]

While maintaining the polytechnical character of the secondary school the 1966 decree also reemphasized the role of academic general education to enable the school to meet the requirements of the "scientific and technological revolution." A revised curriculum for the 10-year general education school was introduced in which "labor," as the subject was now called, was reduced

---

[2] Krupskaya, Nadezhda, K. *On Education: Selected Articles and Features.* Moscow, Foreign Language Publishing House, 1957. p. 167-68.

[3] *Ibid.*, p. 1,294.

[4] *Ibid.*, p. 1,294.

[5] *Ibid.*, p. 1,297-1,298.

to only two hours a week. Previously, this part of the curriculum was known as "production training" (similar to cooperative work/study programs in the United States), which provided work experience for upper level secondary students. The new concept of labor education was more theoretical in its approach, as it was closely linked with the contents of mathematics and science teaching, which were given a practice-oriented slant. Labor training no longer would provide job skills—with the exception of a few schools—but was limited to preparing graduates to choose their occupation. Vocational guidance and counseling, therefore, became one of the major functions of labor training in the school. Career aspirations were to develop through practical work in school workshops or (this was mainly an innovation of the 1970's) in "interschool training and production combines" set up by enterprises and education authorities to cater to students of several schools in a given district.[6]

Another innovation of the curriculum after 1966 was the introduction of electives beginning at grade seven as a means of differentiating instruction in the otherwise uniform Soviet school. Yet another way of catering to special interests and abilities of students were the "special" schools with intensified teaching of individual subjects (similar to magnet schools in the United States, which specialize in subject areas such as mathematics, sciences, humanities) in the upper grades.

On the basis of the new curriculum, the syllabi of all subjects were redesigned with a view of modernizing their structure and contents, getting rid of obsolete material, and encouraging more up-to-date teaching methods. All of this curriculum reform was aimed at the achievement of universal secondary education, lasting at least 10 years.

Glasnost, perestroika, and education—1984-present. Since 1917, the Soviet school system has gone through many changes reflecting the needs of the times. Most of the changes were piecemeal and failed to produce the desired results. The leadership was faced with growing discontent concerning the performance of the educational system, and in 1983, a new reform was announced by Yuri V. Andropov. After considerable debate, the reforms were published in a final document, "Guidelines for the Reform of the General and Vocational School," in April, 1984.

Beginning with the 1984-85 school year, significant changes (which are in place today) in the structure and curricula of the general and vocational-technical school systems were made. The reform endorsed the extension of compulsory schooling by setting the age of entry into primary education at 7 years and emphasized once again the vocational training function of the general school. Another important feature of the reform was the reinforcement of the position of the vocational-technical school. With the exception of teaching training, higher education was not involved in the reform, but in the spring of 1985, the new Party leader, Mikhail Gorbachev, advocated reforming this sector, too.[7]

---

[6]*Ibid.*, p. 1,298.

[7]Traver, Nancy. "Restructuring the 3R'S." *Time* 133:96-97; April 10, 1989.

PUBLIC EDUCATION IN THE U.S.S.R.

All citizens in the U.S.S.R. have the right to an education. This right is guaranteed by free, universal, compulsory primary and secondary schooling and by a system of state stipends for students considered likely to be of greater service to the state as a result of their education. Schools are opened, approved, and run by the state. The state determines the curriculum and methods of instruction to ensure that education is in line with party and state policy and that it will be uniform throughout the nation.

In the following section, preschool, elementary, secondary, and higher education will be discussed.

Preschool education. Both nursery schools and kindergartens are provided for children throughout the U.S.S.R. The nursery schools were first established for children of working mothers and now will accept any child, provided there are facilities available. Children can enter the nursery school at 2½ months of age and remain until the age of 3. The school operates under the minister of health of each republic. Usually the director is a doctor or trained nurse. Fees are charged according to the parents' income and/or the number of children in the family. Fees range from 5 to 20 rubles a month.[8]

Nursery schools usually operate 24 hours a day, six days a week. Program emphasis is on health, group activity, and orientation to a collective society. At the age of 3 children enter Kindergarten, where the activities are similar to those of the nursery schools but on a higher plane, and emphasis is placed on health and speech development. The kindergarten is a four-year school.

In Moscow a kindergarten visited in 1987 operated from 9 a.m. to 6 p.m., and 21 staff members were available for 150 pupils. In Leningrad, there were 18 staff members for 100 pupils, and the school was open from 7 a.m. to 7 p.m. Kindergartens are more prevalent than nursery schools. Some of the kindergartens operate 24 hours a day, six days a week. Medical services and emphasis on health and collective activities remain prominent in the kindergartens.

The Soviet preschool educators express their confidence in preschool education and maintain that children who attend the nursery and kindergarten do better in the primary grades than those who do not have this advantage. The official policy is to invest huge sums in the operation and physical facilities of these preschool institutions, as they lend themselves to "public upbringing" of the younger generation.

Primary and secondary education. The organization of the Soviet school system is illustrated in Figure 1. This organizational pattern is maintained throughout the 15 Union republics and 22 autonomous republics of the U.S.S.R. For governmental purposes, there is tight centralization, with the Ministry of Education in Moscow providing directions for course syllabi, teaching methods, school construction, and teachers' salaries.

---

[8]One ruble equals about $1.62 at the official rate of exchange.

Figure 1

YEARS IN SCHOOL	Outline of Education in U.S.S.R. After Reform of 1958	YEARS OF AGE
18	Research institutes and postgraduate courses	24
17		23
16		22
15	Universities and	21
14	higher institutes	20
13		19
12		18
11	Senior secondary stage / Tekhnikumi / Evening and part-time secondary schools	17
10		16
9		15
8	Four-year junior secondary stage	14
7		13
6		12
5		11
4	Four-year elementary schools	10
3		9
2		8
1		7
	Kindergartens	6
		5
		4
		3

(16-2)

The complete course of the Soviet 10-year general education school embraces both primary and secondary education, and the curriculum is followed by the entire school population with only a few exceptions. For pedagogical and organizational reasons, the course is divided into three successive stages (primary, intermediate, and senior grades).

The curricula for all general education schools are laid down by the republic's Ministries of Public Education and are based on standard curricula issued by the U.S.S.R. Ministry of Public Education—listing the subjects to be taught at each grade along with the number of hours to be devoted to each subject. Table 1, "Curriculum for the U.S.S.R. Secondary General School," illustrates the hours devoted to each subject in the typical secondary general school (the inclusion of grade 11 is for the Baltic states).

As the first stage of the general education school, primary schooling comprises three years. Instruction for the 7 to 10 year olds is characterized by a number of features that distinguish it from the following stages. Half the 24 weekly hours laid down by the curriculum are devoted to learning languages and six to mathematics. "Nature studies" is taught as a special primary school subject from classes two to four with only six hours a week left for the remaining subjects (art, music, physical education, and labor education). At the primary level, all subjects are taught by one teacher, the principle of "departmentalized" subject teaching not being introduced until the fourth grade.

The intermediate stage, which comprises grades four to eight, is made up of subjects that are continued at the upper secondary stage. The emphasis in grades four to eight continues to be on language and mathematics, but many new subjects are also introduced (a foreign language from grade four and the natural sciences from grade five onward). History, geography, biology, physics, chemistry, technical drawing, and "labor and vocational training" (which may include shorthand and typewriting) are also part of the curriculum at this level. A recent drive toward technological modernization of the Soviet economy, including the development and application of information technology and computer sciences, has resulted in the launching of a mass computer literacy program in the schools. The new course entitled "fundamentals of information science and computer technology" began in the fall of 1985 in grade nine and eventually will be taught in grades 10 and 11.

Alongside a demanding academic education, a considerable share of the curriculum is based on a special subject, "labor training," which is supplemented by "polytechnical" contents and applied knowledge in academic subjects. What exactly are school children taught in their labor lessons? From learning to do things with their hands in the three primary years, the pupils progress through an exploratory phase and on to a final, skill-learning phase (somewhat similar to the career education model in the United States). Career guidance is an important component of the courses.

Optional subjects, for which two hours per week are now allowed in the seventh year, three in the eighth, and four in the ninth and tenth, are frequently work related. Auto mechanics, shorthand, and typewriting, for

---

[9] O'Dell, Felicity. "Vocational Education in the U.S.S.R." in Sorrentino, Frank, and Frances R. Curcio, Eds., *Soviet Politics and Education.* New York: University Press of America, 1986. p. 390.

Table 1

Curriculum for the U.S.S.R. Secondary General School

Subjects	1	2	3	4	5	6	7	8	9	10	11	Total of weekly hours
Native language and literature	7	9	11	11	11	9	6	5	5	3	3	80
Mathematics	4	6	6	6	6	6	6	6	6	4/5	4	60.5
Fundamentals of information science and computer technology	—	—	—	—	—	—	—	—	—	1	2	3
History	—	—	—	—	2	2	2	2	3	4	3	18
Fundamentals of Soviet state and law	—	—	—	—	—	—	—	—	1	—	—	1
Social studies	—	—	—	—	—	—	—	—	—	0/2	2/1	2.5
Ethics and psychology of family life	—	—	—	—	—	—	—	—	0/1	1/0	—	1
Getting to know our environment	1	1	—	—	—	—	—	—	—	—	—	2
Nature studies	—	—	1	1	1	—	—	—	—	—	—	3
Geography	—	—	—	—	—	2	3	2	2	2/1	—	10.5
Biology	—	—	—	—	—	2	2	2	2	1	1/2	10.5
Physics	—	—	—	—	—	—	2	2	3	4/3	4	14.5
Astronomy	—	—	—	—	—	—	—	—	—	—	1	1
Chemistry	—	—	—	—	—	—	—	3	3/2	2	2	9.5
Technical drawing	—	—	—	—	—	—	1	1	—	—	—	2
Foreign language	—	—	—	—	4	3	2	2	1	1	1	14
Art	2	1	1	1	1	1	1	—	—	—	—	8
Physical education	2	2	2	2	2	2	2	2	2	2	2	22
Premilitary training	—	—	—	—	—	—	—	—	—	2	2	4
Labor and vocational training	2	2	2	2	2	2	2	3	3	4	4	28
Total	20	22	24	24	30	30	30	30	31	31	31	303
Obligatory												
Socially useful and productive work	—	1	1	1	2	2	2	3	3	4	4	23
Electives												
(facultative courses)	—	—	—	—	—	—	2	2	2	4	4	14
Work experience (days)	—	—	—	—	10	10	10	16	16	20	—	

Source: U.S.S.R. Ministry of Public Education (February 12, 1985).

instance, are subjects taught in some schools.[9] Although evidence is sparse of traditional business education subjects being taught in the general secondary school in the U.S.S.R., this writer observed typewriting being taught in School No. 77, an eleven-year school in Tbilisi, Georgia. The class had all girls, and they were learning commercial typing. Economic geography is also a course that is often included in the curriculum of secondary schools.

Vocational Schools. Another type of secondary school is the *tekhnikum*, which is a specialized secondary school intended to train "middle-level" specialists, in three-, four-, or five-year courses. Approximately one in ten ninth-graders enters one of the *tekhnikumi*, where the child is prepared for a single specialized skill. These schools also provide a general and theoretical education. The best students may proceed to higher education from this type of school.

There are *tekhnikumi* with courses in economics, management, finance, bookkeeping, and clerical work.[10] The majority of the *tekhnikum* graduates go straight into appropriate jobs on completion of their courses.

---

[10]Grant, Nigel. *Soviet Education*. Fourth Edition. New York: Penguin Books, 1979. p. 97.

Vocational technical schools, which are sometimes referred to as "trade schools," or by the old name of "labor-reserve schools," also provide a lower level of vocational training than the *tekhnikum*. The main emphasis is on learning a particular trade. General subjects are taught 15 to 20 percent of the time, with the rest being spent in the field or workshop. Courses may last from six months to three years, and students are paid at apprentice rates. The course culminates with the award of a trade diploma. It is theoretically possible to go on from these schools to higher education, but to do so, the student will be at a distinct disadvantage because of the meager amount of general education offered in the programs.

Administratively, these schools are separate from the rest of the educational system and come under the jurisdiction of the state committee of the U.S.S.R. Council of Ministers on Vocational-Technical Education.

Clerical training. Training for many less highly skilled occupations is still given on the job, not in school. Clerical training is generally considered a type of on-the-job training in the U.S.S.R. Often, the management of each economic enterprise, department, or agency conducts its own training programs for new clerical personnel as well as provides courses for improvement and upgrading of its regular employees.

What about the future of business education at the secondary level in the U.S.S.R.? There is little doubt that it will require greater emphasis than it has received in the past. The move toward a free enterprise, competitive business system and the need for people trained in the information processing areas will mandate that change. The reader must understand, however, that the Soviet secondary school, patterned after the German gymnasium, will require a massive dose of *perestroika* (restructuring) and a good deal of *glasnost* (openness or open-minded thinking) to make the necessary changes.

HIGHER EDUCATION

The main task of higher education in the U.S.S.R. is the training of highly qualified personnel for the economy and the various spheres of cultural life. Its structure, organization, and curricula are closely related to the demands of the employment system. Training is for a specific job, and the planning of enrollments is an integral part of national economic planning. Higher education institutions, numbering 892 in 1984, are divided into three main categories according to different functions, the range of disciplines taught, and research activities. At the apex of the system there are 68 universities with 601,000 students (1984). Some are places of learning and research of high distinction and long-standing traditions, e.g., in Moscow and Leningrad; others, especially those in outlying regions, have been set up more recently by upgrading an existing lower level institution to university status. In the universities a variety of disciplines are represented; programs focus on preparing future researchers and teachers for secondary and higher education. Universities have the right to confer academic degrees. Competition for entry into some of the leading universities, especially those in Moscow and Leningrad, is particularly fierce.

The 61 polytechnical institutes are large establishments in the technological sphere and are mainly engaged in training future research personnel and engineers for various specializations. There is little difference in status between them and the more prestigious universities, and both are engaged in fundamental as well as applied research. The word *VUZ* (*Vysshee Uchebnoe Zavedenie* or Higher Educational Institution) is popularly used to refer to all types of higher education. The balance of the higher educational entities are known as institutes, about which more will be written later.

Admission to the universities, polytechnic institutes, and other lower level institutes is restricted to those holding a certificate of completion from a general secondary school or *tekhnikum*. However, possession of this certificate does not give all holders the right to enroll. The students are selected for each institution on the basis of an entrance examination that includes written tests (native language and mathematics) and an oral test selected on the basis of the specialty chosen for study. The number of places available in each institution and each specialty is determined in relation to general manpower planning.

Priority is given to students who have previously spent two years working in an enterprise. In the higher technical institutes, it is a rule that candidates must have spent a minimum of two years working in an enterprise before being admitted.

After a rapid increase during the 1960's, student numbers in higher education rose more slowly in the 1970's and had begun to drop slightly by the mid-1980's.[11]

On the whole, higher education is regarded as capable of satisfying the demand for specialists, but despite the central planning of student numbers, there is a noticeable imbalance between the supply and demand of people for certain occupations. Thus, future development is expected to focus on the redistribution of proportions among disciplines rather than just turning out more graduates, some of whom can't find a job.

About 55 percent of those who apply are admitted to a VUZ. Although representation of manual workers in higher education tended to rise in the 1970's, they continue to be under-represented in terms of their proportion in the total population, while the children of white collar workers retain their superior position.[12]

Women enjoy virtual parity in access to a VUZ. Although percentage of female students enrolled is 53 percent, they are over-represented in certain disciplines (education and fine arts, 71 percent; economics and law, 69 percent) while their proportion in agricultural courses is only 35 percent.

The duration of VUZ courses is between four and six years; in the majority of disciplines, five years. The academic year is divided into two semesters (fall and spring), at the end of which there are tests in which failure may mean the repetition of a semester or year. For all specialties taught at VUZ's

---

[11]Kuebard, Frederich. "Union of Soviet Socialist Republics," in Kurian, George T. *World Education Encyclopedia*, Vol. 3 New York: Facts on File, 1988. p. 1,312.

[12]*Ibid.*, p. 1,313.

(about 450) there are curricula approved by the Ministry of Higher and Secondary Specialized Education. Fundamental ideological subjects (history of the Communist Party of the U.S.S.R., political economy, Marxist-Leninist philosophy, scientific Communism) are an obligatory component of all curricula and make up between 10 and 15 percent of the course time. A foreign language and physical education also are required. Apart from compulsory subjects, the student is given some choice in attending special classes related to his or her specialization.

Tuition is free and most students are provided a stipend as well as free room and board. Students are counted as being state employees, and therefore, on the completion of their courses, they must take up designated employment in their specialty for a three-year period.

Graduate work. Although students receive diplomas instead of degrees on completion of a university course, there are two postgraduate degrees—the candidate and doctorate. The main purpose of advanced study is to prepare for a teaching position or for a place in a research institute. Graduate students are known as "aspirants" and are older than the average student, having completed a four-year degree and at least two years' work in their specialty before returning to the university or higher institute to work for an advanced degree. Applicants for admission to graduate work present an original research paper and take examinations in the Russian language, the history of the Communist Party, and their special field. Aspirants study for three years, and get a stipend of about 100 rubles a month. They take special graduate courses, carry on approved individual study and research, and write a dissertation. The dissertation must be approved by the department, published in the press or as a monograph, and defended before a committee of the faculty.

If the aspirant is finally passed by the Learned Council of the institution, he/she is awarded the title of candidate. A candidate who has worked in an institution for several years and has published several papers may be awarded the title of *docent*. All of the higher educational institutions are qualified to award the degree of candidate.

Special doctorate institutes (*doctorantura*) have been set up in a few universities and higher institutes that are permitted to award the doctor's degree. Students who hold the degree of candidate must be nominated by their university and must be approved by a joint commission set up by the Ministry of Higher Education and Culture and the Academy of Sciences of the U.S.S.R. in order to study for the degree. After several years of additional work, writing, publishing, preparing, and defending a doctoral dissertation, the candidate may be awarded the title of doctor. Holders of such degrees may be given positions as professors, or may hold high research positions. There is also the possibility that an academic with long service and a distinguished publication record could attain the position and rank of professor even without the doctorate. Predoctoral students are paid higher stipends than precandidate students. No tuition is charged for postgraduate work.

Universities and higher level institutes (Polytechnic) do not have a College of Business. Their emphasis is on highly specialized technical training for a definite occupation or profession. Of course, many of their graduates eventually become managers of their enterprise and would likely do a better job if they learned managerial skills as part of their training. Economic theory is taught at the university level.

The "institute" system. Higher education for business is left up to the lower level institutes and is provided primarily in institutes of economics. More than 25 of these institutes train the large number of managerial people needed for the planning and management of the elaborate machinery of the Soviet industrial and agricultural system.[13] One will not find any type of "clerical skills" courses being taught in institutions of higher education.

Teacher education. The teacher education institution preferred in the Soviet Union today is the pedagogical institute, which offers a five-year course (four years for elementary teachers) based on completion of the secondary school. These schools are on the university level, and the entrance requirements are the same as for universities. In selecting students for teacher training, the institutes give preference to those with the highest grades in their special subjects at the secondary level.

The course of study for each subject is uniform throughout the country. A secondary teacher is prepared to teach two or three related subjects, e.g., Russian language, literature, and history; or mathematics and technical drawing.

Second-year and third-year students spend six hours weekly in practice teaching; in the fourth year they spend eight weeks; in the fifth year, 12 weeks. After graduation from the pedagogical institute the students take the state examinations. They do not get a degree but a certificate and the title "secondary school teacher."

Training of teachers in the Soviet Union has two main purposes: first, to make certain that they are politically reliable and loyal to the teachings of the party; and second, to ensure that they are prepared to illustrate in every way the relationship between general education and the economic life and labor of the country.[14]

Teachers are paid for a basic week of 24 hours, with additional amounts for overtime. They may earn from 85 to 120 rubles a month, although a few get as much as 140 rubles. Salaries vary according to years of teaching experience and the teaching location. A typical Russian language teacher with more than 10 years' service, teaching a 24-hour week, is paid 113 rubles, plus 8 rubles for correcting homework, plus 7.5 rubles for the responsibility of a home room—a monthly wage of 128.5 rubles. A science or typewriting teacher might be paid from six to 15 rubles in addition for supervising a laboratory. Teachers who work in remote areas—the far north or the far east—may receive an additional 20 to 100 percent above the base pay, e.g., in the Irkutsk region this amounts to 20 percent; in the Kuril Islands it is

---

[13]Grant, Nigel. *Soviet Education.* Fourth Edition. New York: Penguin Books, 1979. p. 132.

[14]Cramer, John F. and George S. Browne. *Contemporary Education: A Comparative Study of National System,* 2nd Ed. New York: Harcourt, Brace & World, Inc., 1965. p. 462.

100 percent.[15]

Like all Soviet citizens, teachers are eligible for old-age pensions at the age of 55 for women and 60 for men. Special pensions are paid for extra-long service. Teachers who do not wish to retire after 25 years' service may continue to teach and draw 40 percent of the pension as well as their regular salary. When they retire, they get the full pension.[16]

The real income of the teacher is increased by social service grants provided to all Soviet citizens—social insurance, grants to widowed mothers, grants to mothers with many children, stipends to university students, free medical and dental care, and free higher education.

During the two summer months, the teachers are on vacation with pay and may spend much of this time at tourist resorts provided by their union, to which about 98 percent belong. Their union fund also provides sick benefits, old-age and disability pensions, allowances to widows, maternity allowances, summer camps, rest homes, and children's sanatoriums.

Teachers who work in villages (usually on collective or state farms) get their houses rent free, with free utilities. Among urban teachers, it is estimated that rent and utilities amount to about 8 percent of their monthly budget.

Business education teachers would be trained in the pedagogical institutes and would receive additional training in skills subjects from an enterprise.

New developments in education for business. With the restructuring of the Soviet economy, there is a growing need for better trained managers. The concept of competition in business is new to the Soviets, and managers must learn to deal with it. Trimble explains that business, once a dirty word in the Marxist-Leninist lexicon, with all its overtones of workers' exploitation and obscene profits, has become the latest economic rage.[17]

A few specialized managerial training institutions—many with generous help from the West—have recently sprung up in the U.S.S.R. to capitalize on this interest. Chief among them is Moscow's Higher Commercial Management School. Competition is fierce for admission to this school with 80 applicants for 12 openings per term. The tuition is high with fees ranging up to 3,500 rubles ($5,670), 10 percent of which must be paid in a convertible currency such as dollars or Deutsche marks. In most cases, the students are sponsored by the enterprise where they are employed and are given leave to take the course.[18]

Business education. Westerners (either from the United States or the Continent) will find education in the Soviet Union to be quite different from their own. There is a greater similarity to the continental system because the former Russian Empire patterned its developing educational system after those of the French and German systems. Because their models emphasized the liberal arts at both the secondary and higher education levels, the Soviet schools followed the same pattern. Although business education was and

---

[15]Grifkov, Ivan. "Economic Status of Teachers," *U.S.S.R. Magazine*, October, 1960. pp. 25-28.

[16]*Ibid.*, p. 28.

[17]Trimble, Jeff, and Karen Breslau. "Moscow Tackles Its Manager Gap." *U.S. News and World Report* 107:40; July 31, 1989.

[18]*Ibid.*

is provided in some instances, it is the "second choice" even for a student population in a so-called proletarian (or workers) society. As is true in the United States, parents aspire for the most prestigious education for their children—and that usually means following (or attending) an academic secondary education program and going on to higher education. Business education as a separate discipline does not exist in the U.S.S.R. At the secondary level, some shorthand, clerical, typewriting, and computer courses are being offered as part of labor training programs (vocational education). At the higher education level, business education consists of management training to run a state enterprise. Aside from a few management institutes that have opened on the heels of the *perestroika movement*, business administration, as we know it, is not offered.

SUMMARY AND CONCLUSIONS

The Soviet economic system and the Soviet people are seeing the results of poor economic planning and incompetent management of enterprises. The Soviet leadership has been forced into restructuring their economy away from central planning toward free enterprise.

A better delivery system of business education at the secondary level and education for business at the higher education level will be one of the factors that should help the Soviet economy in the years ahead as they move toward a free and open economic system. Competition among enterprises will demand the training of better, more productive office workers and managers. A business education program that follows the Western model can provide that training.

CHAPTER 18
Business Education Programs in Taiwan

LARRY E. CASTERLINE
State of Ohio Department of Education, Columbus, Ohio

As one thinks about business education from an international perspective, countries such as Germany, England, or France may come to mind first. Taiwan, a country that most people cannot find on the world map, might be far from consideration. However, Taiwan has become a potent force at a time when a nation's economics is a more powerful device than its military. How has Taiwan grown so dramatically, and what role has vocational education—specifically business education—played in its economic development?

BACKGROUND ON TAIWAN

Geographics. The tiny island of Taiwan is approximately 120 miles off the shore of mainland China and 220 miles north of the Philippine Island of Luzon. Taiwan is shaped like a tobacco leaf, with the tip pointing toward Japan. It is 250 miles long, and about 80 miles wide at the broadest point. Within its 13,735 square miles live 20 million people. Most of the population live on the western plains.

The island has few natural resources; however, the country has achieved enormous economic success during the past 40 years. According to a report presented at the 1989 American Vocational Association convention in Orlando, Florida, Taiwan is envied by developed countries for its foreign-exchange surplus of more than 75 billion U.S. dollars. Taiwan had a per capita income in 1988 of over 6,000 U.S. dollars, and has become a model for developing countries.

Historical perspective. Taiwan was occupied by Japan from 1895 until 1945 when Allied forces won World War II and restored Taiwan to Chinese rule. The Chinese launched a movement in Taiwan in the late 1940's that led to the island's phenomenal economic growth. They overhauled Taiwan's educational system and sent thousands of students abroad to study new technology and scientific developments.

Then, in 1949, Taiwan became independent from China under the leadership of Chiang Kai-shek. Both the Nationalist Republic of China (which governs from Taipei, Taiwan) and the Communist People's Republic (which governs on the mainland) still claim to be the sole, rightful government of all China, and view Taiwan as an integral province of the Republic of China. However, the Nationalists rule according to the precepts of capitalism and free enterprise; in contrast, the Communists utilize the centrally managed, authoritarian policies of Marx and Lenin. Both governments wish to reunite Taiwan and mainland China under their own system.

Governmental support for education. The Taiwan Central Government (i.e., the Nationalist Republic of China), regional governments, and local governments place a high value on education. Taiwan's constitution requires that 15 percent of the annual central government's budget be spent on education, science, and culture. Therefore, as the national budget increases so do the dollars spent on education. Education in Taiwan is regarded as an instrument of the overall national policy. The master plan for vocational education in Taiwan corresponds with the nation's priority for economic development.

One of the major factors contributing to Taiwan's successful economic development during the 1980's was the quality and quantity of well-educated, highly skilled workers provided during the past four decades by the nation's vocational education schools and vocational training institutions.

Since the 1960's, Taiwan has achieved an annual economic growth rate of approximately nine percent, which is considered an economic development miracle. Although it is hard to measure vocational education's effect on economic growth, it is generally agreed that one of the decisive factors in Taiwan's success has been the government's emphasis on education and a sufficient supply of technologically skilled labor.

Growth of vocational education. The current vocational education system originated and expanded during the fifties and sixties under the free-enterprise philosophy of the capitalist government. During this time, many private and independent vocational schools were established to offer industrial and business education programs. During the seventies, free public education was extended from six years of elementary school to include three years of junior high school. Vocational education was phased out at the junior-high level and placed at the senior-high level. Curriculum standards were revised in 1974 in the country's six major vocational education areas—agriculture, business, health and nursing, home economics, industrial education, and marine and fishery. To supply the needed human resources to support the nation's major construction and industrial projects, senior academic high schools were converted into comprehensive high schools with industrial and business education programs. To recruit and train qualified teachers for vocational education, a new teachers' college was founded to prepare teachers for industrial education, business education, and vocational counseling. The new teachers' college admitted only graduates from the vocational schools. The number of programs and the enrollment in vocational education programs continued to grow until 1980, when such enrollment accounted for 68 percent of the total secondary schools' enrollment.

TAIWAN'S EDUCATIONAL SYSTEM

Route to higher education. Figure 1 illustrates Taiwan's four levels of education, starting with early childhood. Education is now free and com-

Figure 1

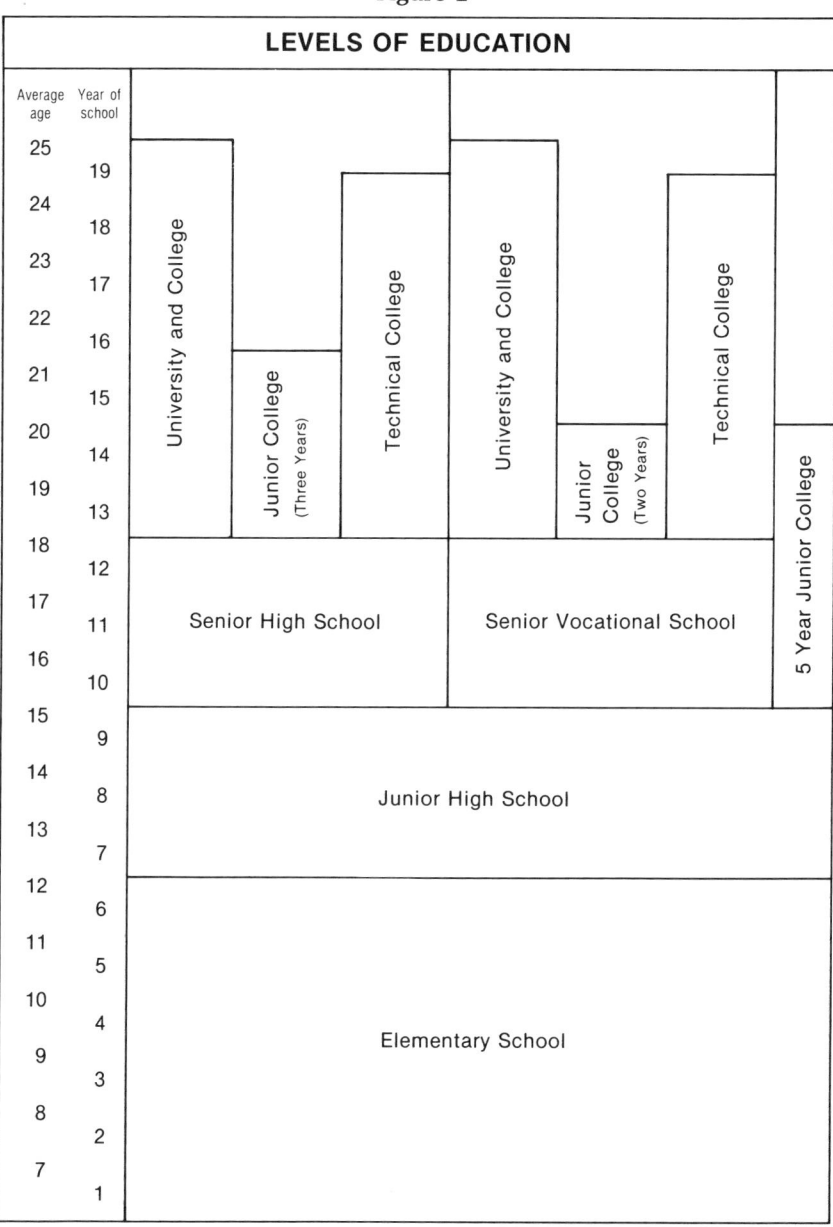

Average age	Year of school							
25	19							
24	18	University and College		Technical College	University and College		Technical College	
23	17							
22	16							
21	15		Junior College (Three Years)					
20	14					Junior College (Two Years)		
19	13							5 Year Junior College
18	12	Senior High School			Senior Vocational School			
17	11							
16	10							
15	9	Junior High School						
14	8							
13	7							
12	6	Elementary School						
11	5							
10	4							
9	3							
8	2							
7	1							

pulsory through the ninth grade. At the end of the ninth grade, students have various options. These are to:
- Attend a senior high school for three years.
- Attend a senior vocational school for three years.

- Go straight from junior high school to a five-year program at a junior college.
- Drop out of school completely.

Which alternative is chosen is somewhat dictated by the results of required tests taken in the ninth grade, in the 12th grade, and at the end of the college or university program. All these tests include English. These tests put excessive stress on students to perform satisfactorily, as do those in Japan. There is a national effort to lessen this pressure, especially at the ninth grade level.

When a student enters a junior college, he or she does so within one of several different time frames. Which time frame applies depends primarily upon the student's high school preparation. If students attended a senior high school and did not participate in a vocational program, and choose the junior college option, they will be in a three-year program at the junior college. If students attend a senior vocational school and choose the junior college option, they will be in a two-year program at the junior college. Or students may elect to drop out of school at the end of the ninth grade and attend a junior college, which would require them to now be in a five-year program at the junior college.

Articulation between secondary vocational programs and the junior colleges appears to be much stronger than in the United States. Part of the reason for the emphasis on articulation is that the leadership for the secondary schools is appointed by the central government, which can mandate this relationship.

Teacher education. A student wishing to become a business education or marketing education teacher must have participated in a business or marketing program in either a senior high school or a senior vocational school. Furthermore, he or she must attend National Changhua University of Education, the only institution on the island that prepares business education teachers. This university offers a comprehensive program for potential business education teachers. Its large staff teaches the technical and professional courses. Students encounter various experiences that are similar to those at an American university.

If a student wishes to attend graduate school, he or she must study in another country because currently Taiwan has no graduate programs in business education. Thus, many Taiwan students study business education at major universities in the United States.

BUSINESS EDUCATION IN TAIWAN

I toured Taiwan in December 1989 at the invitation of Ming-Fa Shih, chief of the Division of Vocational Education, Taiwan Provincial Government. The primary purpose of the visit was to deliver a paper on trends in business and marketing education in the United States. However, I also visited numerous public and private schools and witnessed business education programs in different settings, the results of which are reported in this chapter.

The business education program plays a major role in Taiwan's vocational education system. An examination of student numbers reveals that industrial education is the largest of Taiwan's six vocational education programs, and business education is second. Taiwan's business education programs are similar to those in the United States—a result of Taiwan's historical efforts to expand its educational system by having many of its business education leaders attend graduate school in America.

Curriculum and instruction. The curriculum observed included traditional business education courses. All the business schools visited taught keyboarding to all students. The schools also taught data processing, accounting, and word processing. In the early stages of their high school career, all students took a course in using the abacus. Even though Taiwan is known as an electronics exporter, many of its people use this simple device in their daily entrepreneurial affairs. Students were eager to demonstrate their skills on the abacus and to compare their speed with that of a calculator.

Nonbusiness academic classwork is an important part of the curriculum even though the entire school may emphasize business education. The senior test is important to students' future success; thus, students must be prepared academically as well as occupationally.

In both private and public schools, the faculty and staff accept the responsibility for preparing teaching materials. The sophisticated materials, including elaborate visual aids, are a source of pride at each school. However, teachers and administrators believe that the central government should be playing a larger part in developing instructional materials.

Most of the business schools have programs for students with physical or mental disabilities. No programs were observed for students with economic disadvantages.

Facilities and equipment. In selected situations, the available business education equipment consistently reflected modern technology, but many schools used a combination of both antiquated and state-of-the-art equipment. For example, it was not unusual to visit a large classroom equipped with rows of outdated typewriters on old typewriting tables and in the next room see a small class equipped with a computer terminal for each student and state-of-the-art instructional equipment, including a large-screen television. Incidentally, most typewriters had both English and Chinese on the keys.

Instructional staff. The instructional staff appeared to be well-trained and to enjoy their high status as educators. They had their students' respect and showed enthusiasm regarding their subject area. The traditional business education teacher instructs three hours a day. After that time, the teacher is free to prepare lessons, counsel students, or leave for the day.

A national concern is that teachers are spending the afternoons trading on the stock market. Because the Taiwan stock market is so successful due to the rapidly growing economy, teachers can earn more money playing the market than they do teaching. There is also an overall concern in the schools about providing inservice education for the teachers, which is especially necessary due to rapid changes and innovations in electronic equipment. One of the major inservice events is an annual business and marketing education conference held at the National Changhua University of Education in December of each year. Business education teachers representing the country's various schools are selected to attend the five-day conference along with a large representation of administrators. The conference offers an extensive equipment show and other inservice activities.

There is a business education association for Taiwan teachers and administrators who wish to join. Although the association appears well organized, it has difficulty obtaining membership, maybe because it tends to be dominated by administrators rather than teachers. The Taiwan association annually invites representatives from Japan's business education association to attend its annual meetings. One objective is to also involve representatives from the United States' National Business Education Association in its activities.

Students. The business education students demonstrated a high level of respect for their teachers; were extremely polite and well disciplined; and exhibited a genuine interest in the subject matter. Students in Taiwan attend school six days per week with a half-day schedule on Saturdays. Some schools are residential, and most require uniforms.

FUTURE DIRECTIONS

Taiwan is a very aggressive country that is a world leader in manufacturing and exporting. It enjoys a growing economy despite having a large population, limited land, and few natural resources. Taiwan gives education a high priority in all levels of its government, and perceives vocational education as an important element in the nation's economic development. Business education is a significant part of its vocational education system and appears to have a prosperous future.

As the vocational education enrollment has grown in Taiwan, many issues have arisen that are similar to those in the United States.

In a report titled *Efforts in Improving Flexibility and Efficiency in Vocational Education and Training in Taiwan: Republic Of China,* Tien-Jin Chang, president, National Taipei Institute of Technology, identified 10 efforts to improve Taiwan's technical education and training system:

1. A more flexible vocational education system must be planned. More institutes of technology at the university level are proposed to be established, and distinguished senior vocational high schools must be promoted to technical colleges. This would deliver more business education at the postsecondary level.
2. Programs and departments should be efficiently integrated by utilizing a survey of occupations and an analysis of trades. This implies the need to cluster certain programs in business education. In many states, business education is already being organized into clusters such as information processing, accounting, data processing, and administrative assistance.
3. Curricula and teaching materials must be revised. Flexibility and diversification in curricula are necessary for graduates to cope with the changing job market.
4. There must be teacher training and long-term and short-term continuing education to advance teachers' professional knowledge and skills.

5. An increase is needed in the quantity of modern equipment to improve vocational education and training.
6. There is a need for more efficient school management and administration. Computerization and an efficient school-evaluation process, both already instituted, may accelerate better school management.
7. Educational laws need to be reviewed because rapid social and economic changes have caused some of them to be outdated.
8. A skill-certification system needs to be further developed and enforced. This may secure employment and higher pay for certified students.
9. Service-personnel training needs to be promoted as larger numbers of employees engage in the service industry.
10. Lifelong education and career education through vocational education need to be promoted and expanded.

Taiwan, like the United States, must continually evaluate the direction of its vocational educational systems. With constant evaluation and adjustments, the needs of the students, labor market, and economy will be served.